A Strange Breed of Folks

A Strange Breed of Folks

Tales from the World's
Second Oldest Profession

Mel Lavine

Best wishes,
Mel Lavine

Beaver's Pond Press, Inc.

ISBN 13: 978-1-59298-196-0
ISBN 10: 1-59298-196-8

Library of Congress Control Number: 2007933278

Book design and production: Mighty Media
Cover: Anders Hanson · Interior pages: Chris Long

Front cover photo of Nixon and author by Buster DeBrunner.

Printed in the United States of America

First Printing: September 2007

11   10   9   8   7   6   5   4   3   2   1

7104 Ohms Lane
Edina, Minnesota 55439 USA
(952) 829-8818
www.BeaversPondPress.com

To order, visit www.BookHouseFulfillment.com or call 1-800-901-3480. Reseller and special sales discounts available.

For Donna and Chris,
my biggest supporters

Contents

Author's Note

I am indebted to Lorraine (Rainey) Sykes and Chris Brown for their abiding faith and help and for the help of Barbara Archebeque, Robert Beetem, Minelva Faye Boyd, Margaret Carson, Richard Cohen, Gene Farinet, Janet Gardner, Tom Goldstein, Avrum and Beverly Gratch, Mort Hochstein, Penn Kimball, Charles Kuralt, Henrik Krogius, Bud Lamoreaux, Jennifer Manion, Myra Manning, Bill Moran, Shad Northshield, George Osterkamp, Robert Pierpoint, Selwyn Raab, Jane Murphy Schulberg, Jonathan Schulberg, Doug Sinsel, Stuart Sykes, Pam Thomas, Al Tostado, Carolyn Vines, Dorothy Walker, Robley Wilson, and Fred Zehnder.

I've tried to remember everyone, but some names have eluded my best efforts to recall from the past. Should they happen to come by this book, I hope they will accept my gratitude. May I say, too, that I can't begin to remember all the published material that helped broaden my knowledge of the business of spreading the news. Some of those that stick to my memory are:

Charles Kuralt's America by Charles Kuralt, G. P. Putnam's Sons, 1995.

How to Talk with Practically Anybody about Practically Anything by Barbara Walters, June Callwood, Doubleday, 1970.

A Reporter's Life by Walter Cronkite, Alfred A. Knopf, 1997.

The Today Show: an Insider's Look at 25 Tumultuous Years, Colorful and Controversial People by Robert Metz, Playboy Press, 1977.

The Tin Kazoo: TV Politics and the News by Edwin Diamond, M.I.T. Press, 1977.

Beyond Glory: Joe Louis vs. Max Schmeling and a World on the Brink, by David Margolick, Alfred A. Knopf, 2005.

Prime Time, The Life of Edward R. Murrow by Alexander Kendrick, Little, Brown and Company, 1969.

Edward R. Murrow, An American Original by Joseph E. Persico, McGraw-Hill, 1988.

Timebends: A Life by Arthur Miller, Grove Press, 1987.

The story, "Red and the Tribune" first appeared in the *North American Review* in the January/February 1997 issue in somewhat different form. The story about Richard Nixon was first published in somewhat different form in the Spring 2003 issue of *Television Quarterly*.

Introduction

For many years I kept a notebook of my everyday experiences as a newspaper reporter and later as a television news writer and producer. I had only a vague idea that I might be creating a book. Jotting down conversations, impressions, encounters of the day was a compulsion. Deadlines, rivalries, the tyranny of editors and producers were all grist for my mill, as were memorable characters, felicitous turns of phrases, and the ever-exhilarating scoop.

A Strange Breed of Folks is a book of portraits of journalists with whom I have shared the last half century. Some, such as Barbara Walters and Walter Cronkite, are well-known. Others are not well-known but are no less memorable. The theme is rather a stark one: gifted people with dreams in a struggle to survive in a world ruled by money. In the end, a few are crushed. Hardly a bulletin, but there it is, exclusive by an eyewitness.

Some years ago, Tom Wyman, a then-new chairman of CBS, summoned the distinguished network correspondent Eric Sevareid to his office. Among the divisions of the corporation for which Wyman was now responsible was CBS News; with its proud history, it was the most prestigious department in broadcast journalism.

Wyman, a businessman, knew nothing about the ways of a news gathering organization or about the men and women who took up this line of work. But he wanted to learn. What, he asked Sevareid, makes journalists tick?

Sevareid replied:

Journalists are a restless, curious lot, always wanting to know what's ahead and around the bend, and, generally speaking, they're a cynical lot, certainly skeptical. Really, the best of them are healthy skeptics. By and large they're liberals, identifying with the underdog, with whom their natural affinities lay. And by and large they don't take kindly to authority figures – believe they can't be trusted – and consider it their job to make politicians answerable to the public and keep the feet of the mighty to the fire. Journalists may well have an exaggerated regard of their own importance. But there it is. Money is the least of it. By and large they're not in it for the money. Except for a lucky few there is no big money in journalism. So that's rarely a motivation for most people. A strange breed of folks, indeed.

On the day in November of 1985 when Sevareid related this incident to me, he had been retired for eight years from CBS and, in fact, had just observed his seventy-third birthday.

My purpose was to interview him for a book I was planning to write about the journalists who had been part of the CBS team led by the legendary Edward R. Murrow during the Second World War. Sevareid was one of the stars of that illustrious company.

The project I'd undertaken was never finished. I found myself hard-pressed to take time away from a stressful job as a CBS News producer. When new books about Murrow and his men began appearing, I abandoned the project altogether.

A few years ago, now retired, I set out again to write a book about journalists, where they work, and what they work on. But this time I chose reporters, editors, and producers whom I knew intimately, people with whom I had worked and shared many experiences – a strange breed of folks, indeed.

Mel Lavine
Berkeley, CA

The Investiture

I began in journalism with a blessing.

When I was sixteen, my mother led me upstairs to my grandfather's room in the attic of our house on Beals Street. It was horrible and I hated going up there because it was a cramped place and because of the smells: an old man's foul flesh, crumbling old books, and stagnant cigarette smoke.

I balked and resisted but my mother said it was important, taking me up to see Zayde. And what she was doing, what she insisted upon, was the silliest thing I'd ever heard of, the silliest and the most embarrassing (should any of my friends ever find out). Here we were ascending the steps to my grandfather's inner sanctum. My mother deemed it of the first importance that I secure the holy man's blessings before starting a new job, my very first. As we ascended, I only hoped none of my friends would ever get wind of it.

•

I pulled away but she, as I say, clamored for it. This was important, this step I was taking in my young life, and it should be consecrated; her devoutly religious father, a pious, saintly man (there was no one in her range of acquaintances more devout than he) had the credentials to seek the Almighty's favor on my behalf. Indeed I was fortunate – "blessed" would not be too strong a word – to have a grandfather so learned, so pious. We must enlist his aid. He was one in a million.

What caused all this fuss on my mother's part was the fact that I'd landed a job as an office boy at the AP in Boston. I'd hounded her until she called her best friend, Marcey Connolly, whose brother was the New England sports editor for AP.

Marcey agreed to talk me up with him. Next thing I knew, Bill King asked to see me.

He was one of those colorful characters one associated with the sports world, especially prizefighting and horse racing. A natty dresser in dark glasses, he wore a skimmer at a racy angle.

"So, kid, you think this is the racket for you?" Bill King said when we finally met.

"Oh, yes," I said.

"What makes you think so?"

"Well," I said. "What one does in this business is nothing less than recording the history of our time." I rambled on a bit in this highfalutin way.

"You know," said Bill King, the handicapper, interrupting me. "You're not going to get rich in this racket."

"I'm not in it for the money," I replied.

"Well, that's one problem you won't have around here."

When I began thanking him profusely (he was going to put in a word on my behalf with Ben Wickersham, the bureau chief) he raised his hands in self-defense.

"Whoa, kid," he said. "There'll be plenty of time for that once you know what you've gotten yourself into."

I'd been in the news game before. In grade school I'd published my own newspaper on a mimeograph and called it the *Brookline Variety* in honor of my mother's brother, Sam Shain, a writer at *Variety*, the show business newspaper. My paper sold for a nickel a copy. I took ads and subscriptions from family members as well as classmates.

The appeal for this line of work was furthered by Uncle Sam's example. He was a newspaperman, which to my mind meant going around all day hobnobbing with famous people. After all, he'd attended President Roosevelt's news conferences and used to go on about FDR. "Such shoulders. You never saw such powerful arms and shoulders. Why, you forget the man lived in a wheelchair."

•

I recalled all this as my mother and I climbed the attic stairs. We'd arrived a few minutes early and huddled in a corner while my grandfather finished his morning prayers, his face all but hidden in the folds of his shawl. He prayed with glowing intensity, bowing towards the east, his voice frequently rent by sobs and cries.

When he worshipped at the plain, ultraorthodox synagogue a few blocks away, where women were segregated from the men, he sped through the ritual as he was doing now, as if saying to others: look here, see for yourself. Am I not a wonder? I know the prayers backwards and forwards. My diction, my sense of rhythm, my pitch: are they not flawless? One couldn't but recognize his scholarship and uprightness of character.

When he finally gave my mother leave to speak, she said, "This is a day for rejoicing. Melvin is starting out on his new career in journalism."

And she told him about my new job.

The old man said, "What is this Associated Press?"

"It is a news organization, Papa, the largest in the world," she said in an even voice.

"But he'll never know the Talmud, propound God's laws. Why doesn't he seek the religious life?"

My grandfather's ambition had been to become a rabbi but he had been poor and had to provide for a growing family. He'd married young, at sixteen or seventeen; my grandmother had been fifteen, possibly younger. There were eleven children, three of whom died in infancy.

He looked to his sons to become rabbis in his stead, an obsession that caused both Joe and Sam to flee from home. The youngest, Samson, or Archie as everybody called him, could not escape his father's grasp.

But he had rebelled to a degree. Fresh out of Harvard, Archie enrolled in a course of rabbinical study under Rabbi Stephen S. Wise, leader of the reform movement in the United States and an avowed Zionist.

In his father's eyes the son was as good as an apostate.

Then came the day when Uncle Archie was to assume his first ministry at a synagogue in Sunnyside, Queens. There was concern about Zayde; but surely, the family thought, he would behave himself on so momentous an occasion.

But it was not to be.

My uncle had barely begun his homily when my grandfather rose up and denounced him and the congregation as blasphemers. Ignoring the pleas of congregation members, he preached his brand of hellfire-and-damnation Judaism, then stormed out of the temple of the Philistines.

"What can I say? Journalism is what the boy wants, Papa."

"He doesn't know the Torah. To this day he is ignorant of the Mishne and the Gemara. You have brought up only half a Jew." My mother, the blood draining from her face, replied in a quaking voice, "Please, Papa, don't start. Melvin is a good child. He loves Torah, the holidays, the Sabbath. You have been his teacher, his inspiration. He reveres you."

.

For most of my childhood, my grandparents lived apart. During this time Zayde was living with us in Brookline; my grandmother was keeping house for Sam and Archie in New York.

When both grandparents found themselves together, at Passover or Rosh Hashanah, for example, they rarely spoke. And when they did it was through surrogates, principally the grandchildren, in Yiddish and English.

My grandmother tended to belittle the "old goat," or so she spoke of him, calling attention to his low origins as the son of a water-carrier. She, on the other hand, was accustomed to reminding him of her descent from a distinguished family of rabbis.

Zayde, according to the family, was one of her father's prize students. My grandmother was a beauty, a prize herself, given to Jacob out of his mentor's regard for his brilliance. The story gets muddled. The best I can surmise is that my grandmother, Sarah, was young, no more than fifteen, and that my zayde, Jacob, a few years her senior, was head over heels in love with her. A father with many daughters, the rabbi may have concluded life would be less of a burden for him with one less mouth at home.

GRANDMOTHER (*addressing grandchild, in Yiddish and English*): Tell your zayde he's had enough wine. I don't want a shickah at my table. He can drink himself to death for all I care, but not at my table. He's behaving like the son of a water-carrier. (*By contrast she is a learned rabbi's daughter.*)

GRANDFATHER *(to grandchild)*: Tell the old woman I will no longer honor her as my wife. I can get myself a sixteen-year-old girl any day of the week.

GRANDMOTHER *(convulsed in laughter)*: Imagine, what young girl would have an old goat like him? But tell him to go, hurry, and good riddance!

Their estrangement dated from a time when Bubbe drove Zayde away; much as he implored, she refused to let him into her bed. According to my Aunt Rhoda, Bubbe panicked at the thought of his ever touching her again.

In his frustration, Zayde went around their house slamming doors at night, terrorizing the family, and keeping everyone awake.

•

My grandfather made his living as a mohel, one who performs circumcisions on Jewish male babies on the eighth day. Money was scarce; everybody had to pitch in. All year, the children brought home money from doing odd jobs. Summers my grandmother ran a boarding house and kosher restaurant at Nantasket Beach.

When a bris (circumcision) fell on a Sabbath, my devout grandfather, eschewing trolleys and automobiles, would set out on foot for his appointments.

On one such Saturday, as he passed through the Irish ghetto of South Boston, he was set upon by a band of children. "Evil spirit!" "Devil!" "Christ killer!" they cried out. A few hurled rocks. Fortunately, the stones landed harmlessly on the cobblestones. My grandfather gave chase and captured one of his tormentors, lifting the urchin off the ground and pressing his young, rosy face against Zayde's, an old, grizzled one.

As my grandfather told it, he wanted to enlighten the deluded youngster by posing a question that would show the child the error of his ways.

"Tell me," said my grandfather. "Do I really look 2,000 years old? Do I really look old enough to have killed your Christ?"

The child failed to recognize the fallacy; instead, he howled so uncontrollably my grandfather was obliged to put him down and continue on his journey.

If my grandmother was Zayde's principal antagonist, Rabbi Epstein, a distinguished spiritual leader in Brookline with a liberal bent, was Public Enemy Number One. It was especially galling for Zayde to discover my grandmother among the rabbi's admirers. Whenever she came to visit my family she made it a point to attend services at Epstein's fashionable synagogue, eschewing the one my grandfather favored, a foul-smelling house, maintained by a toothless couple and frequented by working-class Jews. When Rabbi Epstein published a book, arguing that the time had come for Jews in America to follow the civil divorce laws rather than the religious code of their ancestors, my grandfather dipped his pen in vitriol.

A tragic event close to home provided my grandfather with a cause. Rhoda, his youngest daughter, had just lost her husband to cancer. It was my grandfather's contention that she should be given in marriage to a brother-in-law in accordance with the ancient law.

Mother and daughter rebelled: the old law was for a desert people; this was America.

Besides, my grandmother said, what was Rhoda doing marrying a man who already had a wife; further, the brother-in-law in question was a flat-footed, dim-witted chicken farmer.

•

My grandmother's gift for ridicule fired him all the more.

So great was the store of his wrath that he spent year after year writing polemic after polemic denouncing his rival, Rabbi Epstein. In the end he put his rage in a book published at his own expense. Except for those few copies he bestowed on disciples (a tiny band of Hassidics who looked upon him as their leader) all seven hundred copies remained in the basement, unread.

•

"The way of a Jew is to swear allegiance to God, the one and only Father in Heaven," said my grandfather, striking his writing table.

"Yes, Papa."

"Let him go to the Associated Press, but let him love God above all else."

"Oh, yes, Papa."

"He must live an exemplary life, keep a kosher house, obey the commandments."

"We will, Papa. I swear it."

My grandfather placed his powerful hands on my head and bestowed his blessings. It was in the same sobbing, high-pitched voice in which he'd recited his morning prayers.

"Pray," my grandfather said.

"Pray," said my mother.

And I did. My prayer was that none of my friends would ever hear of this, ever.

•

My mother came to this country in the early years of the last century from Lithuania where Jewish people lived pent-up in ghettos and where she knew little of the outside world. Her worst nightmares, which continued into old age, were of the Russian police swooping down on her neighborhood on horseback, ransacking stalls, shops, and homes, and attacking innocent people.

She was eleven when she arrived here, the third of eleven immigrant children, speaking no English, knowing nothing at all about the strange, new land called America.

The openness of the new country won her confidence. She was eager to be accepted, taken as just another American. My mother may have been born on December 25 but no one really knew. When she came through Ellis Island she had no birth certificate, no document attesting to a date and place of birth. But the lack of it did not keep her from setting foot in America. People moved about with far fewer restrictions than they can today. Functionaries often could not spell, let alone pronounce, the strange names so, in many cases, they simplified life for everyone. (My paternal family's name was unreadable as well as unpronounceable. The immigration agent made it Levine, as in La-*veen*. Years later, my father and others in the family would change it to Lavine, as in La-*vine*, in an inheritance dispute, but that is a story for later.)

Once my mother and her family were settled in Boston, the young girl took note of how the world was magically transformed at Christmas with lights and ornaments and music. Children began life anew with presents of boots and coats, caps and sweater, skates and sleds, and all because of Christmas. But her family shunned the holiday. And so my mother faced a quandary. She wanted to be in step with her splendid new country, especially on that most wondrous of days. She resolved the problem by taking December 25 for her birthday. And we always celebrated it on that day. That's how she got around the taboo, got her presents and parties on this special day, but she never called it Christmas. Not even after my grandfather died in 1950. Not ever really, not in all my mother's remaining years, and she lived to be a ripe old eighty-seven, or thereabouts, when she died in 1982.

She put herself through law school, inspired by the progressives of the day. Theodore Roosevelt, Woodrow Wilson, Oliver Wendell Holmes, Benjamin Cardoza, Louis Brandeis were role models. She practiced criminal law for a time; later was a lawyer for a Federal loan agency, and still later, a minor figure in Massachusetts Republican politics.

The Boston Republican party of my mother's day was moderate, if not liberal. A Colin Powell would have been at home there. At an early age I learned from her example to show respect to people of different racial and cultural backgrounds. Nevertheless, and as much as she tried, she couldn't make me into a Republican. Franklin Roosevelt's charm and oratory had cast too strong a spell. Nonetheless, when I was about ten, she confessed, though I was never to breathe a word of it to my father, that she once voted for a Democrat, Roosevelt, over Alf Landon, the Republican, in 1936.

Although she liked Landon's stand on the issues, the Governor of Kansas was much too common for her tastes. Roosevelt was still too slick for her but, at least, she whispered, he was an aristocrat.

She wanted me to be a lawyer. She would open doors, she said, and introduce me to all the right people; a brilliant career was all but assured. But when I began writing for the University of Maine paper and the *Boston Jewish Advocate* she capitulated and made the rounds of Boston newspaper offices with samples of my work. "Does he have talent? Does my son have a future in this line of endeavor? I want him to follow me into the law but he is determined to follow your example," she importuned one editor after another. At length she reported, "Your peers of the Fourth Estate are unanimous in their opinion that you indeed have a future in journalism. My darling son, I am so terribly proud of you. Don't be angry with me, please! In no way have I embarrassed you. On the contrary these fine gentlemen, each and everyone, are looking forward to making your acquaintance in the near future. When you are a parent you will know how much your child's happiness means to you and you will do no less for them!"

∙

Of all my possible role models, my Boston-born father was dead last. No one in the family ever held him up as an anything exemplary. No one seriously respected him. He was a kid at heart. He did things that one might put up with in a teenager but not in a man past forty with a wife and family. He drank, he palled around with lowlife, got into brawls, was unfaithful, and all the rest.

A flooring contractor and lumber salesman, he was a rough-and-tumble man and, unlike my mother, did not believe in meddling with my choice of a career. "Melvin," he said, "should do what he wants, whatever it is that makes him happy."

He was a man of, by, and for business. A fastidious dresser, even during hard times, he was what was then known as a "lady's man." His time was the First World War. A first sergeant wounded three times, awarded the Croix de Guerre and the Silver Star Medal for gallantry in France, he lived in the glories of the past. He was driven by a wanderlust that led him out on the road, beating the bushes for flooring contracts, for lumber sales. He loved the road. In town, he was an habitué of the YMCA on Massachusetts Avenue. The eternal boy, he defeated men half his age at handball; he was past forty when he won a New England championship.

In the depths of the Great Depression he made a decent living, in good part by currying favor with the politicians who controlled the money for public works. We lived in the two upper floors of a house we owned at 85 Beals Street in Brookline. The McMunns, an Irish family, occupied the first floor. The house next door, at 83, was to become a national monument as the birthplace of John F. Kennedy. By the time we'd moved in, the four-year-old future president and his family had moved to a fancier part of town.

The important Kennedy then was Joe, the father, who was making a controversial name and fortune as a banker, broker, and speculator, chairman of the Security and Exchange Commission and ambassador to England.

Visitors are surprised to find that our 35th president, born May 29, 1917, lived his first few years in a modest, three-story house on a leafy residential street. People think of the Kennedys as fabulously rich and so they became, but in his Beals Street days Joe Kennedy was not yet the magnate he was to become.

"Often people will blow right by the house, expecting to see a mansion or castle," the park ranger tells visitors.

Rose Kennedy, the president's mother, bought back the house in 1966, and gave it to the country after restoring it to its 1917 state. (She died in 1995 at 104.)

I've been to the Kennedy house in recent years, but I must confess, I felt a little sad to find it remade into a museum attraction. The first family that I remember living there were the Myersons, who made their money manufacturing false teeth – which I thought was very funny until my father said it was a very profitable business and that the laugh was on everybody else.

I first learned of such elitist games as golf and tennis from seeing the two Myerson boys running down their front steps with tennis rackets and golf clubs. Eventually, like the Kennedys, the family that made dentals moved on to a more affluent address.

The new owners at 83 were an older couple and their granddaughter, Audrey, who had lost her parents in a car crash. When I first knew her, she was a little girl of whom I took no notice. But I looked again when we both were in our teens and I began taking her more seriously. She introduced me to jazz and Fats Waller. I still remember the metronome beating the time as she practiced dutifully on the piano.

From her bedroom window, my mother spied Audrey and me one night exploring each other's anatomy on Audrey's front porch hammock.

"I can see what you're doing, Melvin. Stop right now," she said and ordered me home.

I fancied myself in love with Audrey. When I went away to the army, she sent me an extravagantly glamorous photo of herself, which I prominently displayed on my locker, to the envy of the other fellows in the barracks.

But Audrey and I never really clicked romantically, though we remained pen pals. By the time I came home, she was engaged to a young student of pharmacy. I guess they eventually got married but I don't really know.

I have only been back one since 83 was designated a national monument and made to look as it did on the day JFK was born. I looked around. It was all wrong, too Catholic. It was as if the Jewishness had been washed away in Oxydol. When Audrey and her grandparents lived there, there were no gate leg tables, ornamental vases, or fancy ancestral glass and porcelain and silver flatware. Instead of mantel vases there had been menorahs and brassy Passover plates. Those toothy Celts peering from wall pictures were alien, hostile. And what was this? JFK's christening dress handmade by the Franciscan Missionaries of Mary in East Boston. Sacrilege! I stayed only a few minutes. But I left with a postcard of the Kennedy house to always remind me of Audrey and Fats Waller.

·

In February of 1936, my brother Irvin and I were gravely ill. Irvin, eleven and three years older, succumbed in a few days to spinal meningitis for which there was then no miracle drug. I was stricken with a streptococcus infection for which there was a new sulfur drug.

When my brother's body was taken from the house, my father buried his head in my lap and sobbed, "Sonny, don't you die, too. Please, don't you die, too." Dr. Harris, an austere figure, laid his cold hands on my feverish forehead and pronounced, "I don't give this boy a plug nickel's chances." In defiance I rallied and lived.

My parents drew apart that year and my father began spending more and more nights away from home. And then he would be gone for whole days at a time. And then he was gone for good. My mother shut herself up in an upstairs room mourning for her oldest son.

I spent the better part of that year at my grandmother's where she was keeping house for my Uncle Joe, a bachelor doctor, in Stamford, Connecticut. We grew close, a bond that would only end with her death many years later.

When I came home, my mother cast uncle Harry, my wayward father's older brother, as a surrogate father. He relished the role and shook his meaty head in sorrowful wonder at how far my father had strayed. "Even the best of families have their black sheep," he said. "Alas, your own poor Dad is the prodigal son in this family."

It was Harry I was to listen to, go to with my questions, and look to for guidance, Harry being a successful man of affairs, an executive with Equitable Life, a family man with a reputation for probity and wisdom.

At Thanksgiving and Christmas he took a bully's pleasure in conducting inquisitions of the nephews gathered round his wife's copious table. To the general glee of family members we were grilled on our progress in school. (Uncle Harry took pride in the fact that he'd never read a novel; he relied on periodicals, particularly *Life* magazine, for information of the contemporary world.)

Amid such a gallery of elders I searched for role models.

These were the possibilities in order of seniority:

FATHER'S SIDE
Uncle Harry. As noted.
My father. As noted.
Uncle Percy. Cigar-smoking, silky talking merchant.
Uncle Bill. Narrow-minded do-gooder.

MOTHER'S SIDE
My grandfather. As noted.
Uncle Sam, of the estimable periodical *Variety*. As noted.
Uncle Joe. Dyspeptic, misanthropic pediatrician.
Uncle Archie. Sweet rabbi but feckless.

•

To be sure my mother's brother Sam, glamorous Sam with his newspaper bylines, Sam, a friend of famous people, was a source of inspiration but in those difficult, adolescent years I had a need for towering examples.

I discovered the martyred Lincoln who, like me, was well over six feet, plain of face, ungainly in manner. In the sixth grade, I committed to memory a milky essay of twenty thousand or so words about the Great Emancipator ("The Perfect Tribute"). The recitation so amazed my teachers that they marched me before numerous classes for repeat performances.

And I rallied to President Roosevelt. He'd triumphed over infantile paralysis (as I would triumph over Uncle Harry) and filled my

Republican-loving father's family with fear and foreboding. His voice so thrilled me that I began imitating it, so well in fact that I caused my parents, to say nothing of my father's family, great distress. Just imagine the tyranny of a teenage boy blasting forth in orotund tones à la FDR from the sanctuary of a toilet seat!

My maternal grandmother, however, took a keen delight in these fulminations (and spoke up in my defense whenever she visited) as both she and I were unreconstructed New Dealers.

The Army, the Professor, and the Leggy Blonde

At eighteen, with high school and a semester of college behind me, I was anxious lest I not be accepted into the Army. The prospect of rejection, being branded 4-F, was an inglorious destiny for a youth who sought adventure and acceptance as a regular guy.

Over my protests, my mother had asked the doctors for letters describing the state of my health. On the day I was to appear for my physical, she entrusted me with documents attesting to asthma and chronic bronchitis, and susceptibility to colds, sore throats, and multiple allergies. Note was also taken of hernia operations when I was a few months old and at eleven years. When I got a few block from my house, I hesitated, then reached inside my coat and tossed the letters into a trashcan.

I was sent to Fort Knox, Kentucky, for eight weeks of basic training in the field artillery. Afterwards I was asked what theatre I wished to serve in. The options were Europe and Japan. Having heard that the Army never gave you what you asked for, I opted for occupation duty in Japan, thinking this was a sure-fire ticket to Europe. But when the orders were cut I found out that I would be remaining stateside. Instead of romantic Europe or exotic Asia I was being shipped to Fort Lewis in dullish Tacoma. My training as an artilleryman was wasted and I was assigned to a medical battalion. Though I put my mind to it, I never could get the hang of making a good tourniquet. Mainly, I remembered that a medic's first duty was to treat the wounded for shock. No matter how grievously crippled, the poor fellow was to be assured that he was going to be all right.

The U.S. was at peace during the time I served, 1946–47. Army life was a lark, a summer camp, a paid vacation.

My boon companion was a fellow New Englander, Paul Christopher Giblin, a laughing shoe salesman from Worcester, Massachusetts. He often made more of our weekends into town than the facts warranted, as when he spread the fable that I'd flattened a first lieutenant at a public dance. The way Paul put it, horselaugh and all, I was romancing the best-looking girl in the room when the officer, a strapping paratrooper, laid claim to the girl. Well, to hear Paul tell it, I knocked the poor sap on his keister. The truth of the matter is that when the lieutenant tried to break in, I drew on courage contained in a couple of beers and told him to get lost. End of story.

Paul was a prankster, pure and simple. But his buffoonery rubbed some of the men wrong. "Don't mess with me," he warned, "or you'll have my buddy, Mel, to contend with." Unbeknownst to me, he retailed the following fiction:

In civilian life, Mel, his great buddy, was an up-and-coming boxer, albeit an amateur, but there was serious talk of his turning pro after he left the army. The guys scoffed. Paul advised them to observe when I soaped in the shower. Note the wrists, "powerful wrists, lightening reaction." "Mark my words, you'll hear plenty about him one of these days." At six feet four and 190 it's conceivable I could have been mistaken for a contender. In the previous year I'd played football and shot the put at college and gone through a couple of months of rigorous basic training. But, Giblin's fable notwithstanding, I shunned confrontation.

When Giblin's shocking story caught up with me, he greeted my alarm with that infectious horselaugh of his.

"What's the harm?" he said.

For the moment I conceded I could see none, but I had not reckoned with the commanding general of the Second Infantry Division ("Second to None").

In the general's opinion the troops were drifting into purposelessness nine months after Hiroshima and needed firing up. With the end in mind of boosting morale, he announced the commencement of a boxing tournament. In his directive, the general said he knew there was great ring talent in the ranks and ordered his commanders to recruit it. A day or two later I got word to report to the company commander.

Captain Woods looked up from his desk. "No need playing coy," he said. He'd heard the scuttlebutt. He was relieving me of KP, guard duty, field exercises, even reveille, so I could get back in shape. All I had to do was say the word. "How's that, champ?" he said. Until that moment Captain Woods had been a remote figure, a martinet with a trim moustache. Now he was going to be running my life. I was tempted to spill the beans but said I'd give the matter serious thought.

"By all means," said Captain Woods. He'd taken it better than I expected.

•

I went around like a condemned man, doomed. Either I had to climb into the ring and put my life in jeopardy or come clean and risk disgrace. But then I came upon a posted notice advertising for an experienced reporter on the division newspaper, the *Spearhead*. As the general's imperious personality led him to promote a boxing tournament, so his vanity led him to publish a newspaper. Lying shamelessly to the editor, a Chicago journalist, I claimed to have covered all sorts of momentous events for the Associated Press in Boston: shootings, murder trials, political scandals, and hurricanes. In fact, I had been a mere high school boy, running copy afternoons and weekends, and never left the newsroom save for errands after cigarettes or beer and sandwiches. So great was my panic, though, that I'd have sworn to having won a Pulitzer.

But I talked myself into the job and wound up writing up the tournament from ringside on a portable typewriter. In the end a promising brawler from Brockton, Massachusetts, who'd damaged his right in a previous match, won the heavyweight title with only the use of a left hand. Often have I recalled that night when Rocky Marciano and his opponent traded murderous blow after blow, thinking there but for the grace of God and journalism.

•

Today one can hardly pick up a newspaper without reading stories of young people who have been sexually assaulted by respected clergy, pedagogues, and other community role models. But in those *Spearhead* days, around 1950, such crimes rarely, if ever, were broadcast. To be sure, there was the occasional rumor but, as a rule, scandals of this nature were hushed up. Lawyers drew up confidentiality agreements as money changed hands to compensate the victims.

Matters like these were far from my mind when, once my army time was up, I returned to the University of Maine at Orono and resumed my studies. Although journalism was my calling, I enrolled in a creative writing course with the idea that a semester or two of fiction would make me a better writer and help my career in journalism. Both the professor, Walter Whitney, and the course were widely popular, and I gained admission after appealing repeatedly and submitting samples of my work. At this stage of my life I thought I was pretty sophisticated and knew just about everything there was to know about people. I could see that the professor already was sympathetic towards me. I simply had to keep plugging away and he would be impressed with my work.

Walter was reputed to have been an editor for the *New Yorker* but, in fact, he had been a reader at the magazine after earning a master's in English at Harvard. He had never said he had done anything important at the magazine but people were always conferring significance to his *New Yorker* years. In an isolated, rural college like the University of Maine, it was not unusual for people to make something of a modest employment at a glamorous place.

Walter liked my stuff. He wrote on an early paper, "How does someone so young gain so much knowledge of life?" He urged me to send the story to the *New Yorker* at once. Such chutzpah produced my first rejection slip. We became friendly. I often was invited to his house where I met local artists, writers and other professors.

At the start of my last semester, Walter told me he was planning to take a sabbatical at the end of the term. His plan was to drive to California where old friends owned a cabin in Ventura, which they were offering him rent-free as a refuge, a place to write. Since I would be graduating at the same time, he asked if I would be interested in going along, sharing expenses and the cabin with him. He had a play he wanted to write. Surely I had things of my own in mind.

To family and friends, my mother said, "Mel's professor is taking him to California where Mel is going to write his book. Can you imagine? What a compliment the professor is paying my son!" She paid no attention when I said that I was paying my own way, that he wanted company, and would be busy with work of his own.

•

Soon after graduation Walter drove down to Boston in his new 1950 Studebaker. He chortled that the car gave very good mileage, twenty-six miles to the gallon. After a sumptuous meal prepared by my mother, with help from aunts Annie and Rhoda, I saw him back to his hotel. "Come in the room," he insisted. He wanted to show me things he'd bought for the California idyll. As he laid out a colorful robe on the bed, he said, "Exquisite, don't you think?" He invited me to run my hand along the silky garment. As I did so I felt Walter's hand on my knee. I look up and said something like, "What the hell are you up to?" He immediately removed his hand, but purred like a beast in passion.

I'd heard rumors about Walter but didn't take them seriously. He was my literary mentor and good friend. He'd never pulled a stunt like this before. Later, when I was back at my mother's apartment, I couldn't get to sleep, debating whether I should make the trip at all. Maybe I should stay home. But where was home now? Surely not in the folds of a family I'd been running away from since graduating high school. I was hot to break free in California. But how could I think of living in a cabin on a beach with someone I feared, someone who, as I now felt, may have encouraged me to think I could write serious fiction when his purpose was to lure me into what I then thought would be a perverted relationship?

We took off in the morning for Washington, neither of us making reference to the incident in Walter's room. But we were no longer the friends we had been for a year. The kidding and intimacy were gone.

In Washington, we were the overnight guests of a fashionable couple, both about fifty, Walter's age. The husband was a writer. He had known Walter when they were undergraduates at Bowdoin, or perhaps at Harvard or maybe the New *Yorker*. Anyway, now he wrote speeches for Vannevar Bush, president of the Carnegie Institution, an eminent figure who'd made his name as developer of the first analog computer, and who, during the war, served President Roosevelt as a scientific adviser. The pair heartily castigated the current occupant of the White House, Harry Truman, thinking it tragic that so ordinary a person now inhabited that seat of power.

The hostess, handing me a cocktail, steered the conversation. She'd been drinking rather a lot. She sat down with her cocktail in hand. "May I ask Walter's friend a personal question?" she smiled. "Something's bothered me and perhaps I can ask him? Perhaps he knows the answer." I looked up at the smartly groomed matron. She continued, this time addressing me. "I've never felt comfortable in the company of Jews. I must say I do not feel comfortable sitting here with you. Is this because we know so few Jews? I don't believe we have any Jewish friends. This may be due to my lack of knowledge of Jews. Is there something about Jews I should know? Something you can tell me? Have you ever been told this by other people? I simply have to ask."

Walter and his old friend chided her, made light of her questions, and we went into dinner. Next day I suffered a bad attack of asthma; fortunately I'd packed plenty of adrenalin and got through the crisis.

Inasmuch as we were traveling in winter, we followed a southern route all the way across the country. In eastern Tennessee the rain came down so hard it was difficult to keep track of the road. By mid-afternoon we began looking for a place to spend the night. Motel after motel was full. Eventually, we spotted a vacancy but the place looked so forbidding that we kept on going. We drove on for several more miles in the face of terrific winds, and then decided to turn back. Walter dashed inside the motel with the vacancy sign. He came out looking miserable. "One room," he reported through the crack in the window. "And one bed." He'd asked for another bed, a cot, and a sofa. There was only the single bed. Without other options, we took the room.

That night in the dark I lay awake, my body coiled, prepared to strike if Walter should try something funny. Once or twice an arm or leg made contact. I stirred. "For heaven's sake, relax. I'm not going to touch you," Walter said dryly. The next morning, with the wretched night over, we found to our relief that the storm had passed.

Early on Walter had talked about his intention of going into California through the desert and stopping at a mining camp where he was meeting someone from South Africa. The individual was a body builder, in fact a Mr. South Africa. He wasn't the current Mr. South Africa, but had won the title several years before, and had competed for the Mr. Universe title. Presently, he was working in a gypsum mine. Walter hadn't ever met him, in fact did not know him, but he was the person we were driving out of our way to see, interrupting our journey; the camp at Trona, on the western edge of Death Valley National Monument, was a good many miles from Ventura.

The object of Walter's desire was a strapping young fellow with a stubble of blond beard on a red face. He had just driven back to Trona from Seattle to keep the appointment. When we sat down for lunch in the company mess it was obvious, though they spoke guardedly, that the details of the tryst had been worked out through third parties, that Walter had chosen the South African from pictures, and that the money had already changed hands. Mr. South Africa was weary from his trip but promised Walter he was up to fulfilling his part of the bargain. But I presented a complication. What role did I play in the arrangements? he asked. Walter shook his head, saying something like, "Oh no, he has nothing to do with any of this." But my presence raised a question about where the assignation could take place. They could not go to where Mr. South Africa lived, in closely watched company quarters. Walter was quick to say they could not go to the motel room either, which Walter and I were sharing. Mr. South Africa snickered when the feasible location came down to the back seat of Walter's Studebaker. Walter's woeful eyes confirmed that they had no other choice. Late that night Walter answered a knock on the door, slipped out of his bed, and went outside to meet Mr. South Africa. I could hear them getting into the Studebaker. It was a very warm night, and they must have rolled down the windows for I also could hear Walter's heartbreaking cries.

•

In Ventura the clatter of two portables filled the cabin. Walter worked on a comedy that he'd had in mind for years about two families who have a falling out. He succeeded in getting them to stop talking to one another by the end of act 1 but was having a difficult time getting them back together in act 3. He kept to a writing schedule of three hours, nine to noon, five days a week which, he found, was the optimum time for creative work. I clung to the notion that the longer one worked, the better. As my father liked to say, "What you put in is what you'll get out." Nonetheless I had only a vague notion of what I was trying to say.

One afternoon, walking the long, flat beach I ran into a neighbor, a bearish Oklahoman named Jim. He was full of questions. What brought Walter and me to Ventura? What kind of work did we do? How long had we known one another? People wondered about us. Nothing would do until I'd met his wife, teenage daughter, sister-in-law, and aunt, all living in a ruined dwelling nearby, and promised to go honky-tonking with them.

Walter grimaced when he learned what lay in store. "You can count me out," he said.

But I urged him to reconsider. "They're neighbors. We have to be diplomatic."

A few nights later Walter and I and the neighbors crammed into Jim's jalopy for the ride into town. Walter, a debonair type she had never encountered before, fascinated Jim's sixty-year old aunt. A countrywoman of small stature, she came out for the evening heavily made up in a flashy dress with a low neckline, which called attention to her melon-sized breasts. Walter endured her flirtations, even getting off his high horse to dance a foxtrot with her. Of course, when he could catch my eye he glared with unconcealed fury. On the way home everyone sang, even poor Walter.

•

Neighbors snooped on us. The Oklahomans pestered us to go honky-tonking with them again. Walter and I quarreled. In the end, we closed up the cabin and went into San Francisco where we amiably parted company. Walter moved in with an artist friend on Green Street and I found a room on Columbus Avenue in North Beach.

•

To be sure the Beats, led by Jack Kerouac, poet and novelist, with their vehement rejection of middle-class life and values would not be heard from until later in the decade with Allen Ginsberg's *Howl*, Kerouac's *On the Road*, William Burrough's *Naked Lunch*, and the ferment nurtured by Lawrence Ferlinghetti's City Lights Bookstore.

But, in 1950–51 before the Beats, San Francisco was already a city of literary distinction identified with writers like Mark Twain, Bret Harte, Ambrose Bierce, Kenneth Patchen, William Saroyan, and others. Enough of their fame was in the air to lure aspiring writers to town and there were the crusading newspaper, the *Chronicle*, and the great columnist, Herb Caen. Before long, however, I found living in a cold room and patronizing cheap places for meals and company a wretched existence. Asthma laid me low. Walter's painter friend brought me to his doctor at 450 Sutter Street. Dr. Seymour Farber was a lanky fellow, in his late thirties. As I was led into his examining room, gasping desperately for air, he stood a few feet away and said sharply, "Stop it! Cut it out!" I did, and immediately began breathing normally.

·

I should point out that I was free to roam the country that year thanks to a $1,000 gift from my father's younger brother, Bill, co-owner with another brother of a prospering appliance store. The money, to be used for education or travel, came in monthly checks of $100. Uncle Bill made a similar gift to another nephew who, like me, was moving into the world in straitened circumstances.

My father was now living with a new wife in Los Angeles. He suggested my making a move down there. The warmer weather would be easier on my health, and he would help me find an affordable hotel where I could go on with my writing.

·

I did my drinking at a Los Angeles bar a door or two from my hotel on Alvarado Street next to MacArthur Park. The bartender was a convivial Irishman whom everyone knew as Les. Les's place became my classroom. Here I took for my models the flotsam of society, the drifters, people who had no real homes, people who were on the lam from creditors, spouses, and the law. When I mentioned my strategy to one of the patrons, a stout, fiftiesh whore, she replied, "You're still wet behind the ears. You have to do a heap of living before I'd spend a red cent on any book of yours."

I found her memorable.

One of her regulars was a famous sculptor whom she visited once a week at his estate. The assignations followed a pattern. First, she would sit down to a fancy lunch on the terrace with the artist and his mother. Second, after coffee, the mother would rise up, kiss her son on the cheek, bid the whore a warm farewell, and retire inside her mansion. Then the whore and her client would rise up from the table and repair to the latter's studio, a hut on the grounds. After they undressed, the artist led the whore to a padded covering on the floor. He would lie in a supine position. She squatted over him; her knees bent, the weight resting on the balls of her feet, she'd pee directly into his mouth. Less than half an hour later, she was back on the freeway, bound for Alvarado Street.

•

Small-town merchants, artisans, clerks, waitresses, and pensioners lived in my hotel. The one notorious character was Jake, the bellman. On learning that I was a literary person, Jake sought my expertise in the composition of a few urgent letters. Inasmuch as he was the street's principal pimp and loan shark, I thought it prudent to do it gratis, and refused his money. But when he proposed sending a beautiful girl to my room as compensation, I yielded.

She was indeed lovely, with lustrous black hair, flawless, milky skin, and a dainty face. When she got ready to leave she asked for money. I handed her ten dollars.

Jake was livid when I mentioned it. "The bitch," he said. "She already got her cut. She got no business putting the bite on you. I owed you. Now she owes both of us."

"I don't want to get her in trouble," I said. But Jake shook his head crossly. She would hear from him.

A day or so later, the beautiful girl returned to my door. "I want to make it up to you," she said shyly, slipping into the room.

•

In the neighborhood, it seemed almost everyone gambled and played the numbers. My friend, Jake, operated a numbers game along with other rackets. The horses caused the most excitement. Eddie Rodriguez, who ran a chili joint at the corner, was the most unforgettable horseplayer I've ever known. He was a benign fellow and I took a liking to him. Eddie handicapped the races daily, keeping up with the Racing Form, and tuning in on the radio. He was in the dumps or on cloud nine, depending on how his nags fared. Yet, as I was to learn, he never bet on any of the races. He couldn't. The bookmakers wouldn't take his money until he'd paid off a large debt that he'd run up from races past. True, the amount of money he claimed he'd "won" or "lost" was fiction. But there was no mistaking his moods. Money may not have been at stake, but he was incapable of faking his joy or despair. Eddie lived through every race as if, in truth, he had real money riding on the nose.

•

I met a leggy blonde from St. Louis at Les's. We hit it off from the start and I guess you could say she became my girlfriend. I knew what business she was in, but I tried to keep an open mind. Then one day she needed a place to leave things, to get away from her madam, a place nobody knew about. She never stayed for long and never used my room for business. I never knew where she lived or if she had a permanent address, and never asked.

The problem for me was that she was always in a hurry. There was little time for lovemaking but she was always promising. She would find time tomorrow or next week, she'd say. But when tomorrow or next week arrived she'd beg off yet again.

One fine day, however, she'd successfully hid an hour or two away from madam, only to find me in a dysfunctional state when she stepped across the threshold. Wasn't I glad to see her?

"Of course, but ..."

"But what?"

"The president," I said. "President Truman is speaking on the radio." She looked confused.

"North Korea has invaded South Korea, and we may be going in to drive them out. Who knows, if China gets into it, this could be the beginning of World War Three."

As earth-rattling as the news was to the world at large, she took it personally. It was if I were rejecting her.

But I had no intention of neglecting her, I said. I could listen to Truman and pay attention to her, too. "But, as a journalist, I have to know what's going on in the world."

She waited impatiently while I fiddled with the radio.

"Hold on," I said, listening carefully. "Truman's ordered the Air

Force and Navy to Korea. He's approved military action by the United States against North Korea."

While Truman discussed the crisis I gave half my attention to the girl and half to the president. At times I was obliged to interrupt our tryst in order to catch a word from the radio. My partner expressed dismay, but resigned herself. Truman couldn't go on forever and, mercifully, he didn't.

•

My allowance was running out, and I had to think about the future. Jake Saks offered to speak to the hotel manager. Maybe I could catch on as the night clerk. But I discouraged him. I'd not yet heard of Nathanael West, a Jewish compatriot, who took employment in a seedy hotel in the 1930s as a way to gain knowledge for his acclaimed books. My idea then of a role model was Hemingway, who'd served an adventurous apprenticeship as a newspaperman before going on to literary glory.

I wrote Professor Jordan at the University of Maine. In his reply, he noted there was the prospect of a job on a weekly in Sanford, Maine. If I was interested – the pay was modest but the experience valuable – he advised me to act quickly. I kept the Maine job to myself for a long time before telling my beautiful call girl.

I knew she cared for me but I thought the room was what mattered most to her. She'd really be sore about losing the room. I kept putting off telling her my news until we met for dinner in Les's the night before I took off for Boston.

I blurted it out. "I have to go back East for a job interview," I said. "It's on a paper, a weekly, but it's a start. It's an opportunity. I'll keep you posted, care of Les. Who knows? It may not work out."

"When are you leaving?"

"In the morning."

"What time in the morning?"

"First thing, first plane."

"You think you're going, and that's the end of us?"

"Whoa. What do you mean?"

"You're not going to run out on me."

"What are you talking about?"

"So that's it, is it? You're going to walk out on me – just like that, get on a plane and fly away, scot-free, clear across the country? Well, you have another thing coming. I've got friends. They'll take care of you. You'll never leave town."

"Now don't act like this. Be reasonable." She was making a scene. "People are staring."

"Let them. You're not walking out on me."

I spent a restless night, fearful of her goons breaking down the door, and paced, chiding myself for my folly in getting involved with a woman from the demimonde. It was still dark when the phone rang. It was she.

"I've called to apologize," she said. "I'm ashamed at the way I behaved. I wish you a good trip, and good luck."

"I was going to tell you sooner," I said. "But, quite frankly, I didn't think you'd care. It never occurred to me. I never thought I'd feel like this, too, so lousy leaving you and L.A. I've really been happy here."

"That's the way it goes sometimes, kid."

Kid? I said to myself. She was twenty-eight or twenty-nine but I'd just turned twenty-three. "I was afraid you'd do something terrible to yourself."

"Not on your life. I'm OK."

"I'll be back. I'm only going for a little while. We'll keep in touch through Les. Whatever happens back east, I'll be back before you know it."

Red and the Tribune

I got to the *Tribune* up in Maine in the fall of 1950 by way of my journalism professor to whom I'd written about job prospects. He'd said that the weekly in Sanford would prove "short on money but long on experience." The remark, he hastened to add, was not his but came straight from the publisher.

"I'm not making any claims for the *Tribune*, one way or the other," he wrote. "Other than that it strikes me that Sanford is a place where you can get your start."

It was a job I needed badly after graduating from the University of Maine. I'd spent a footloose spring and summer in California cavorting with pimps, prostitutes, gamblers, and assorted underworld characters, believing I was soaking up dynamite material for a big book. But when I sat down to write, nothing came of it.

I was coming home to journalism, my true love, and ready to scale the barricades armed with a philosophy I'd rehearsed before a kindly soul I'd met years earlier at the *Boston American*, a Hearst rag of all places. Win Brooks was the managing editor but he put me at ease. I'd known him since I began making the rounds of papers as a teenager, when he'd let me run on about dreams of a conquering career. Now, when I dropped in on him before boarding the train for Maine, he asked, "Why the dickens do you want to get into a business like this?" he asked. He pointed out there were a lot of bad things about journalism, and very few good: the hours were long, the pay miserable, and proprietors a highly manipulative, bloodsucking lot.

I was taking no notice of this side of the news business, the low pay, the broken careers, the reactionary publishers, the power of advertisers; none of this entered my picture of the future. Appraising the busy street below from his office window, I replied, "The thing that draws me to journalism is the opportunity to see how a community ticks, and trying to foster the cause of democracy; getting inside institutions and the lives of people, coming to grips, if you will, with the human comedy."

Win, puffing on a cigarette, said, "Why don't you marry a rich Jewish girl? If I were you that's what I'd do, and then you could do whatever you damn please."

"I got to be in love," I said.

He shrugged. There was no cure for the likes of me.

•

Sanford, less than an hour's drive from Portland, was a New England mill town famous for its Palm Beach suits. Half Yankee, half French-Canadian and with a handful of Italian, Jewish, and Greek families, it was typical of many factory towns in the region in the early 1950s.

The *Tribune* office was down on Water Street, around the corner from Main. It was an unprepossessing building that could have sheltered any one of a score of enterprises. However, the clutter, the dilapidated furnishings, the wretched quarters … all this should have given me pause. But as I was making my way up the well-worn staircase to the newsroom all I could think of was that I was finally answering my life's calling. Indeed, I regarded my $27 a week salary as a windfall.

In an office at the top of the stairs and leaning back in his chair, arms folded across his chest, was a man past fifty with a mop of hair that had once been red but was now almost entirely white.

Norman "Red" McCann, the editor, said, "Any experience?"

"Not really."

"Not really? What in God's green earth is that supposed to mean?"

"Well, I wrote for the college paper. And I contributed a column entitled 'Up in Maine' to the *Boston Jewish Advocate*."

"Do you know anything about baseball?"

"Oh, sure. I'm a Red Sox fan."

"Football? Basketball?"

"Certainly."

"Can you score a game?"

"I can score a baseball game."

"No shit?"

"Absolutely."

"If my legs were willing I'd come over there right now and kiss your goddamn ass."

Red had had polio as a kid and it left him a cripple. But there was nothing wrong, he said, with his commitment to the First Amendment. He'd put his passion for justice and fair play up against that of any other editor in the land.

"Let me tell you," he said. "The press is the last outpost in a republic. Once the bastards get control of the government, once they get the courts, there's nothing left but the press. Believe me, boy, we're democracy's last line of defense. Are you ready to roll up your sleeves and go to work?"

Irish on one side, French-Canadian on the other, he was – for the most part – the tempestuous Irishman when he swung into action on behalf of journalistic principle. Be it with a clergyman, a shopkeeper, a selectman, crank or agitator, he more than held his own, giving better than he got by sticking to his principles.

People would troop up to the newsroom looking for some favor or special consideration. Red squared their requests with his notions of honesty and fair play, and if they squared, the petitioners went away happy. If not, they left empty-handed.

He was denounced regularly, sometimes on the phone and sometimes in person. On occasion, after work, I'd sit with him in his car on Main Street. People would come up, some to praise, some to give him hell. Once a Catholic parent came up to him and denounced Red for devoting more space in the *Tribune* to Sanford High than Saint Ignatius. In his eyes, Red was anti-Catholic. Red laughed. How could he be anti-Catholic when he was the offspring of a French Catholic mother and an Irish Catholic father? He was, however, a staunch supporter of public school education and the separation of church and state. And he bitterly complained against the French-speaking faculty for treating English as a second language and poorly equipping their students, who came from French-speaking homes, to compete in the outside world. Red relished the beefs. He could yell as loud as any of his critics and out-point them all on the merits.

He was a larger-than-life figure to me, although I had to be around him awhile before realizing how smart he was. His face was red and fat like a drunkard's, though he didn't drink, and he wore knockabout garments and was always picking his teeth. In fact he had been first in his class at Bates and could have gone on to something more remunerative than journalism, but newspapering was in his blood and I believe that's all he ever wanted to do.

In sum, Red was a lightning rod for controversy, and consequently had more than his share of enemies.

This was OK with him.

"You don't go into this racket to be loved. You're in it to afflict the comfortable, and see that the little fellow doesn't always get screwed." First Amendment issues, the people's right to know, and so on, these matters were not just so much rhetoric to Red. Why, this is what a newspaper was all about, he'd say, and this was the real compensation in running the *Tribune*. No one in his right mind went into journalism for the money.

Soon after I hit Sanford, the local proprietors sold the *Tribune* to a Boston firm that had many business interests in addition to newspapers. When the takeover took place the new owners said they were not contemplating any changes, that everyone's job was safe, that we were all considered essential to the company's future.

•

This was how matters stood one blazing morning in August when I looked up to find Red on the phone furiously taking notes. I was typing out a late item from Rotary. Isabel O'Connell was filling up her Woman's Page.

When he hung up, Red's face was flushed with excitement.

"Guess who was in the hoosegow Sunday night for drunken driving?" Isabel made a few suggestions.

I took a stab.

"None of the above," cried Red. "Fred Nutter. Now can you beat that?"

"Arrested? Fred Nutter?" Isabel, a Sanford native, was breathless.

"Booked 'n' everything," said Red shaking his head.

Fred Nutter was the prodigal son of the family that operated the mills, Sanford's principal employer. He was a nuisance after a few drinks but the cops always saw to it that he got home safely.

"It had to be the new cop," I said.

Red nodded.

The arresting officer was a rookie, a young man from Tennessee who'd married a local girl and just moved to Sanford. "The sonofabitch didn't know any better," said Red.

"Who's that who called, the chief?" I asked.

He nodded. "But I can't start making exceptions now," Red said, mopping his brow beaded in perspiration.

The next day, Tuesday, we got wind from Roger Wilcox, the young publisher, that the Nutter family was appealing to the owners in Boston to kill the story. They were afraid of shareholders hearing of the boy's problems, an embarrassment that could adversely affect the value of the stock.

Red picked his teeth.

"We're ready for them," he said at length.

And he was. When he got the call he was beautiful. He looked over to me a few times and winked. He lectured his caller (a company lawyer) on the glorious history of the *Tribune*, how it reported the news fairly and fully, how it enjoyed the regard of fair-minded people in Sanford and the journalistic community at large. With every story the *Tribune*'s credibility was at stake and that had to count with proprietors as priority number one.

And, he went on, he was personally fond of young Nutter – he expected he'd straighten out one day and be a credit to the town – but as editor of the *Tribune* Red plainly had no choice; he was obligated professionally, ethically, in every principled way, to run the story.

"There, that ought to settle the matter," said Red supremely pleased with himself when he hung up.

The company lawyer was on the phone again the next day.

Red said, "For God's sake, everyone in town knows young Nutter's a drunk."

The Boston lawyer must have said something like, "If everyone in town knows all about Fred Nutter, the prodigal son, then why do you have to run any story at all?"

Red flared, "But you forget something. There's a world of difference between something that's just talked about and something that's written up in the *Tribune*."

And *bang* went Red's phone.

•

Red often lost himself rewriting my stuff.

In fact, my early stories were often impaled on Red's spike. He'd say, "You'll get the hang of it one of these days. It takes awhile. This won't do," and went on to re-write the story in its entirety.

When I asked for criticism he'd say, "Just do it the way I do. Read my stories, read my leads." Red was notorious in Maine journalism circles for his interminable leads. His idea of good news writing was to cram every conceivable detail of significance into the very first sentence, or failing that, into the first paragraph. There were lead sentences in the *Tribune* that went on for more than 100 words, opening paragraphs that ran four and five inches deep. At the same time Joe Adler, the shop foreman, liked to put as many stories as possible on page one, the combined result being that the *Tribune*'s front page might feature only the opening four or five lines of two dozen stories.

But never mind all that. Red got his high grades from his peers because he was an editor of character.

•

The Boston lawyer was on the line again insisting the story be killed. Why, replied Red, he'd be a laughing stock if he took a dive, never be able to look people in the eye again.

And then he threw a Hail Mary pass. "There's twenty years of a man's life tied up in this rag, doesn't that count for anything?" As if the people down there had a heart.

But Red would be flexible. OK, no big deal, no end-of-the-world headlines. OK, an item, two lines, three at the most somewhere deep inside the paper. Look, if he'd have got to Nutter before the dumb cop, he not only would have driven the poor sonofabitch home but would have tucked his ass into bed.

"They've got to give me a break," said Red, turning to Roger when he was off the phone. Red and Roger went back a long time.

Both grew up in Sanford and Roger, a genial New Englander in his thirties with thinning hair, had taken over as publisher when Red was already an institution in Sanford. "They owe me the courtesy. With all due respects, I'm the *Tribune* to the folks in this town," Red emphasized.

He'd gone the extra mile. No headlines. (Nothing like "Town Father Found Drunk in Cemetery!" the time a selectman was found sleeping it off at Myrtle Grove. Nothing like that.) A brief item. Inside the paper. Deep.

Now Roger said, "The *New York Times* and the *Boston Globe* – I bet they have their sacred cows. It's not like it was, Red. We're working for different people. These days you've got to be adaptable."

Roger was pleading with Red to get off his high horse.

•

We were putting the paper to bed the next night when the lawyer was back on the line with the final word. The new owners wanted the story killed, period.

"If I hear you right, you're really asking me to quit; after all the song and dance, that's what this all boils down to," Red bellowed as if he'd been physically assaulted.

Roger took the phone from Red. "Might there not be a reprieve? Might we not find a way to keep Red?"

The lawyer thought of one approach the proprietors might find acceptable: dropping reporting petty and misdemeanor crimes, reporting only felonies.

"Leave it to a big city lawyer," snorted Red.

Then Roger told Red, "They're willing to let you stay on as editor. But you have got to restrain yourself, learn to take orders. Leave policy matters to the proprietors. No more discussion. That's what they said. There you have it."

Red silently picked his teeth.

Roger said, "You can still save your job."

Red scoffed.

"People will understand. They'll forget."

"Too many enemies. Too many noses rubbed in the dirt. The people in this town would never forgive me. They'd forget nothing. I sold out, that's what they'd remember."

At length he gathered himself up from his desk littered with newspapers, copy paper, mail, pop bottles, coffee mugs, and, waving away the insects, started down the staircase, his body swaying as if on a shifting deck. He moved under a terrible strain, for his body was man-sized but his legs dwarf-like, supported by steel braces. As he made his way down to the street he kept saying, "Time to haul in the flag. The last bastion of liberty has been breached."

We drove around to Main Street where the cooling sidewalks had been "rolled up" for hours.

Until now, said Red, we'd been the last line of defense in Sanford and York County. But all that was changed. The absentee proprietors had just trampled upon the First Amendment and no one in town seemed to care.

"Roger was going down to the composing room to tell Joe Adler to kill the Nutter story," I said.

Red shrugged. The paper was no longer his responsibility.

"You know what? You're free now to go after the *Boston Globe*." Red's dream was to cover sports for a metropolitan daily like the *Globe*.

"You ought to call the *Globe*. They know you."

Red was the *Globe*'s stringer in southeastern Maine, a job worth an inch or two of space in the big metropolitan daily every other month or so and for which they threw him a few dollars.

"It's a pipe dream. A paper like that'd never hire a cripple to cover sports. Can you imagine them sending someone like me to Fenway or the Gardens?"

"I'd keep after the *Globe*," I said.

"Maybe I'll do some time for my brother."

His older brother, a successful restaurateur in Florida, owned a sporting goods store in Sanford. He'd been after Red to give up the paper and run the place for him. Red wasn't going to starve.

As for me, I was torn. One part of me wanted to quit in protest and solidarity. "They shouldn't be allowed to get away with it. They take twenty years of a man's life and throw it out the window." This was the part of me saying that if I didn't quit I was betraying Red.

"I'm going to quit," I said. "I don't want to work here anymore. I'll tell Roger in the morning."

"Whoa, hold on," said Red. "This thing has nothing to do with you."

"I'll find a daily," I said. "I'll get a little more experience and get a job on a daily." There was a daily in Biddeford, another mill town, not far from Sanford. The Biddeford paper, with a broader interest in the world, was something to strive for.

"With what I've taught you so far, you can do better than Biddeford." Red considered any paper in the *Tribune* circulation area, weekly or daily, an unworthy competitor.

"What about Rochester?"

He began to smile.

Our prime competitor was another weekly just across the state line in Rochester, New Hampshire. The two papers covered much of the same territory. Red was always muttering about his opposite number, wondering what he was up to next, and warning me to be on the lookout for any scoops he might attempt to snare from under our very noses.

Most weeks the *Tribune* bested its rival, and Red gloried in the triumphs. "They didn't lay a glove on us," he'd chortle, holding up both front pages. He liked to picture his rival as going around in frustration, muttering, "How do they do it? One scoop after another, week after week?"

But one week, the week leading to Easter Sunday, Red beckoned to Isabel and me, saying, "Run up the white flag. They've topped us this week."

He held up the Rochester paper. In the boldest type it proclaimed, "CHRIST HAS RISEN!"

Now he said, "You're just eccentric enough to go to Rochester."

"If I go to Rochester I'll get revenge for what they've done to you."

"How do you propose to do that?"

"Scooping the *Tribune* every week."

"Every week?"

"I won't have to go to the courts or the cops for my headlines. I'll get 'em all in church."

"You would, too," said Red, grinning widely. He was a great atheist.

Nothing changed so far as my job was concerned. I continued to cover police, court, school board, selectmen, service clubs, and sports from Little League through high school and American Legion baseball, where I often doubled as the official scorer.

On Thursday mornings when the paper came out I still helped out in the back shop inserting the shoppers' guides and delivering the papers to the stores, and collecting the week's sales from the merchants.

Funny thing, but I began doing my best work after Red left. People in town even remarked on my pieces, quoting them, and this, along with the new editor's compliments, spurred me on. Where Red had been downright contemptuous of my stuff, editing harshly, Elizabeth Mitchell was extravagant in her praise and ran almost everything I wrote just as it came from my typewriter. A conscientious Yankee of middle age, she lacked Red's humor and passion but she was not an apologist for the Boston company that owned us. She simply tried to cover the news as best she could, and she went about it in a very professional manner.

Of course I resented her terribly, but Elizabeth took that in stride.

"I know how you feel about Red," she said. "It was a shame how that business turned out, and I sympathize with Red, but the world is an imperfect place. No one is indispensable. Red was living in a cocoon."

Isabel, who'd known Red all her life, said, "Red has a lot of good qualities but he's also pig-headed – and vain. He's had his own way so long he's forgotten his place."

She thought I was behaving like a kid.

The new editor hoped I'd stay on in Sanford. Addressing my new dream of finding redemption back in California, she said, "Sometimes it's better to be a big fish in a little pond than a little fish in a big pond."

It wasn't what I wanted to hear.

Nonetheless, I began writing better, feeling more confident, covering my beat more aggressively. The cops were furious with me for writing up a bungled arrest, and when next I dropped into the station, they waved little American flags in my face. (This was progress.) Another time Judge Marshall called me into his chambers to admonish me for ridiculing a defense lawyer in a criminal case. The lawyer was young and finding his way. "You know more criminal law than he does right now, you're more familiar with the proceedings. He's still learning." (I was taking hold.) After reading an impassioned column I'd written on behalf of Junior Legion baseball, a shopkeeper told me, "Now I know the pen is mightier than the sword." (A taste of glory.)

I kept up with Red, making a point to drop in from time to time at the Dugout, the shop he managed for his brother. The store was squeaky clean with sporting goods of all descriptions arrayed on racks and tables. The tables were covered with action sports scenes. Red sat next to the register hopelessly miscast in his role of Main Street merchant. Whenever I showed up he took to razzing me, especially when hangers-on were present to hoot him on. He'd say, "How can you stand working for the sons of bitches? I thought you were an honest reporter. How long are you going to let 'em keep putting your name in the paper? Where's your pride?" And so on. My visits provided him with a few welcome laughs.

·

I spent my last night in Sanford with Red in his Ford up on Main Street. It was late October. We joked a little, he teased me some, and then, turning to me during a long silence, he said, "So it's California or bust."

"Yep. Things will be better out there. It's still a young state."

"Land of opportunity."

"That's what I figure. Got to be better out there. I'm going to find a courageous paper. One with guts."

"They're out there. You just got to put in the legwork."

"I will, even if I have to dig ditches to tide me over."

"They're bound to be out there. California is a big place."

"You'd do the same, wouldn't you, if you were my age?"

"I'd find an honest rag, one that wasn't afraid to speak out. And have the time of my life."

"Boy, wouldn't that be something"

"I'd pull no punches."

"No sacred cows."

"My God," said Red, "think of the time we could have right here in Sanford if only we had proprietors who believed in the U.S. Constitution!"

Hodge and the
Humboldt Times

Most people had an alibi for living in Eureka. Mine was to escape another Maine winter.

My first choice was San Francisco, for which I'd set out from Bangor on a Greyhound bus in the fall of 1951.

I carried a letter of introduction to Jack Foisie, a *San Francisco Chronicle* reporter. It was from Dave Golding, my boss of two summers in the publicity department of the New York City offices of 20th Century Fox when I was still a student at the University of Maine. Jack and Dave had been reporters on *Stars and Stripes* in Europe in World War Two. I had written Dave of my dream of covering the news in a city like San Francisco for a paper like the *Chronicle* and he wrote Jack.

I arrived in San Francisco in the afternoon, the city awash in white sunlight. Although battered from lack of sleep after five days on the Greyhound, I was yet brimming with anticipation.

In those days the bus was a common way of travel for millions of Americans. (The ubiquity of the automobile was still a few years off.) Following the example of other travelers, I shaved and washed as best I could at the depot. Then I dug into my duffle bag for fresh clothes, slipped into them, and walked directly over to the newspaper.

After a moment or two of small talk, Jack, wiry with eagle eyes, led me out of the newsroom deciding I needed a square meal. We ate at Bernstein's Grotto, a sumptuous fish house, close to the din of Powell and Market.

After satisfying Jack's curiosity about his old comrade, I said,

"What's Abe like?" Abe being Abe Mellinkoff, the *Chronicle*'s city editor. "I'm not expecting anything," I lied. "It's just swell of you to run interference for me."

"He's a little guy with a Napoleonic complex," Jack said. "I don't think he'll hire you – you've got two strikes against you. One, you're over six feet. He likes little guys like himself. Two, you're not an Ivy Leaguer. He's partial to Ivy Leaguers. Well, you're already here," he shrugged. "You've got nothing to lose. Who else are you going to see?"

I told him.

He whistled. "William Randolph Hearst, Jr. How'd you fix that?"

"My uncle, Sam Shain. He knows everybody or knows the people who do. It was Sam who got me the summer job at Fox with Dave Golding."

"I'd say you've got a pretty good pipeline. I'm flattered to be included on your rounds of important people."

We had a laugh: a kid dead broke with next to no experience rolls into San Francisco from Bangor, Maine, on a Greyhound bus with a letter of introduction to the crown prince of one of American's newspaper empires.

"Tell me, what did your uncle say, beyond 'Dear Junior?'"

"My uncle didn't write the letter. Someone else did, a Hearst lawyer. A guy in New York. Ed Weisel."

Jack said, "You know Ed Weisel?" Ed Weisel was a big-time New York lawyer and a political power broker.

"No. My Uncle Sam does. If Hearst asks me about Weisel I'm supposed to act as if I know him."

"What are you going to say?"

"I don't know. I just hope he doesn't bring it up."

When we stepped out into the street, he said, "You want to look rested when you meet Abe tomorrow."

"Oh, I'll be fine," I said.

"What are you going to do now?" It was getting dark, past six o'clock.

"Oh, I don't know. Look around, I guess." Although I'd set foot in the city before, all I really knew about San Francisco was what others had said: Like Rome built on seven hills. Facing the Orient. Romantic past and present. The Gold Rush. Mark Twain. Sam Spade. Charlie Chan. Joe DiMaggio. One of my favorite songs was Billie Holiday's "I Cover the Waterfront." Someone told me that the lament was written about San Francisco.

"Get yourself a hotel room," Jack said. "You want to be at your best with Abe."

He placed a five-dollar bill in my hand.

I'd left Bangor with limited funds, arriving in San Francisco with $18, hardly a munificent sum even in those days. There was no money from home. My dad was a transplanted Bostonian still living in Los Angeles with his new line of work and family. My mother's circumstances were modest. But I was confident of catching on somewhere. Jobs were plentiful if one were willing to work.

Before Jack added to my funds I was seriously concerned how I was going to spend the night. But his generosity helped make up my mind.

I checked into the Devonshire, a small hotel off Union Square, for eight dollars, and got into bed before ten. My body ablaze for adventure, I nonetheless heeded Jack's advice.

⋅

Abe Mellinkoff was a little high-octane engine. Swarthy, in vest and tie, he strutted about the newsroom, issuing commands right and left. Now he admonished, now praised, now shared a laugh with a privileged staffer. When I drew up, he threw his head back and tendered a limp hand. "I hope you didn't come all this way thinking you were walking into a job."

"No," I said. "Jack made that clear in his note. 'No promises.'"

"That's right. Things are tight. I'm afraid I have to send you away empty-handed."

"Well, I'll keep in touch. I've always dreamed of working here."

"You couldn't have picked a worse time to come looking for a job. I hope you have other irons in the fire."

"I'll keep in touch. Through Jack."

"Do that."

He turned to glance at copy, pick up the phone, shout a command across the room.

"Thanks, Abe," I said, but he paid no attention. Maybe he didn't hear me.

I made my way past a row of desks in the *Chronicle*'s packed newsroom until I came to Jack's located in a far corner. Jack wasn't surprised. Nor, for that matter was I, but I was hurt.

"I warned you," said Jack.

"You did," I said.

"That's Abe for you. Sorry."

"That's OK."

"You're sitting pretty, though. You've got William Randolph Hearst, Jr. in your pocket."

"I will tomorrow."

"We'll figure something out."

His phone rang. I watched him chip away at his caller, drawing him out, feeling his way to the peg of the story and then to the story itself. He spoke easily, patiently, unfailingly cheerful. Jack was the real thing.

When he hung up, he said. "You're not counting on Hearst? You should try the California Newspaper Association. They're a clearinghouse for jobs. Meantime, you'll need something to tide you over. I know the postmaster, one of my innumerable sources. I'll see what I can smoke up."

"Thank you."

"I suspect it won't be pretty. Probably handling sacks of mail on the Embarcadero for ships going to our boys in Korea. You look as if you can lick your weight in mailbags, though. You'll be making as much or even more with overtime than a journeyman reporter. Hell, I'll know where to go for a loan."

"You're worried about getting your five dollars back."

"I wasn't going to mention it," said Jack.

•

Ushered into his office by a secretary, I was struck by the son's resemblance to his famous father.

"Well," said William Randolph Hearst, Jr., showing me to a chair. "How is our friend Ed Weisel?"

"Oh, fine."

"A wonderful man."

"Oh, yes."

"When did you last see him?"

"Oh, not that long ago."

He asked about my newspaper experience.

"I've just put in a year at the Sanford *Tribune* in Sanford, Maine. A weekly. But I did everything. Sports. Police. Board of Selectmen. Wrote editorials. Delivered papers to the stores. Before that I worked on the college paper, University of Maine, and wrote a weekly column in the *Boston Jewish Advocate*."

"Oh, if it counts," I rattled on in my nervousness, "office boy at the Boston AP nights and summers during high school. Brookline High. Brookline, Mass. Ha, ran my own newspaper in the eighth grade, a nickel a copy. Took ads."

"As a matter of policy I don't hire the reporters," Hearst replied. "I leave that to my editors. I don't believe it's my place to interfere. This is their domain and they know best what their needs are. You are free to see them, but I don't think you have enough experience for a reporter's job on a metropolitan newspaper, not yet."

It was obvious that he was seeing me as a courtesy to Ed Weisel.

Then, after pausing to consult the Weisel letter, he said, "But I'd be happy to offer you a job writing about television. You don't need any experience. It's not something my editors care about. They hold their nose but I think the public would buy it. The job's open."

Looking back today on that scene in the office of William Randolph Hearst, Jr. I'm abashed and amazed at how I behaved. But, in fact, I spurned his benign gesture. I rose up to my full six feet four and protested.

"I am a newspaper reporter," I naively declared. "I did not travel across a continent to write about a horrid new fad." The electronic medium then was a no-class upstart for a starry-eyed journalist like me.

•

My chutzpah landed me on the docks of San Francisco loading those sacks of military mail for the Far East that Jack had in mind. I soon gave up hope of ever working on a San Francisco paper and began looking into less fantastic possibilities at the California Newspaper Association.

There were two openings, one in Tulare in the rich Central Valley, in hot desert country that never knew snow, and one in Eureka, far up on the North Coast in wet, fogbound, redwood forests. Snow fell in the mountains.

"Too bad," said the Tulare editor when I called. "From the sound of it, you would have been my choice, but I hired a fellow yesterday. Try me again in a few months if you're still in the market for a job. No telling how long he'll stick around."

I held off calling Eureka because it was far enough north of San Francisco to raise my concern about snow. If at all possible, I wanted to dodge another glacial winter. People told me that it rained heavily in Eureka but that the snow fell in the mountains. It rarely, if ever, reached sea level.

It had been three months since I began a term at hard labor in the Embarcadero mailroom and I was tiring of the sport.

The *Humboldt Times* in Eureka remained the only paper advertising a vacancy.

"Let's give it a whirl," Elmer L. Hodgkinson, Jr., the managing editor, said after we'd agreed on a starting salary of fifty dollars a week.

•

For a middle-class person like myself raised on Old Testament and Puritan virtues the rough and tumble life of Eureka in 1952 was a revelation; that is, it was a liberating change from the formal ways of my native New England. With its rows of whore houses, card rooms, and gin mills, and a waterfront teeming with crabbers, trawlers, and ocean-going freighters, Eureka spelled freedom for an adventurous youth of twenty-four.

I don't want to leave the impression that Eureka was in the throes of a second gold rush when I disembarked from yet another Greyhound. It was a pretty settled town with an aristocracy of its own: lumbermen, doctors, lawyers, merchants, and clergy, as well as pioneer families. But, as towns go, it was still fairly young and raw, scarcely 100 years away from the first white settlers. There was a sense of movement, of new construction, of a community on the rise. The county director of the civil defense office summed it up on the day I introduced myself as the new reporter on the beat.

"Out here," he said, welcoming me warmly, "we don't ask a feller where he's been. All we care about is where he's going."

I spent my first few nights in a small, crib-like room, one of about a dozen fronting an alley behind the Vance Hotel. The Vance owned the rooms and rented some of them by the hour to prostitutes and petty criminals.

The paper was up on E Street, four block away, in a two-story wood frame building. Next door was Harriet's, an all-night restaurant, and next to it, the Annex Bar, and then Bill Turk's place. (Bill was a shoeshine man and one of the few blacks in Humboldt County.)

Across the street was the DeLuxe Club, one of two nightspots where it was safe to take a date. In back of the paper's office was a parking lot and looking towards D Street, Roy's Club, a good place for getting Sicilian cooking. The rough bars – the High Lead, the Pride of Humboldt, Jimmy Dunn's, and the Palace – were on Two Street, close to the waterfront. On weekends, these joints rang with the shouts of brawling Swedish loggers, Okies, Italian and Portuguese fishermen, ranch hands, and Hoopa, Yurok, and Klamath Indians. Sometimes knives flashed. The police got plenty of business.

I soon moved to a rooming house where a set of "Though-Shalt-Nots" posted above the bed informed the occupant that he was in a respectable part of town:

1. No radios permitted after 10 P.M.
2. No more than two visitors in a room at any time.
3. During visits of members of the opposite sex your door must be ajar at all times.
4. No visitors permitted after 10 P.M.
5. No eating or drinking at any time.
6. Bathroom use limited to 15 minutes in the morning.
7. No personal phone calls accepted after 10 P.M.

You entered the newspaper office from the street, passed Rhoda, a local ancient who ran the switchboard, passed the classified desk, and passed the publisher's office and, at the foot of a flight of stairs, began the climb to the newsroom on the second floor. You'd find Hodge sitting behind a wide desk in front of a large window that looked out on the street. Every now and then he'd get up to attend to the AP ticker a few feet away. He'd tear off yards of copy, peruse it, toss most of it in a barrel, but retain the news most likely to pique the readers' interest. The staff – the eight or nine of us – sat at desks where we clacked out our stories on typewriters or worked the phones to keep tabs on the ebb and flow of the news around town. Alone among us, Hodge kept his hat on, as that was the custom of his day as a young journalist. You did so in those days, he said, because you never knew when you'd have to drop everything and run out to cover a fire. You didn't have time to look for your chapeau.

The room, glowing in a fluorescent light, was heavy with cigarette smoke but no one ever remarked about it since almost all of us smoked and no one seriously worried that cigarettes posed anything like a mortal threat to our well-being.

Most of the night-time tread of foot traffic on the stairs was bound for the persons who handled sports and society. These beats covered the athletic contests of local schools and colleges and weddings and golden anniversaries to a fare-thee-well.

The photography end of the business was left to a pair of photographers who could be found in a darkroom next to a flight of stairs that led to the alley below, when they were not out shooting the news.

·

Almost everyone on the paper had a story, which, in effect apologized for their winding up in Eureka.

My editor, Elmer L. Hodgkinson, Jr., or Hodge – this is what everyone called him – had fled his native Oklahoma when a sheriff showed up at his father's house with a warrant for Hodge's arrest. The cops wanted him for delinquent child support. He told the officer, "Just a minute, I'll see if he's in," threw some clothes into a suitcase, and skipped out the back door.

He worked on New Orleans' *Times-Picayune* and the *Seattle Post-Intelligencer* but when World War Two broke out – a restless, footloose time for millions of Americans – he chucked journalism for more lucrative employment in a defense plant. This was how he ended up in Eureka, where he'd first found work as a pipe fitter in a local shipyard.

I don't remember exactly what had kept him out of the service but it might have been poor eyesight or flat feet. (In the early 1950s people were still accounting for their whereabouts during World War Two.)

Don O'Kane, the publisher, who came down from Portland, liked to say that he hit Eureka with fifty cents in his pocket but if he'd had another fifty cents he would have kept on going.

Another Oregonian, Ernie Snowberger, had a bit more in his pocket when he set out from Oregon to look for a job on a metropolitan paper. However, during a stopover in Eureka, a Two Street maiden took pains to separate him from his money. So he presented himself to Hodge the next morning. Because of his experience on a small Oregon daily, Ernie was able to talk Hodge into giving him a job.

Al Tostado, the one-man Sports department, came up from his native San Francisco. Back then the city dailies weren't hiring people with names like Tostado.

•

And so it went. Jehanne Salinger, the mother of *San Francisco Chronicle* reporter Pierre Salinger – he later became President Kennedy's press secretary – left a rocky marriage in the Bay Area and came up to Eureka to renew a journalistic career as the *Humboldt* Times' society editor.

There were mysteries for which no explanation was known. The scion of an old Virginia family, Walter Johnston found his way to the *Humboldt Times* in his middle years. A graduate of famous universities, including the Columbia School of Journalism, and a former big city reporter, Walter never voiced an alibi for making Eureka his home.

Andrew M. Genzoli was the only staffer who had no need for one. A local historian and the editor of the farm page, Andy was a Humboldt county native, born in nearby Ferndale. Andy's style was verbose and exclamatory but he wrote with a passion – and authority – about his native heath that none of the rest of us could match.

Getting good people and keeping them was a trial for Hodge.

Consider, for example, the newsman who proved as good as his resume.

In the first few weeks of his employment, the journalist, whom I shall call Roland, scored scoop after scoop, turning out the kind of sizzling reportage one found on big city newspapers. It was before my time, but as Hodge recalled the story, Roland's prose was crisp, pithy, the leads imaginative, provocative.

At the same time, though, Hodge had reason to be distressed. The youngish man – Roland was somewhere in his thirties – came in to work every day wearing the same pants, T-shirt, and threadbare sneakers. The T-shirt only half-covered a furry navel, which Roland was in the habit of massaging while working up to a sparkling figure of speech.

Roland added to Hodge's distress by approaching Hodge and whispering in the editor's ear – as if it were a secret they alone must share – every time he prepared to visit the bathroom. Similarly, on his return, Roland confided in Hodge in the same conspiratorial manner about how he'd fared.

In a matter of a few days, Hodge shrank from drawing near the younger man.

But he took the fellow to task. Roland promised to mend his ways. But nothing changed. Hodge's indignation came to a boil, but his hand was stayed by yet another scoop, yet another display of exemplary news writing.

It gains us nothing to speculate on how long this opera bouffe would have gone on had not a distinguished-looking gentleman made his way into the newsroom one night.

Accompanied by a nurse and police officer, he asked for Hodge's consummate journalist by name. The gentleman identified himself as a psychiatrist from the state hospital in Napa. He had come to take Roland back to the institution from which he'd escaped two months before.

•

Once, when Hodge was reading letters from people asking for jobs, he invited my recommendations. Of the three or four applications, I did not hesitate in picking a prospect.

It was a fellow with degrees from leading universities, big city experience, and a stint or two as a foreign correspondent.

"Hodge," I said, "this is your guy. Look at his resume."

Hodge glanced at the letter again, and shook his head. He didn't think so.

"You've got to ask yourself," said Hodge, "why a fellow with those credentials would be asking for a job in Eureka."

"He's probably tired of the rat race, wants to slow down. Maybe he's an outdoorsman, crazy about hunting and fishing," I offered.

Filing the letter in the wastebasket, Hodge smiled. "Sounds like a drinker to me," he said.

"But how do you know? " I challenged.

He shrugged. He just knew.

Billie Holiday

Hodge was funny about blacks. He resented them, kept his distance. He thought they smelled, looked upon them as an inferior race. He was funny about Jews, too. He used to say, "Hey, boy, I believe you're the only Jew I've ever known who worked for a living."

Until he'd met up with me, all the Jews he'd ever seen growing up in Oklahoma City and later in New Orleans were living off the fat of the land. We got into arguments over that, my pointing out there were plenty of Jews who worked for a living and plenty of poor ones, too.

"You come to New York, Boston, Philadelphia and I'll show you lots of poor Jews, and lots of Jews who do menial work," I said. He scoffed. Jews were merchants, peddlers, haberdashers, people who bought and sold second-hand goods, people who never got their hands dirty.

But blacks were his principal hang-up. When word spread that the famous singer Billie Holiday was coming to Eureka, Hodge turned a deaf ear. It was as if Al and I were foisting something shameful on him when we said she was big-time, a story we couldn't ignore. Hodge was wholly lacking in knowledge of popular culture. A fond boast of his was that he hadn't seen a movie since *Going My Way* in 1944.

Al and I argued but he remained adamantly opposed to opening the pages of the *Humboldt Times*, a family newspaper, to "a colored saloon singer."

If she were half as great as Al and I maintained, then what was she doing in Eureka? The big stars never came up here. The only time you saw them was when they were on their way down.

Hodge said, "She's a story for cities like L.A. and Oakland where there are a lot of niggers, but she isn't news in Eureka and Humboldt County." He conceded that if she were a Metropolitan Opera star he might think otherwise.

"Why?" I persisted. "She is a great name in American music, in jazz and the blues." I followed Hodge to the shoot where he dispatched the last bit of copy of the night downstairs to the composing room. "She's in the same league as Louis Armstrong and Duke Ellington and even you have heard of them. Wake up, Hodge. Billie Holiday may not sing at the Met but she's a lot better known than most opera singers. Hodge, we can't afford not to cover her."

He reached for his coat and started for the stairs. All the way into the street I kept declaiming, "You could look at this way: Billie Holiday is honoring Eureka by coming here. She's putting the town on the map. All I'm saying is give me a chance. Let me interview her. If you don't like the story, fine. But keep an open mind."

I continued pleading my case while Hodge sized up one of Johnny's new pinball machines at the Annex Bar.

Next morning (after getting a conditional OK from him in the Annex) I ran off to the Carnegie Library. Luckily, I found a book about Billie on the shelf, *Lady Sings the Blues*. In the afternoon I walked over to Fred Hamilton's Victory Club on Two Street to meet Billie. She'd be opening there the next night.

Fred, a spent roué, fixed drinks and a heavy-set black man straddled the stool next to Billie. (He was introduced as her manager.) Though she was clad in a smart navy blue jacket, and skirt and big hat, Billie, already running to fat, was not the beauty I'd prayed for.

The door was left ajar, leaving space for a piece of sun from the street to illuminate the front end of the bar where we were sitting. The rest of the room was a cavernous void of glittering tinsel and sham splendor. (In his drinking days, Hodge had spent many a riotous night at Fred's Hamilton's club but now Hodge rarely spoke of him, and never with regard.)

Billy was tipsy and hoarse and chain-smoked using a holder, a saloon singer gone on booze and drugs, just as Hodge said. She complained of feeling miserable, hot and sticky. They'd driven up from Fresno, the trip taking them two days. Both were starved for a decent meal.

A Strange Breed of Folks

It was good I'd done the legwork. It wasn't that Billie was uncommunicative – she was amazed that I'd gone to the library to read up on her – she simply was not given to talking about her early life. I knew from the book about her growing up in a Baltimore ghetto; that as a child she washed the stoops of row houses; that as a hungry child, she sold her love for pocket change.

"Why, you know all about me," she laughed.

That night when Hodge finally got around to reading my copy I tried reading his face. But it was hopeless. Whatever he thought he kept to himself.

"Hey, boy, it's time for you to check the cops," he said, without looking up.

"I did, not twenty, thirty minutes ago. The sheriff's office, fire department, Coast Guard, too."

"Try again. This paper's dying on La-*vine*." It was a favorite expression of his.

Fender-bender, chimney fire, fishing boat adrift was all I could report, nothing important enough to keep Billie Holiday out of the paper or off the front page for that matter.

As usual the front-page proof came up from the composing room a few minutes before midnight. I strode as casually as I could toward the AP printer and then stole a glance as Hodge checked the heads and leads. There was no Billie. Hodge ran the story inside the paper and without my customary byline.

She stumbled through her week of performances. Nonetheless, Fred Hamilton's Victory Club was packed night after night, and people cheered lustily – not for what they heard but for what once had been. Eureka indeed was the end of the line.

Earl Warren

Someone at the paper – I guess Al Tostado, who covered sports but was sitting in as managing editor for Hodge, who had gone rock hunting in Wyoming – had been tipped off that Earl Warren, the Chief Justice of the United States, a former California governor, was stopping at a private home in Eureka for lunch. Al's informant said that Warren had been hunting up in Redwood Creek and was coming here to visit with friends before flying back to Washington.

The lady of the house proved difficult when I phoned. She wouldn't say whether Warren was coming, only that it was a private affair and none of our business. When I held to the contrary, citing the First Amendment, she hung up.

"You better go on out there," said Al. "But keep me posted."

The lady of the house came to the door. As soon as I stated my business, she ordered me around to the back. There she gave me a piece of her mind. "You have no business being here. This is a private affair. If I'd known it was someone from the newspaper when you knocked, I would have called for the police."

"Please, ma'am," I said. "We have information that the Chief Justice is due here today."

She adamantly denied any such thing but it was obvious something important was taking place. Servants were rarities in a place like Eureka; even the rich made do without help most of the time. And by the looks of things the house was set for a banquet, with maids running to and fro. Someone important was paying a call.

The lady of the house, however, ordered me off the premises. I found a pay phone and called Al.

"Earl Warren" he said, "is a public figure. You have every right to be there."

"But she won't let me into the house. She denies Warren's coming."

"Do you believe her?"

"No."

"Go back and charm her. That's why I picked you for this assignment. I figured since she was one of the town's social biggies you were the best man on the staff to sweet-talk your way in."

So I went back.

"You again," she snapped. "Haven't I told you to leave me alone? We're having company. This is a private party. You're intruding, trespassing on private property. I'll call the police."

"But just tell me, ma'am," I said in a gentle manner, "is the Chief Justice coming? Is it he you are expecting?" She shut the door.

"It's no use," I told Al from the pay phone. "She won't even talk to me."

"OK, if it's war she wants, we'll give it to her. We're the press."

He reeled off instructions.

"You've got to stake out a spot on the road. You've got to wait there for Warren's car and before it turns into the lady's driveway, get it to stop, and if Warren is there, tell him who you are and beg, borrow, or steal a few minutes of his time. You'll be on public property – the sidewalk's public, the street's public. She can't bug you so long as you're out there."

So I waited – rather we waited, a photographer and I. We passed the time guessing what kind of car he'd be driving. We counted on a fancy one, Rolls or Jag, or Caddy, or maybe a Lincoln. The guessing went on for more than an hour before a Rolls Royce surfaced on the rising of a hill. There were four men inside in hunting dress.

"Get ready," I told the cameraman running toward the Rolls. "We got to get them before they turn in."

On my frantic approach the Rolls purred to a stop. The passengers peered through the glass. One or two were holding rifles. Then I spotted Warren. He was sporting a stubble of a beard.

"Mr. Chief Justice," I cried. Through the lowered window I told him I was a reporter and wanted a few words with him. It wouldn't take long. Just a couple of questions.

Warren said something to his friends and slipped out.

"Well," he said. "Young man, I'm pleased to meet you. But there's no point in our talking out here in the cold when there's a hot meal waiting inside and perhaps some liquid refreshments."

He took my arm.

"Sir, you should know your hostess doesn't take kindly to me. I'm afraid I've been pestering her; she denies you were even coming."

"I'll be happy to talk with you but I won't discuss any cases before the court, that's my rule," Warren said as we made our way along a path that led to the rear of the house.

"Oh, sir, that's perfectly fine." I would have agreed to almost anything. And I went on to praise his tenure on the Court, saying that I thought the decision in Kansas v. the Board of Education – the ruling that ended school segregation – was his finest hour. "This is what you'll be remembered for for many years to come," I said. "This is what will go down in the history books." He seemed pleased.

We were now at the back door. But before either of us could rap, the lady rose up.

"I'm calling the police," she said, but then recognized Warren.

"Oh, Mr. Chief Justice, you gave me a start. I didn't expect your coming in at the back door. Oh, please come in."

But my way was barred.

Warren turned. "Oh, madam, this young man, he's a reporter from the local paper. Could we sit somewhere for a few questions?"

When we were seated, a maid asked Warren if he'd care for a cocktail. He thanked her and added, "My reporter friend here, I believe, will have one, too."

Now, I would like to say that despite Warren's restrictions, I landed a scoop. But I didn't. When he spoke for the record, it was in guarded generalities, and I wasn't experienced or clever enough to get anything more. The story I sat down to write at the paper was pretty bland. However, with the Chief Justice running interference, the *Humboldt Times* had made a point about the freedom of the press.

And the Chief Justice had made his. Warren, old pol that he was, understood the adversarial relationship between public figures and the press. It would have been unusual for a good politician like Warren to post no trespassing signs on his privacy. The lady of the house notwithstanding, he knew a public figure could not use the press only when it suited his own purposes. The relationship was one of give and take. By giving a few minutes to a reporter he could make the press happy and have his privacy, too.

Marilyn Monroe

Hodge was always on the lookout for stories that the AP might want to run. In addition to his job as managing editor of the *Humboldt Times*, Hodge was also a stringer for the Associated Press. He took his responsibilities seriously. The news from the world beyond our circulation area came thumping, thumping over a Teletype machine only a few feet from Hodge's desk. A local story that "made" the wire not only put Eureka on the map, it also put a few dollars in Hodge's pocket.

•

U.S. 101, also known as the Redwood Highway, was a no-man's land of mountainous hairpin turns and careening logging trucks. All too frequently motorists plunged into ravines thousands of feet below at the cost of their lives.

One intrepid traveler who made it through was Horace Heidt, the bandleader. When he disembarked from his bus in Eureka after an adventurous ride from the Bay Area, the shaken musician suggested that the tortuous highway be renamed for Marilyn Monroe.

Hodge chuckled as he read my copy. Then he waved me over to his desk. An idea was coming to boil.

The next morning readers of the *Humboldt Times* beheld the Horace Heidt suggestion in front page headlines alongside a picture of Miss Monroe in a bathing suit superimposed on a map of the Redwood Highway.

"Horace Heidt," began the story, "after winding his way over Highway 101 this week to keep a Eureka engagement declared that the famed Redwood Highway should be renamed the Marilyn Monroe Highway – for obvious reasons. And for the same obvious reason, and after scanning Marilyn – the map – in detail, the *Times* photographer got busy and came up with the above. Miss Monroe has been notified and we are awaiting her answer – breathlessly. Lots of curves there, son – along the highway, too!"

Before the presses rolled we wired the actress of our intentions and followed up next morning by sending her a copy of the newspaper, air mail, special delivery.

A few days later Miss Monroe replied by Western Union.

I APPRECIATE THE HUMOR IN YOUR WIRE BUT NATURALLY I COULDN'T GO ALONG WITH THE HORACE HEIDT SUGGESTION EVEN IN JEST.

Marilyn Monroe may have declined the honor, but Hodge was not dismayed. His enterprise was rewarded. The AP ran the Monroe story on its national wire, which, in addition to spreading Eureka's glory from coast to coast, netted Hodge $5 or $10.

·

After the paper went to press at midnight, Al Tostado and I, and sometimes Ernie Snowberger, another reporter, or sometimes Hodge, went down to the Annex Bar to unwind. While the rest of us caroused, Hodge would remain in a corner of the room playing the pinball machine. Although Hodge no longer drank, he missed the smoky, uric atmosphere of a bar and was especially fond of the characters drifting in with their pipe dreams. The pinball machine gave him a reason for being there.

But bars and pinball weren't his only amusements. To my surprise, he read fiction. The work of the Norwegian novelist Knut Hamsun impressed him, especially *Hunger*, Hamsun's first novel. But Hodge's all-time favorite was *The Brothers Karamazov*, followed, I believe, by *Crime and Punishment*. I'd never read Hamsun but was well acquainted with Dostoevsky.

The Brothers Karamazov, I said to him once, may well have been my favorite novel as well.

Every so often we discussed books, but those exchanges never matched the shock of recognition of that first time.

Hodge was mainly a loner. Advised by his doctors to give up drinking and whoring after suffering that heart attack, he became a passionate rock-hound, filling up his leisure time looking for semi-precious stones such as amber, turquoise, topaz, and jade. On vacations, he traveled as far away as Colorado, Utah, and Wyoming. He usually went alone, crossing gorges and mountain passes. He put up with great physical discomforts, now and then suffering bruises and scrapes and heat prostration.

Hodge became skilled in stone polishing and carving, often working far into the night in his basement. He made countless pendants, bracelets, and rings from the rocks he'd gathered in the wilds. He gave the jewelry away as presents to his wife, daughter, relatives, and friends. People prized the jewelry as much for Hodge's workmanship as for the value of the stones.

Hodge, the rock hound, rivaled Hodge, the managing editor, with the exception of the paper's Sunday features. Here, like a parent or teacher, he sowed seeds of inspiration.

One day, early in my Eureka career, Hodge led me into a backroom where old editions of the *Humboldt Times* lay under layers of dust.

As Hodge began leafing through the moldy pages he sang the praises of the Sunday features of my predecessors.

"Look here," said Hodge. "This young fellow, Eisenberg, a Jewish fellow like you." He laid open a yellowed page that bore Eisenberg's byline.

The article, illustrated with pictures, focused on a popular spot for clam diggers a little north of Eureka.

"An easterner like yourself. New Jersey. He was crazy for these features."

"Where is he now, this Eisenberg fellow?"

"Last we heard, he was doing features for Cleveland's *Plain Dealer*. Eureka sure wasn't big enough to hold him."

"Why, that paper must reach a million readers."

"These features show what a fellow can do when he's given a chance. There's no dearth of opportunity on a paper our size."

Hodge now pointed to a two-page layout chronicling a whale hunt off California's north coast.

"Isn't it a beauty?"

He ran a loving hand across the page.

"The reporter is with the *Honolulu Advertiser* today. Circulation's got to be in the hundred thousand or more range."

"What happened to the fellow who did this one?" I asked, referring to a picture-page about a working gold mine in El Dorado County.

"Now this fellow had a talent for digging up wild characters. The *Sacramento Bee* grabbed him. These features get around. Editors read them. They're rare for a paper our size, but talent will out, that's what I say."

Sacramento Bee? Circulation a hundred thousand?"

"Oh, it's a good size."

He'd achieved the desired effect. I was eager to try my own hand. But the catch in all this was that Hodge couldn't pay me a dime extra.

"It's fine with me," I said. I didn't see why I should be paid anything extra. It was all part of the job, wasn't it?

"The thing is," said Hodge. "I can only spare you on Sundays." During the six-day week the cops and fire and sheriff and courts and highway patrol and Coast Guard and city council had priority. If I were to try one of these features – and by now he'd made me restless with excitement – it would have to be on a Sunday, my only day off.

Now this was unfair and I said so.

"If it were my newspaper I'd do things differently," Hodge replied. "But O'Kane's of the old school, doesn't believe in overtime. He's guaranteeing you forty-eight hours a week which is better than any union can do for you."

"Sunday's my only day off," I protested.

Hodge shook his head. "I thought you were looking for experience, boy, making a name for yourself."

So, I was dispatched on many a romantic quest into the back country, concerning the lore and rituals of Indian tribes (Hoopas, Yuroks, and Klamath).

On the subject of Indians, Hodge spoke with an extraordinary sympathy. It was not long before I understood the reason. His Oklahoma father was of English ancestry but his mother was half Arapaho. Hodge was fiercely proud of the Indian blood she'd bequeathed him and plainly said so on occasion.

It seemed – and I may be taking undue license though I don't believe so – that Hodge saw himself as something of a missionary in reverse, spreading news of Indian culture among our readership of Swedes, Norwegians, Finns, northern Italians, Welsh, Scottish, Irish, and other whites.

Thus, I spent a great many unpaid Sundays pursuing my visions of Yurok basket-weavers, thousand-year-old sweathouses, Hoopa medicine men, ceremonial feasts, and deerskin dances, and Klamath fishers and waterfowl hunters.

Although stories of indigenous peoples of northwestern California were pet projects, Hodge was a generalist, curious about everything. And so I also explored the Del Loma caves, famed as a bandit hideout during frontier days; investigated microscopic life on the craggy shores of Humboldt Bay; traversed an amazing pygmy forest of pine and cypress in Mendocino County; payed a call on an old lighthouse in a perilous sea off Crescent City; witnessed logging crews felling thundering redwoods; went aloft with steeplejacks to the lips of a lumber company smokestack; even covered the antics of a shepherding rabbit.

Not long after I started doing such stories, I made it a point to send tear sheets of the Sunday features to the editors I'd met on my early rounds of the San Francisco papers. A year or so later, in 1954, I heard from Joshua Eppinger III, executive editor of the *San Francisco Examiner*.

"I've read your Eureka stuff," said Eppinger when he called. "There's a job down here if you want it."

It wasn't the *Chronicle* and Abe Mellinkoff on the line, but it was San Francisco.

I'd been advised by older heads to reconsider. San Francisco was a big jump; perhaps a paper of medium size would make more sense at so early a stage in my career. Jehanne Salinger warned me about Eppinger. She knew from her son Pierre, who wrote for the *Chronicle*, that the *Examiner* editor was temperamental, running through reporters like Kleenex, often giving them only a couple of weeks to turn in a blockbuster before letting them go if they didn't come through. She pleaded with me to ask Hodge to hold my job for a few weeks, as things might not turn out well in San Francisco, and

I would find myself jobless in a strange city. I was reluctant, but she persisted and I found Hodge willing.

Jehanne was our society editor, a position with a quaint job title nowadays when women fill every job description in a news organization. But half a century ago, with few exceptions, women were assigned to the society beat to keep track of marriages, births, wedding anniversaries, church events, women's clubs, and guest speakers. Jehanne hit Eureka like a hurricane. Teas and socials were fine in their place but she broadened her beat to call attention to worthwhile artists and their endeavors in the county, and to promote local theatre groups and cultural activities, especially at Humboldt State College over in Arcata. But hers could be an acid tongue for work that did not please her. Hodge often looked on in utter astonishment as she spoke her mind.

Her father had been a planter in Indo-China, where Jehanne was raised, and a member of the French Chamber of Deputies. In the storied Paris of the 1920s she earned her living as a journalist. She was acquainted with many of the literary lions of the day, and once covered a Hemingway speech. She was more impressed by his he-man, Hollywood looks than by what he had to say. Having been an editor of a French-language weekly in San Francisco she renewed an acquaintance with the Francophile, Gertrude Stein, who grew up in Oakland.

On occasion, Jehanne's son, Pierre, came up to Eureka to see his mother. His last and most memorable visit coincided with the announcement that he had been awarded a journalism prize and praise from Governor Earl Warren for exposés about conditions for inmates in Bay Area jails. The big city reporter was full of himself that weekend. Put off by his lordly manner, Al Tostado, Ernie Snowberger, and I cooked up a scheme. Once the paper was put to bed, we'd entice Pierre to join us on a tour of Eureka's Two Street. Meantime, we alerted the gendarmes. When we rolled out from Jack Perkin's Palace, the police, following the script, nabbed him. A dirty trick, I grant you, but we wanted to make a point. Ignoring Pierre's protests – "You can't do this to me. I'm Pierre Salinger of the *San Francisco Chronicle*" – the cops packed him into the patrol car and sped off to the station. But before he was ever booked, we called off the gag. As he stormed off, Pierre vowed never to talk to any of us again.

●

In San Francisco I was thrown into a city I did not know. In the *Examiner* newsroom I was surrounded by famous by-line names and in awe of one Pulitzer Prize winner whose desk was next to mine.

My writing was labored. One day Eppinger came by and said, "You're choking up, kid. You got to relax." The next day he said, "Why can't you give me the same quality stuff you gave them in Eureka?" The third day he swooped down ridiculing me for writing the governor "flew" to Los Angeles.

"The way you got it, kid, the guy's sprouting wings!" The fourth day he said, "You're a good kid but I may have to let you go." On the fifth day I was fired.

This was the day I rushed into the newsroom with what I was sure was headline news – a double slaying. Instead I got a lecture on what constituted news on the *Ex*. Eppinger began by telling me what was not news. Murders of poor blacks led the index.

"If you're ever going to make it as a metropolitan reporter you got to be hard-boiled. The *Ex* is no place for bleeding hearts. I had hopes for you, kid, but you're not working out."

●

I returned to Eureka in defeat. Hodge acted as if nothing much had happened. For all the thought he gave to my absence I might have been away on vacation or down with the flu.

But I bore my defeat as if I'd been branded with an F on my forehead – for failure, for being no fucking good.

●

At this time – the mid-1950s – the Soviets were the bugbears, the anti-Christs, the creators of the evil empire. Agents of the communist conspiracy or their dupes were assumed to be everywhere: in federal, state, and local governments; in towns large and small; in the house next door. The Reds were in the schools, contaminating the water, and in the churches. And the liberals were the usual suspects. No one was safe, really, only the Yahoos.

In this paranoid, political climate Hodge and I laid bets on the election of 1956. First for five dollars, then for ten, and so on. As the campaign heated up we raised the ante. Before long my entire paycheck was on the line.

"Sure you want to do this?" Hodge would ask.

I remained resolute.

"You haven't been following the polls, boy. They're predicting an Eisenhower landslide over Stevenson."

"I know what they're saying but I've also seen straws in the wind. People are coming to their senses."

"Who you been talking to, Bill Turk?"

"As a matter of fact, Bill detected a shift in public opinion from people you'd never suspect."

Hodge lit a cigarette, the sweet smoke calling attention to his finely chiseled face. "Most folks in this country are not left-fielders like you and Bill Turk," he said. "They like Ike, and they don't want to change." He took a drag on his cigarette. "Sure you don't want to cancel the bet?"

"Nothing doing," I declared.

He typed out the Inquiring Reporter's question of the day and handed it to me. Importuning people on the street with a newsworthy subject was one of my chores. As I was leaving the newsroom, Hodge's parting injunction followed me to the landing. "I don't want your coming back here saying you looked all over town but couldn't find any voters for Eisenhower."

After toiling along Fourth and Fifth Streets for an hour or so I turned in my findings. Hodge read the copy carefully, concluding, "That's three and three, an even split." But he thought Stevenson got the better of the argument.

INQUIRING REPORTER
Today's Question:
"And the next President of the U.S. is ...?"

CLERK
Mrs. Pat Biasca
3527 M Street
"Stevenson. He's got brains, something that's in short supply in politics."

STUDENT
Barbara Watkins
3421 Oregon Street
"Ike. He's a natural leader. Proved it in the war."

CREDIT MANAGER
S. L. Lindeblad
2539 California Street
"Eisenhower. He knows the world is a dangerous place."

STUDENT
John Bukowski
3223 E Street
"Stevenson. Democrats care about people. Republicans are for
the rich."

MILLWORKER
James Strickland, Jr.
Cutten-Elk River Road
"Stevenson. He's for working people."

RETIRED
Mrs. C. E. Price
McKinleyville
"Ike. There's just something about a soldier."

·

"You didn't doctor any of this, did you? Straight from the horse's
mouth?"

"If you don't believe me you can call them. They're all in the
phone book."

Hodge gave me a twisted smile. "A feller can't be too sure. Not
when he knows someone's bet his whole pay check on the outcome
of the election."

The next day as I was coming in to work, the publisher, Don
O'Kane, gave me the unmistakable high sign to drop in, a flicker of
the index finger on the hand with the big diamond. He presided in
a glass-enclosed office on the street floor from where he could keep
an owlish eye on the girls in bookkeeping.

I was not one of his favorites. He'd never invited me to see the pornographic wallpaper that hung in his private toilet. (It was said to portray 69 positions.) Hodge, Al Tostado, the sports editor, and many others had been privy to the scandalous art, but not me.

This is not to say he treated me badly. Not at all. He was always cordial. I'd been at the paper for a month, maybe a little longer, when he invited me to ride with him around town as he pointed out things. (Since I was Hodge's hire, I suspected he felt a little in the dark about me.)

"Now this is Fifth Avenue," he laughed on that tour as we traversed a railroad crossing near a row of fish canneries.

"And up there," he pointed to a lumber mill, "is Park Avenue." He relished the irony.

Since then he'd been pleasantly surprised with my work, and complimented me on a story about a pygmy forest in Mendocino and another on the hidden marine life in the tide pools at Trinidad. When the town was hit by a small earthquake and the *New York Times* requested a few lines, O'Kane sent for me saying, "They asked for my best man."

And yet I was never completely at ease in his company. I'd seen him stoney drunk with his florid face sunk in the mashed potatoes. And I'd seen him lying prostrate in the gutter outside Johnny's Annex Bar during a night on the town.

Once, I'd had the bad luck to run into him quite late in Johnny's. He was still alert enough to recognize me. Over my protestations, he told Johnny to give us a round. Immediately, he began saying that he hoped I would get over my fascination with FDR and Truman and Stevenson, and come over to the true American party, the Republican Party. Otherwise, he said ... but didn't finish the thought. His manner frightened me. I felt he was delivering a warning, that I was under suspicion, a marked man.

For all his nocturnal carousing, his recuperative powers were truly amazing. After only a few hours' sleep he was his sober self again, crisp and enlivened, drawing on one of his delicious Havanas.

That morning when he summoned me into his office, the morning paper was spread out on his desk.

He leaned his great bulk forward, his froggy eyes bleary from the night's excesses. His voice wheedled.

"Sit down. You're not getting fired."

I found a seat.

"It's something you ought to know," he said. "But it's not anything you should worry about."

A delegation of Republican women had descended on him, denouncing me as a communist sympathizer and worse, all because of the morning's Inquiring Reporter.

"They wanted me to fire you," he smiled, drawing the ever-present cigar from his lips. "They're outraged over the free ride you gave Stevenson."

He held up the column.

"Eisenhower got three favorables, too," I said.

"That's right," said O'Kane. "But the ladies think you loaded the dice. Did you? I wouldn't hear of it. And I told them so."

"I was careful to strike a balance. Hodge insisted on it."

"I know. The good matrons live in a cocoon. They don't believe there are three literate Democrats in Humboldt County."

"What would have made them happy?"

"Four Ike's to two Adlai's, maybe. Better yet, five Ike's to one Adlai. I told them, I yield to no one in my devotion to the Republican cause but no one is going to tell me how to run my newspaper." And with that, the proprietor of the Eureka Newspapers, Inc. bid the ladies a good day.

"That's great, Don."

"I haven't told you the half of it. I told them I abhorred your brand of politics but that you were young and there was hope that one day you'd come around."

I was on the point of saying something effusive but he waved me off with his Havana.

"Now, run along upstairs, and we'll talk no more of this. You and Hodge have a paper to put out."

Bill Turk

I'd just climbed the stairs to the newsroom saying, "Something's funny, Hodge. Bill Turk's not in his shop."

Hodge looked up from his pile of wire copy.

"I just went over there for a shine but the place is locked up tighter than a drum."

At that hour, six o'clock on a Saturday night, Bill was always going strong. He'd go to nine or ten or even later to catch the trade.

"What'd you find out?"

"I can't really say. It just felt funny."

When the rhythm of life is interrupted in a small town, people's premonitions are aroused. I began calling around, starting with the hospitals.

Something had happened. Bill had been admitted to General Hospital complaining of chest pains and then he died, just up and died. He must have breathed his last while I was rattling his door.

"Obit?" I said, assuming Hodge wanted the usual death notice, with the listing of next of kin and funeral arrangements from the mortuary.

Hodge shook his head. He wanted a story. Bill Turk was a name in this town. Everybody knew him. He was shining shoes at his hut at E Street and Third before Hodge hit Eureka. The editor didn't share my opinion of Bill as a diamond in the rough but he did get a kick out of him, as did O'Kane, as did most white folks who believed that Bill gave color to the town, and no pun intended.

Amazing. Rising above the hand-me-down prejudices of his native Oklahoma, Hodge was treating the natural death of an ordinary black as legitimate news. "Well, Jesus," I said. "You do think he's a story?"

Hodge said, "O'Kane, you know, the fat sonofabitch downstairs who signs our check, he enjoyed him, thought well of him, for a colored man," he said of our publisher.

"You really are serious?"

"Time's awastin'."

"The pictures, that's what O'Kane went in there for."

The walls of Bill's hut were covered with pictures of lusty, bosomy girls from *Playboy*. Bill liked to say they kept up his spirits and helped him to think positively. At the same time they brought in the big spenders and kept the prudes away.

All I knew about Bill Turk was that he was a genial black with a stubble of beard and a bawdy sense of humor. When the jokes petered out we turned to sports but our real passion was politics and giving the Republicans hell.

"Well, write all that," said Hodge.

"The dirty pictures, that's the heart of it," I said. "They worked for Bill the way they worked for Gauguin."

"Gauguin."

I couldn't resist. "Gauguin, the French painter. He hung obscene pictures on the wall of his Paris stairway. They kept the do-gooders from his door. Bill was like that. An independent guy."

"Get that in there, too," Hodge chuckled.

•

The Inquiring Reporter was a dream assignment for a young, single male. He didn't need an introduction to meet a girl, only Hodge's question of the day. ("In this modern age, should a girl allow a boy to kiss her on their first date?" "Do you believe in love at first sight?" "Do you favor separate vacations for married couples?")

I fell in and out of love with astonishing frequency. And I must have had a "thing" for white uniforms. My great loves were a county health nurse and a physical therapist; but there were countless infatuations and flirtations in between, almost all the result of chance encounters when plying the question of the day,

Sometimes (when time hung heavy and there was little stirring) I'd slip away to keep a rendezvous. Looking up from his desk and finding me gone, Hodge would call over to Al Tostado.

"Where the hell is the kid? Where's he gone now?"

A Strange Breed of Folks

I only learned of Hodge's pique in later years when Al and I reminisced about our Eureka days.

Thus I learned that, one night, advancing on the sports desk, Hodge said, "The kid, he's got girls stashed away all over town. Now don't sit there and deny it. He isn't a drinker. I would have spotted that long ago."

"Beats me," said Al.

When I was on the phone with a love interest, Hodge would be in despair trying to read my lips or catch a telltale word or two. I took pains to wheel far enough around so that all he could make of me was my back. (I'd learned the technique from him.)

It plainly bothered the old Lothario when, looking out his wide window, he'd spot me sprinting across to the DeLuxe Club or ducking into Johnny's or flitting through the alley to Roy's.

"How does he manage it? How does he meet them? I've lived in this town for twenty years and I don't know half as many women as he does."

"Beats me," said Al.

Hodge had given up women when he gave up drinking after a heart attack, but he still fancied himself a lady's man. He was a handsome, courtly southerner who looked back wistfully on his own past amours.

"I got it," he said one night. This time there was conviction in his voice. "The kid's no Gable. There's no mystery to it. He meets them on the Inquiring Reporter, that's how he does it."

Al remained his impassive self.

Hodge swore, "I'm going to take the kid off the Inquiring Reporter if it's the last thing I do."

But he only made these threats to Al.

•

The first payday after the election (Eisenhower won in a landslide), I duly handed Hodge my paycheck, fully expecting him to adopt a fatherly attitude, give the check back, and say something like, "Let this be a lesson to you. In the future if you must bet, do so with your head and not your heart. When you let your emotions get the upperhand where money is concerned, it's going to cost you."

But he said nothing of the kind. He gave me that crooked smile instead, laughed softly, and put the check in his pocket. The whole damn thing.

·

There was a bottomless fear that the Russians were bent on taking over the United States militarily. But how would they come? Where would they strike? The media was full of scenarios. Hodge had one of his own.

A Soviet sub, carrying a small A-bomb, would transfer the device to a trawler off the vast, unprotected northern California coast. Under cover of night, the fishing boat would put in at a cove where the nuclear device would be hoisted onto the bed of a semi trailer. And off the truck would go down Highway 1 to San Francisco.

Hodge looked up from the map, paused to light a cigarette, and to let it all sink in.

"Next morning," he resumed, "just as thousands of people are streaming in to work, the bomb goes off at the Ferry Building. The explosion is many times greater than the blast at Hiroshima. San Francisco's wiped out. World War Three has begun. Well, it could happen."

The sneak nuclear attack, as Hodge depicted it, begged for artwork for which we had no money. But we knew where to turn. A former Hollywood art director was living in the redwoods in the southern tier of the county. To our minds (Hodge's and mine), Bob Usher was just about the greatest artist alive. Soon after he'd moved to Humboldt County, I wrote a welcoming Sunday feature, and more recently, he'd designed – free of charge – blueprints for the new Eureka Zoo.

So, as Hodge said, we knew he was civic-minded.

Bob obliged us. Thanks to his artistry we were, for the moment, in big-time journalism.

THIS CAN HAPPEN HERE
This Article Will Frighten You, And Make You Think –
It Is Not A Fable, But Is Based On Cold, Considered Facts.
What Can We Do About It?

For this fantasy we won plaudits from civilian defense officials in Sacramento and Washington. The local chapter gave Hodge a plaque.

Although we may have added to the hysteria of the times, no one could claim that any real harm had been done.

However, another Hodge idea did threaten to get out of hand, given the paranoia of those times.

You knew an idea was percolating the moment he chuckled softly to himself and lit a cigarette.

"Boy," he called out to me one day. "How many fatalities would you say we have every year? One a week, maybe more?"

He began typing, paused, and looked up, grinning. A new crusade was being conceived.

"High-time," he said, "to do something about highway safety." With a few taps on the keyboard Hodge brought into being a new cause. He'd even come up with a name, Drivers Alert!

ALL-OUT WAR DECLARED ON DRUNKEN DRIVERS!
DRIVERS ALERT! TO BE EYES OF THE LAW

He needled me for a line to go with a montage of auto wrecks and fatalities.

THESE DEAD WERE NOT KILLED IN KOREA

Then, as I wrote the lead, he prompted:

"The Humboldt Times called on Humboldt County's licensed drivers today to join a grass-roots crusade to drive reckless and drunken drivers off our 5,280 miles of roads.

"Drivers Alert! is both the name and the rallying cry of the new volunteer force whose members will function as para-militaries reporting rule-of-the-road violations to law enforcement agencies."

Once again we made a pilgrimage to Bob Usher. In due time he produced a logo for Drivers Alert! Shaped like a pyramid in patriotic red, white, and blue, it was designed for display in the lower right-hand corner of the windshield.

We'd struck a nerve. In a week we collected hundreds of dollars in five-dollar membership fees. We took in more money the following week.

"If the response keeps up this way," said Hodge, "we'll be in the running for a Pulitzer."

The front pages bellowed with headlines aimed at inspiring the public's participation in Hodge's brainstorm. One such article shouted:

DRIVERS ALERT! THE EYES AND EARS OF THE LAW

"Fifty-five highway deaths so far this year, and it's only September. In a county as sparsely populated as ours the death rate from auto and truck accidents already exceeds the toll, per capita, of the Civil War, this nation's bloodiest war. WE MUST RECLAIM OUR HIGHWAYS AND STREETS FROM THE TYRANNY OF RECKLESS AND DRUNKEN DRIVERS. THE LIFE YOU SAVE MAY BE YOUR OWN!"

•

Up to this point in time Hodge, Al, Ernie, and I were frequently broke. (I don't remember what I was making in 1955 – $75 a week, maybe $80, not much even for those days.) To tide us over we were in the habit of tapping Johnny at the Annex Bar for the extra dollars required until payday.

Now, thanks to Drivers Alert! we were solvent beyond our wildest dreams. We had no further need of Johnny. All we had to do was dip a hand into the shoebox – our own bank, so to speak – for this was where the Drivers Alert! money was kept. Our laissez-faire behavior was probably felonious (though we left IOUs behind) but consider: when you've worked till midnight and you're as dry as can be, and the bars close in two hours and you're young and your heart's on fire for adventure and romance, you have to make allowances.

Such was the philosophy Al and I espoused. Ernie did, too, though he was a loner.

Every now and then I'd come across Ernie in a waterfront dive. He never welcomed companionship. A true drinker, he was happy in his solitude.

On the rare occasion when he broke his silence he'd remind me that the town jumped in the old days. When I'd ask him when that might have been, he'd furnish a date, which, as it turned out, was just before I hit town.

"This joint here," he'd say, "it used to be a pretty lively place. The booze was better and cheaper. There were always some good-look-ing babes around. For a few drinks, you could have your pick. This was a fun town in those days."

It wasn't until I knew his story that I found an explanation for Ernie's misanthropy.

Some months before my arrival in Eureka – I now set down what Al told me of that day – the police were looking for a drifter named Gulbranson. A suspect in a triple murder down in Sonoma, Gulbran-son was thought to be headed our way.

Only Hodge, Al and a new cub were in the newsroom when the phone rang. The cub picked it up.

A few moments later the cub, whose name was Ed Neumeir, was trying to get Hodge's attention. The managing editor paid him no heed. Hodge was too busy wheedling free tickets from a circus advance man.

"Gulbranson," Neumeir persisted. An annoyed Hodge turned.

"It's Gulbranson," Neumier said, covering the mouthpiece. "He's at the Log Cabin."

"Gulbranson?"

"Wants to turn himself in. To a reporter."

"Where's Ernie?" Hodge said. Drunk or sober, Ernie was our ace. The cops loved him, never let him fail. But his desk was vacant. Then Hodge remembered; Ernie had gone off for his laundry, or so he had claimed.

Hodge hesitated. No telling when Ernie might return – or in what shape. Al couldn't be spared from the sports desk; Hodge couldn't leave, and someone had to remain in charge. That left the cub.

"You better go," Hodge told Neumier. He was a spunky young man, and took to newspapering naturally.

Neumeir was already at the door when Hodge cautioned, "Don't tell anyone what you're up to. And get back here as soon as you can. Just remember, you're dealing with a fugitive from justice, a man wanted for murder, so don't do anything foolish."

Hodge paced. A half-hour past before the kid called.

He's the McCoy, Neumier said, over the phone. But shaky and miserable, he hasn't eaten in days, Hodge learned. Neumier was keeping an eye on him. No, Gulbranson wasn't armed – the kid was certain. The old guy's just scared and hungry. After a square meal, he swears he'll talk.

"All right," said Hodge. "Be careful. Bring him here to the paper. Act as nonchalant as possible. You don't want to give people the idea that something big is going on. Better you come up through the back door. You want to be careful."

After hanging up, Hodge glanced at the clock over Al's desk. He wondered whether to call the cops.

"Call the cops," said Al, "and you'll risk losing the scoop. Everybody in town, everybody on the coast, would be in on the story. Get the Gulbranson confession first. Worry about the cops later."

"But what if the guy's violent, turns on us?" Hodge responded.

Al said, "Trust the kid. He says the guy's beat. Gulbranson's turning himself in – to us. It's every newspaperman's dream."

Hodge fretted, saying that he'd feel a lot better if Ernie were on the story.

The cub, following Hodge's instructions, came in through the alley; that is, through the composing room and up the stairs, past the photo lab and into the newsroom.

Far from being a menacing figure, the murder suspect was an object of pity, frail and sickly.

"Hodge," announced the young reporter. "This is Gulbranson." Hodge mumbled a few pleasantries but did not offer his hand.

"He won't talk until he's had something to eat," said Neumeir.

As he, Neumier, and Gulbranson started down the back stairs, Hodge called over to Al, "We're going over to Harriet's. We shouldn't be long."

As they settled in the restaurant, Hodge asked the fugitive to sit with his back to the other patrons. He wanted to minimize the risk of Gulbranson's being discovered.

"Order whatever you like," said Hodge. "It's on us." (When he submitted his expenses, Hodge wrote, "Five dollars. Entertaining a murderer.")

Once the suspect had eaten his fill and they'd returned to the newspaper, Hodge selected a spare room, away from the newsroom, where the young reporter could take Gulbranson's confession. Hodge stood by to help with the questions and double as security.

Never having been alone with a murder suspect before, Hodge – by a later account to Al – was fidgety.

A large pair of scissors lay on a table. Anxious that the fugitive might, if aroused, seize them as a weapon, Hodge wanted to get them out of sight, but he dared not move for fear of provoking Gulbranson. During all the time he and the young reporter were taking Gulbranson's confession, Hodge never took his eyes off the scissors.

Eventually, Ernie returned to the newsroom. By this time, Gulbranson was being led away by a sheriff's deputy, and Neumier, the cub, was furiously typing up the scoop, which, by right, should have been Ernie's.

·

Gulbranson's surrender and murder confession to a *Humboldt Times* reporter got big play in newspapers all along the West Coast, and on radio and TV. A few months later the Pall Mall television program, *The Big Story*, awarded its $500 cash prize "for courageous and enterprising journalism" to Ed Neumier. An actor played him in a re-enactment of the confession.

Hodge begrudged the kid neither the money nor the glory, but thought the managing editor deserved better in the TV treatment. A camera crew shot Hodge leaving his house, getting in his car, coming into the newspaper office, editing copy, walking the length of the newsroom; but on the air there was only a fleeting glimpse of him in the "tease" footage leading in to the story.

The actor playing Hodge not only had a bit role but also came across as the heavy.

Ed Neumier wasn't long for Eureka. Even before *The Big Story* aired he had been hired by the *Honolulu Star*.

·

COUNTY TOLL DOWN:
DRIVERS ALERT!
SEEN AS FACTOR

"Humboldt County Sheriff Albert Nichols yesterday declared that preliminary studies showed a decline in fatalities on county roads last month as compared with figures from a comparable period of the year before."

"Those are county roads. Not killers like 101 or 299," scoffed Ernie Snowberger who, it was said, had developed a sardonic attitude towards life ever since the Gulbranson story.

"Besides, Nichols's up for re-election. You and Hodge have turned a lot of nuts loose, and the question is, how are you going to get the genie back in the bottle?"

Ernie was right – Hodge's vigilantes were taking to the highways and city streets – running after drivers, swamping the police with complaints; in some instances, taking the law into their own hands and making citizens' arrests. Worse, night after night crusaders tramped up to the newsroom besieging Hodge and me with notions on how to bring wayward drivers to justice. We were spooked. We wanted out. But how? What could we do? Hodge and I were news-types, word people, not organizers. What did we know about leading a movement that numbered in the hundreds and was still growing?

We sought out Bob Usher. He'd know what to do. Hadn't he been a success in Hollywood?

From the start Bob, a long-limbed figure, had expressed concern about promoting a Big Brother mentality with Drivers' Alert! Now, after reminding us of this fact, he said, reassuringly, that yes, there was a way out, a way that moguls resorted to whenever they found themselves under siege.

"There's no need for panic," said Bob. "You've done your job. You've raised an issue of concern to the community. Now it's time to give the job to others."

His suggestion was that we name a blue-ribbon committee composed of the top people, the most prominent in the county, and let them run it.

"But appoint them now while Drivers Alert! is still popular and there's glory in it for them."

Now? Hodge and I exchanged knowing looks. We couldn't do it now. At least not immediately. What about the money? We had to replenish the shoebox (stowed in a filing cabinet) before we ever could give thought to a blue ribbon commission.

In time we did. But it took several weeks, several diligent, self-sacrificing weeks, before we were able to make good on all those IOUS. Once purged of guilt, however, Hodge and I got busy and named a committee.

The group we brought forth included the chairman of the county board of supervisors; the mayors of Eureka and Blue Lake; the district attorney; the head of the local state highway patrol; Eureka's chief of police (the biggest crypto-fascist in town); an advertising executive; and representatives of the Eureka and Humboldt County chambers of commerce, including businessmen, lawyers, a medical doctor, a dentist, and a veterinarian.

A car dealer was chosen president. In his acceptance speech he said, "The job is a tough one, but I can't imagine one that is more important to the welfare of all our people. We need the best brains of the county and the professional assistance they can give us – lawyers, insurance men, automobile dealers – and I am confident that we are going to do just that."

Hodge, preoccupied with the paper, entrusted me with responsibility for keeping things humming.

DRIVERS ALERT! SAFETY
GROUP FORMED HERE
Leaders Enthusiastically
Endorse Plan to Halt
Slaughter on Highways

"There was little doubt," the *Humboldt Times* commented next morning, "that from now on the eyes of the state and perhaps the nation would be focused on Humboldt County."

Make no mistake. Drivers Alert! was the most spectacular idea that Hodge ever had.

Anne-Marie

Ever since I hit Eureka, my mother was on guard lest I fall prey to a gentile. Bubbe urged her to give up Boston and relocate in San Francisco once I'd landed my newspaper job so she could be closer to her only child. Perhaps Bubbe could recall the circumstances when my newspaper uncle, Sam, had strayed into the arms of a gentile in the Midwest. This was a dark period in the family's history, unspoken history about which nothing was ever said within earshot of the grandchildren. Bitterly, no doubt, she recalled how he'd showed up impoverished on the steps of the house in Dorchester with a wife and baby girl. A family council was convened. My father was one of those opportuned to contribute to a fund to enable Sam's bride to return to the plains with the child. (Long afterwards my father would complain that Sam never paid any of the money back as he had promised.)

Several months after I'd landed in Eureka, my mother sought law work in the northwestern California city with the idea of relocating there, but nothing came of it. The several years I lived in Eureka she would stay put in San Francisco, 300 merciful miles away, where she found employment badgering delinquents for a loan company.

Too often my mother would announce that she was planning a Eureka weekend. I did my best to discourage her, making up excuses. But sometimes, when she persisted, I yielded. At the time of one visit I was staying in a rooming house where the landlady stipulated that one's door must be left ajar at all times when a visitor was in the room. When I engaged a room across the hall for my mother, the proprietress waived the restriction.

I was there to greet my mother when she pulled in at the Greyhound depot. After a dinner of her favorite fish, broiled halibut, and a favorite dessert, apple pie à la mode, at an excellent seafood restaurant, I brought her to her room and bade her goodnight; then I raced uptown to Anne-Marie's. I hadn't breathed a word to her about Anne-Marie or, for that matter, about my mother's coming to Anne-Marie. Anne-Marie would want to meet my mother; my mother would be stiff-necked and disdainful meeting the woman in my life. Were they ever to meet, my mother surely would treat her badly.

There the matter lay, unspoken, as Anne-Marie and I proceeded to get stinko on a Saturday night. When we drank heavily we usually wound up at each other's throat.

We fought over a future together, of her fear of being used, of her growing old, of my sexual demands, of her need for time away from me. And then she cried, "I don't want to see you again. Please, I beg you. It's over!" And she drove me from her house.

Many of our nights had ended in this ghastly fashion. That night with my mother across the hall, I slept fitfully as I always did following such self-slaughter marinated in alcohol. And I vowed, as I always did, that this was the finish, I was not going to take her abuse any longer, no ifs ands or buts about it, promises I had made to myself a hundred times. (I mistakenly believed that if I could abstain from any contact with Anne-Marie for as long as three days, or seventy-two hours, I would be set free from her.)

In the morning, past ten, I finally fell into a deep sleep, when I was startled by a rattling sound. Someone was tapping on my ground-floor window.

It was Anne-Marie, still half-drunk, still in love. Seeing her cheerful eyes I knew all was forgiven, the nightmare past. She laughed at the sight of my disheveled astonishment.

"I'm coming in," she said.

"But you can't," I protested. My landlady didn't permit visitors into the house until noon. I was also concerned lest my mother find us together. "Wait," I pleaded. "I'll be out in a minute.

I slipped into a pair of jeans and a jersey and paused to scribble a note: "Dear Ma, off on a story. Don't expect to be long, but one never knows in the news game. Love, Mel." I had barely made it back to my room when I heard a thud, as if a sack had dropped. Wheeling around I found myself face to face with Anne-Marie. She had climbed into the room through the street window.

She looked worn, older than the age I took her for. Our breaths reeked of alcohol. No matter; we kissed greedily.

"It's all right. I'm here," she said comfortingly.

"Everything is going to be all right," I said.

"We mustn't fight like that again."

"Promise."

"Melvin!"

A familiar cry sliced through me like a knife. My mother, dressed for the day, was waiting on the threshold. She took no notice of Anne-Marie. If I didn't know her better I would have sworn she didn't see her.

"Melvin," she said. "I've been waiting for hours to go to breakfast. I'm famished."

"Mother, I'd like you to meet a good friend."

ANNE-MARIE (*warmly, with dignity*): Hello. I've heard so much about you from your son, Mrs. Lavine. I'm so pleased to meet you at last.

MOTHER (*stiffly*): Hello.

ANNE-MARIE: Mel didn't tell me you were coming up. If I had known I would have arranged a better welcome. I hope you will let me make dinner for you.

MOTHER: I don't see how it can be arranged. We have so much to do. I don't see my son very often.

ANNE-MARIE: If you change your mind, don't forget, you have a rain check. Just give me a ring. Have fun, you two.

When I drove off with my mother, she said, "That woman is much too old for you. You're just having a good time? You're not serious?"

MEL: We're friends, Ma.

MOTHER: But you can't be serious about her. You have your whole life ahead of you. You can't tie yourself to an old woman, and a gentile, no less!

MEL: Her family fought in the Norwegian underground during the occupation. She herself helped Jews get away from the Germans. She saved Jewish lives! She's a good person.

The argument failed to move her.

With Anne-Marie I roamed the old beaches of the northern California coast, swam and camped near the site of an old mine on the other side of the mountains, hiked through fir and redwood forests, took pleasure in wildlife, plants, and flowers. Anne-Marie shared my disdain for tradition. My most memorable Thanksgiving was spent with her at the quiet, foggy Boat Basin, feasting on crab and beer, far from my family's traditional board and ponderous company.

Anne-Marie, this tall, supple, frizzy blonde immigrant who labored as a physical therapist at the General Hospital, sometimes questioned my reporting. After reading my story of the police capturing a man wanted for armed robbery, the interrogation went on like this:

ANNE-MARIE: Why do you only take what the police say? Why don't you talk to the other people? There must be more to it than what the police say.

ME: We're a small paper. We depend on the cops for the news.

ANNE-MARIE: It's not right that you collaborate with the police. Your job is to tell the truth. If people cannot trust what you report, what are we to believe?

I argued she was not being realistic, that in a small town like Eureka everyone has to get along. The *Humboldt Times* is not the *San Francisco Chronicle*. What I didn't say was that I was afraid of the cops, the chief of police, Ced Emahiser, in particular. He, especially, intimidated me. A wiry, humorless fellow, he seemed to intimidate almost everyone, including members of the City Council. Rather than admit to Anne-Marie that Emahiser frightened me, I referred to him as a crypto-fascist who was liked by Don O'Kane, the publisher, and Hodge.

"The chief holds all the cards," I said. "If you don't go along with them they'll withhold the good stuff, give it to one of our competitors (the afternoon paper, or a weekly or to a broadcaster) and in Hodge's eyes I would have fallen down on the job. I can't let that happen. The cops know how to play us."

Anne-Marie, thrusting her hands in the pockets of her dress, said, "But how can they do this? How can they get away with it?

You must show more backbone. You have such wonderful ideals. What do you care about them? If you lost your job here, you can find another, and a better one, maybe."

Except for Red McCann, no one had ever spoken to me like this before. Appealing to Hodge was an exercise in futility, I said. Hodge was not like my old editor in Maine. Cautious, fearful Hodge saw his role as a facilitator; his goal was to please O'Kane, to spare O'Kane from stress. O'Kane had spared Hodge when the latter was drinking heavily, and when he made Hodge managing editor of the morning paper Hodge became his indentured servant for life.

Anne-Marie would not be appeased. "Do something about it," she said.

So we argued about journalism in Eureka, often parting in a storm of angry words.

•

As I reflect on the days with Anne-Marie, I see myself at twenty-four as a flashy success in a small backwater, in danger of becoming a pompous boob. Along with offering her critiques about journalism, she re-awakened my slumbering interest in the arts – in literature, painting, and classical music – by holding up such models of excellence as her great countrymen, Ibsen and Munch and Grieg, and the German Thomas Mann, the Spaniard Picasso, and the Austrian Mozart. I countered with my own gods, Thomas Wolfe, Hemingway, Scott Fitzgerald, Walt Whitman, and then, running low on titans, pressed Ring Lardner and Damon Runyon into service. Valiant efforts, but I was overwhelmed by her legions in which Johann Wolfgang von Goethe, Johann Christoph Friedrich von Schiller, Sigrid Undset, Hans Christian Anderson, Johann Sebastian Bach, and Ludwig van Beethoven also figured prominently.

Before immigrating to this country, Anne-Marie had been married for ten years to a successful lawyer in Oslo, and bored with her life. An older sister urged her to move to northern California where she was living with a new husband, also a Norwegian immigrant. Soon after her arrival in 1949, she enrolled in school to study physical therapy. I first met her plying the question of the day on the street for the Inquiring Reporter, smitten by her Scandinavian beauty.

Our romance coincided with the harrowing heyday of the demagogue Joe McCarthy. He frightened us both. He and his fellow reactionaries reminded her of Hitler and the Storm Troopers. She was suspicious of the U.S. government's motives in the Cold War. She believed the big capitalists in America used communism in much the same way as the fascists used fear of communism in Germany, Italy, and Spain, and the communists in Russia and China and elsewhere used fear of the fascists and capitalists, all to suppress their populations, all to perpetuate themselves in power.

"You must read Arthue Koestler," she said. "You must know *Darkness at Noon*, a great novel about the totalitarian state. Yes, something like this could happen here." Pacing, she thought it was already happening. In Norway she had seen reactionaries gain power during the German occupation when the Quislings moved into the positions of authority. Irwin Shaw's *The Young Lions* was another book I must read, and Shaw's *The Troubled Air*, a story about curtailing free speech by purging liberals from the airwaves; it was a prophetic work in Anne-Marie's estimation, since just such a thing was happening then in America.

During this time my patriotism was suspect and I was shunned by friends. People we knew believed McCarthy's lies about a communist conspiracy inside the White House, State Department, and Army. Liberal-minded professors who refused to take loyalty oaths lost their jobs. Actors, writers, and artists, suspected of disloyalty, were blacklisted and lost their careers. In this poisoned climate Anne-Marie and I spoke guardedly when around other people. We were like two souls locked in a mad embrace while the world outside had gone to the dogs, howling outside the door.

•

Hodge looked up from his desk and said, "This newspaper is dying on La-*vine*." This was the managing editor's way of saying, "We're short a good local story for page one; high time to make another check 'round your beat."

I walked over in the damp fog to the police station. As always at night, the brilliant florescent lighting came as a shock. Captain Carey, a beefy, slow-witted Irishman, was at the counter, idly perusing *Playboy*. As I scanned the report sheet, I heard a commotion in the alley. Carey read my mind. "A drunk, an uppity spic they found down at the Northwestern Pacific tracks. He's been giving the boys nothing but a hard time."

The two cops came in with their prisoner, handling him roughly. When he objected, they fell on him. Then they stood him up against the wall and started throwing punches. One of the cops, bespectacled, bookish-looking, was an amateur lightweight. He took aim and hit the drunk repeatedly. The Latino wet his pants. The cops went wild, especially the bookish one, until, at length, the cops tired of the sport and tossed the bedeviled fellow in a heap on the floor of a cell where drunks and petty offenders were locked up for the night.

I bounded upstairs to the newsroom to pour out my eyewitness account.

Hodge shrugged. "We get a lot of good stuff from the cops. We don't want to get them sore at us. O'Kane would never go along. He likes Emahiser."

"Hodge, we're talking about police brutality, a savage beating of a defenseless human being. I saw it with my own eyes. They're so arrogant, they let me watch them!"

"O'Kane would never go for it. The man's a transient, a Mexican. He doesn't live here, has nothing to do with Eureka, has no family here, no job, and pays no taxes. Why should we jeopardize our relationship with the cops over something like this? If he lived here and worked here, well, maybe that'd be different."

I could have predicted Anne-Marie's response. "You have to tell the world," she said heatedly. "You have to write it for the *San Francisco Chronicle* or the AP. People need to know. Isn't that a reporter's job? To tell the truth?"

"You're not being realistic," I told her that night when I recounted the episode to her. I couldn't betray Hodge and O'Kane.

"You could resign."

"With no job to go to?" As reasonable my reply, I nevertheless felt diminished, that I'd made myself smaller in Anne-Marie's eyes.

●

One early morning after a night of heavy drinking, too upset to sleep, I got out of bed with the intention of fixing myself a cup of coffee. The contents of Anne-Marie's purse, which lay in a heap on her dresser, caught my attention. I looked over at Anne-Marie. She was still sleeping soundly. Her driver's license was in plain sight. It confirmed (Anne-Marie never spoke of her age) what I'd feared most – a great difference in our ages. When in twelve years I reached her present age of thirty-six, she would be a matron of forty-eight. When I reached forty-eight she would be an old woman of sixty!

Nonetheless, I wanted the relationship to go on. But as time went on, our rows grew fiercer and more frequent. Before long, Anne-Marie's attitude turned harsh. "What's wrong?" I said. "Why do you want to end things?"

She retorted that I gave her no time for herself, no time to breathe. She was suffocating. "I want my freedom," she cried.

I kept asking to see her, even after she began dating other men.

"You're only looking for a place to put it," she screamed as she drove me away from her modest but attractive cottage for the last time.

Years later I would hear from a person who'd known us both that Anne-Marie had in fact been in love with me, but was angry because I wouldn't marry her. I was shocked to learn this, and for a long time in despair over my loss.

A Lumberjack Abroad

At twenty-four I was feeling as if the world had passed me by, my misfortune being that I came along too late to play a role in World War Two, the great watershed in the lives of uncles and older cousins and family friends. When I was drafted in 1946 the war had been over a year, a tranquil time. Korea still lay in the future.

But to make it as a newsman I decided I needed more life experience.

In the spring of 1955 I began looking for a ship. My quest led to Rolf Larsen, the San Francisco agent for the Goteborg-based Transatlantic Company. Larsen occupied a tiny office in a huge warehouse on the docks.

He listened sympathetically but had become wary of writer-types begging for a term at grunt labor to see the world from the deck of a freighter. They all talked big and backed out at the last minute or became so disillusioned they paid off in Australia or Singapore which may have been where they were headed all the time.

I was not like the others, I said. He would not be wasting his time helping me.

"But there is nothing now," he said. "A vacancy occurs when someone gets hurt or jumps ship and I have to fill the job immediately. If I call you'll have to come at once."

I kept after Larsen, but he never had anything to say other than that his news was not encouraging and that he had no idea when he would have something.

Looking for a berth on an American ship led nowhere. The union men I met discouraged me with talk of interminable delays over waiting lists, and seniority rules, and the scarcity of openings for apprentices.

I dug into my modest savings and booked passage on a British freighter due to sail from San Francisco for England by way of the Panama Canal in July.

But how was I going to afford to live? I'd really not given it any serious thought. Hodge was alarmed and got to scheming. My idea was to write a column about my travels, my adventures and misadventures. Surely that would pay for expenses.

Hodge wisely saw it differently.

"That won't do," he said. "O'Kane would never go for it." If I was to get some pay from the newspaper, we needed to come up with an angle, a gimmick.

Days passed. The sailing date was drawing near.

Then Hodge lit a cigarette and began typing. He'd hit upon a scheme to persuade O'Kane to keep me on the payroll.

A SPARKLING NEW FEATURE:
A LUMBERJACK ABROAD

He stabbed away at the keyboard:

"Staff Writer Mel Lavine leaves by freighter in a month on a roving international assignment, and so will begin a sparkling new feature exclusive in the *Times*, 'A Lumberjack Abroad.'

"While in Europe, Lavine will call on as many relatives and friends of our readers, as time and itinerary will permit.

"If you have a relative or friend whom you think would make interesting reading locally, fill in the information requested below and send to the *Humboldt Times* 328 E Street as soon as possible."

"We can't promise that your suggestion will be used but we will give it every consideration. And please omit packages, parcels, or presents of any kind."

Hodge's face burned with the intensity it always did when he was consumed by the brilliance of one of his ideas.

"Look," he said, tilting his head at an angle to address me. "Our circulation area is full of Swedes and Finns and northern Italians. Sentimental folks, always talking about the old country, taking vacations there, sending money to the old people. I bet we'll get five hundred letters."

"Which means I'll be visiting God-knows how many friends and relatives? It's not going to work." I could see myself having to give up Paris and London and Rome to trek to somebody's Aunt Helga in a glacial hamlet.

"We're not saying how many people you're going to talk to," said Hodge, marking the copy to run on Page One.

"Shit."

Hodge looked up. "Find half a dozen that work. The rest of the time write anything you like. We have to worry about that fat son of a bitch downstairs. I've already talked to him and he's agreed to pay you fifty dollars a week."

As Hodge predicted, readers were enthusiastic. There were requests to visit relatives and friends throughout Scandinavia and northern Europe: Switzerland, Spain, Portugal, Italy, France, even Luxemburg.

"Figure where you're going to be and take a bunch of the most promising letters with you. That's the way to do it," said Hodge who'd never set foot outside the country. "If you do one or two relatives' stories a month nobody's going to make a fuss."

"Hodge, have you ever factored in the distances between cities in Europe, the time it's going to take, the money it's going to cost?"

"You make it easy on yourself. If there's a relative of one of our readers in the neighborhood where you happen to be, take a minute and drop in for smorgasbord or pickled herring. You'll have a ball. They'll greet you like a long-lost brother."

"It's not going to work," I said.

With my sailing date a month away, Rolf Larsen was unexpectedly on the other end of the line. He had a ship but I had to be aboard the next day in San Pedro, 800 miles away. The freighter sailed for Australia the following day.

I panicked. "I can't possibly make it," I said, pleading for more time to wind up my job, move out of my apartment, store belongings and my '49 Chevrolet.

"I thought you were sincere," he said. There was reproach in his voice.

"I am," I said.

'Your ship sails in forty-eight hours," the agent said. "If you are not going to be there you must tell me now, immediately."

"I will be there," I answered flatly.

"You better tell O'Kane," said Hodge, when he heard of my new departure date.

I found O'Kane downstairs in his office.

"I have this chance to work my way around the world on a Swedish freighter. They're holding a job for me but I have to leave right away. Tonight."

O'Kane listened with an amused look. When I finished he drew on his cigar, slowly exhaled the luxurious smoke and said, "Bon voyage."

My landlord and his wife told me not to worry. They had plenty of closet space where my things would be safe until I returned. Joe Coggins and Stan Stremka, the pressmen, put my car up on blocks in the building that housed the presses. Clyde Mooney, the bookkeeper, handed me $100 advance.

That night I caught the last Greyhound to San Francisco, and in the early morning rode another bus to Los Angeles.

Hodge informed our readers that Staff Writer Lavine was already on his way to Europe, albeit by way of Australia and as a member of the forty-five-man crew of the Swedish freighter, Parrakoola. His "Lumberjack Abroad" column would be appearing soon.

.

I went to sea as massup, or mess boy. The pay was $44 a month, plus a nightly ration of beer. My afternoons were free, and I spent them tapping out columns for Hodge. I shared a cabin with a young Dutchman of my own age, Jeffrey De Jong, who was also doing double duty as a journalist for a hometown paper. He was working his way back to Europe after eighteen months of disillusionment as an immigrant in Australia.

In Liverpool I got my first look at Europe and was shocked. I found a rundown city, pitch-black and crumbling ten years after the war. "So this is Europe," I said sarcastically, as we passed into the harbor. "Yes," said Jeffrey. "Isn't it beautiful?" I thought he was kidding but when I turned his face was streaked with tears of joy.

During the year abroad I only wrote about the things that interested me. I saw but one relative of our readers. Everybody else, it seemed, lived up a fjord or on a mountaintop; in any event it would be taking time away from London, Paris, Rome, Israel, and other enticing destinations, something I was reluctant to do. Consequently, I found fault with every prospect: too banal, too remote. The sole interview I took the trouble to pursue was with Jack London, an ex-heavyweight champ of the British Empire, the brother of a mill worker in Scotia in Humboldt County.

I found the ex-fighter in a Manchester nightclub keeping body and soul together as a glad-hander and bouncer. In his prime, Jack London was a highly regarded pugilist. A big, bluff figure with a cheerful face, he was so delighted to hear news of his brother that he invited me home where I met his wife and their two boys. Both stood over six feet and were professional boxers. The oldest, Bryant, a heavyweight at twenty-one, had beaten champs of Ireland, Spain, and Belgium. Over cutlets and ale Jack said Bryant already was a better fighter than he ever was. "I was soft-hearted," the ex-champ of the ex-British Empire said sadly. "This boy, though, has the killer instinct, and that is what it takes be the champion of the world." To my knowledge, neither son's career ever matched the dad's.

•

On my return from my travels, Eureka never looked more wretched than when I'd staggered down from the Greyhound. Such a small town! Such a backwater! My instinct was to turn around and flee. But my conscience wouldn't permit it. I owed Hodge, and O'Kane, too, at least a year.

Donna

June 23, 1956 of a Saturday night. The paper had just gone to bed, and I'd crossed the street to the Deluxe Club to wait out a cocktail waitress I was seeing. As I nursed a bourbon and water Herman Bistrin, a local businessman, came over to the bar and said, "How would you like to meet a beautiful Yiddisha shiksa?" He meant, "How would you like to meet a beautiful gentile who digs Jewish boys?"

I put down my drink and followed him across the room. His wife, Patti, herself a Yiddisha shiksa, gave me a warm hello although I scarcely knew her. I asked the lovely friend to dance, but she declined with a broad smile. She'd come with someone. When I counted only three at the table she laughed and said her date had gone for cigarettes.

A few minutes later Herman was back at the bar. "So, what did you think of her?" he said.

"Oh, she's lovely but there's nothing there for me. She's got a guy."

"Oh," said Herman. "He's just an old friend. Nobody to worry about. Would you like to see her again? Tomorrow night?"

I hesitated. "There's a complication."

Look, Herman said. He, Patti, and Donna were having dinner at the Goodmans. "Why don't you join us?" I knew Max, a physician, and Bernice, his wife, and liked them.

"But I've made other plans."

The complication was this: I'd made a date with a friend of the girl I'd been seeing. We were rendezvousing at the Sportsman's up on Fifth Street where she worked. But meeting Donna changed things. Ever since I'd come back from globetrotting I swore I'd give up whoring and settle down with the first good-looking, respectable girl I met, someone I wouldn't be ashamed to introduce to friends and family.

•

I'd taken Donna for a dazzling redhead but in broad daylight I was staring at a sparkling blonde in a pillbox. Herman tossed me the keys to his Cadillac after dinner. "Why don't you and Donna get better acquainted?" he asked. He and the others were intent on playing bridge.

I headed for the waterfront, a part of town respectable people shunned after dark, counting on my familiarity with Eureka's demimonde to make an impression. We hit a few bars, rapped with barflies, bartenders, and gamblers, and danced at the raffish Log Cabin. By the time we'd said goodnight I knew my life was going to be different. I'd also learned that Donna and the Bistrins had been out the previous evening celebrating her interlocutory decree from a husband to whom she'd been married ten years. It marked the start of a year of separation before either party would be free to marry again. But only much later would I learn that the Bistrins were considering romantic prospects for Donna when I walked into the nightclub.

•

Growing up in Gadsden, an industrial city in northwest Alabama, Donna was the oldest of four children. Her father, a grocer and butcher, was indifferent to religion, but her mother, Fanalou, was plainly a God-fearing Christian. After proposing to Donna, I'd met them both but separately in Oregon where the family had long been living. It was a stressful time, as their marriage of more than thirty years was breaking up.

As Donna and I were leaving her mother's home in Salem, Fanalou startled me by stopping us at the door to implore us to think hard on what we were contemplating. "Search your hearts. Be absolutely sure you're doing the right thing," she said. If we would do this, and could still answer yes, we would have her blessings. But if there was a shadow of a doubt, she begged us to drop our plans or at least put off the wedding. She would still love us both and we would have her blessings. The worst thing we could do was to take this serious step without having searched our souls.

"Mother," Donna said, with some heat, "we've known each other

A Strange Breed of Folks

for almost a year. There is no question in my mind." Fanalou turned to me.

"There is no question in my mind."

"Then you're sure?"

"I am," said Donna. "I've never been so sure of anything before in my life."

"And me, too," I said.

And so she blessed us, and said we would be in her prayers for a long and happy life. Nonetheless, I never quite forgave her for raising the questions.

When I told my mother the news, she wrote that Donna, a divorced woman who at thirty-one was my senior by two years, was not the right wife for me. She didn't have a college degree. She had no skills. She worked at a lowly job as a receptionist in a lumber mill. My mother recruited my Uncle Harry, my father's oldest brother, and Uncle Archie, my mother's younger brother and a rabbi, to admonish me in separate letters against marrying outside my religion. By marrying a gentile, said Archie, I would be forsaking my heritage.

It seemed to me an unnecessary concession to my mother but Donna made up her mind to convert to Judaism. Were we to have children, she thought, they should be raised with a religion. Soon after Donna told Lillie, the matriarch of the Bistrin family, of her intention to marry me, the older woman took Donna in hand and commenced a course of instruction in traditional Jewish dishes. Lillie also made it a point to compliment me. Taking me aside, she said that Donna had helped make her first husband rich by persuading him to give up his high school coaching job and go into the lumber business. "She is a smart girl," Lillie said. "You are lucky. She will put money in your pocket."

After consulting with her rabbi brother whose ministry was in Lancaster, Pennsylvania, my mother hired a San Francisco rabbi, Sol White, of the conservative wing, to initiate Donna into the faith. For many weeks Donna drove from Eureka to San Francisco, a three-hundred-mile trip, much of it over mountain roads, for lessons in Jewish culture and the Torah. Archie wrote approvingly of what she was doing.

Although he hadn't been expected, my father showed up in San Francisco on the day of the wedding, June 23, 1957, a year to the day that Donna and I first met. His sudden appearance took everyone by surprise. Once she recognized him, my mother metamorphosed into a coquette. It was the first time she'd seen him in twenty years.

"Oh, Dave," she said. "Is it really you?" She dared to touch him.

He put out a protesting hand. "Stop the dramatics, Sarah Bernhardt. There's nothing between you and me anymore." He'd come up from Los Angeles to see Donna and me get married and to warn her in plain English against meddling in our lives.

•

When Rabbi White asked if anyone objected to the marriage, he (or she) should speak now or forever hold their peace. I suppressed a cry welling up in my chest, and imagined myself in the manner of an actor in a play or movie, saying, "I don't know if I love this woman or not. I don't know if I want to marry her. Everything's moving so fast. She says she loves me, and wants to marry me, but does she really know me? Ladies and gentlemen, I'm not what I seem. The night before last I shacked up with a divorced friend, and not for the first time, either." As the speech played out in my mind, I asked myself why could I not say this. If I could, I would be a free man.

A month or so before the wedding, I'd begun sleeping with the ex-wife of an advertising salesman at the paper. After I'd confessed to dreadful anxieties about my impending marriage, she persisted in asking, "You mustn't go through with it. You must pull yourself together. Why are you doing this?"

"I couldn't live with myself if I walked out on Donna."

"You're crazy. You can't love her or you wouldn't be with me."

"I don't know if I love her. I probably do, but then I'm not sure. But I gave her my word. I couldn't live with myself if I walked out on her."

"You're crazy."

One day soon after, Herman's younger brother, Harry, hailed me on the street. Harry, whose attitude toward Donna was one of condescension, said, "This marriage with Donna," he said. "You can't be serious."

"But I am."

"She's very sweet and very pretty but you don't have much in common. Your interest is in books, politics, and ideas. I can't see the two of you as husband and wife."

"Look," I shot back. "If Arthur Miller can marry Marilyn Monroe, I can marry Donna Wilbanks."

•

After the ceremony, my father hugged Donna and me, and wished us a happy life together. "Love yourselves," he said. "And remember, you only get out of something what you put into it." With that, he moved hurriedly down the steps of the temple to his car. My mother called to him and then ran after him, but he paid no mind to her whatsoever.

•

Our original intention was to head for Mexico immediately after the wedding and find a cheap and idyllic spot where I would write my big book. I was saying goodbye to Eureka for good. But Hodge importuned. My timing collided head-on with his plans to go rock hunting in Wyoming. With both of us gone at the same time, he said, the paper would be left unprotected, in the care of irresponsible journalists.

Hodge proposed a deal. He'd put off his vacation a few days, giving me enough time to get married and squeeze in a honeymoon. But then he wanted me back in town so he could start on his vacation. He was only asking for three more weeks of my time. After that, I could do whatever I pleased; go to Mexico or New Mexico, for all he cared.

"Tough apples," said Donna. "He's known of our plans for months."

But I owed Hodge and O'Kane. They had taken me back after the *Examiner* had canned me. They held my job when I was away at sea and paid me for my columns. I did, however, wonder whether Hodge was playing the Jake Burns character, that his bid to bring me back to Eureka after the wedding was a ploy to keep me from quitting the paper.

But it turned out not to be the case. In late July, when Hodge got back from Wyoming, my bride and I finally set out for Mexico in a lumbering Dodge sedan mounted on treadless rubber, which well-to-do friends of Donna had donated to our cause.

•

During our failed Mexican idyll I aspired to be a second Hemingway or Thomas Wolfe – I was never sure which. And there was the problem of settling down in a foreign country that was prehistoric by our standards, a strange, scary place which neither of us knew. We were down there because it was cheap, because we figured, or really I figured, my $700 in life savings would stretch nearly a lifetime. Married life, too, was something I absolutely hadn't thought through. Two months from the day we crossed the border at Nogales, we were writing (to my mother mainly) for money. Four months later we were back in the U.S. I'd suffered two bad asthmatic attacks, one so bad after attending my first bullfight I had to have oxygen before I rallied. The slaughter in the ring didn't upset Donna, but she suffered from diarrhea, which she'd brought on herself by refusing to heed warnings about the water. We were flat broke but I swore I wasn't going back to journalism, that I would stick it out doing odd jobs until, I guess, I was discovered by Maxwell Perkins.

When we passed through Los Angeles we discovered that my Dad and Gertrude, his new wife, had split.

Gertrude was living with a married daughter and her family. My father was alone in their house on Kerwood Avenue in Los Angeles. "You'll find him there," said Gertrude, wan and troubled. "He just sits there, brooding. I can't reach him. Nobody can. The war is taking his life," by which she meant the old war, the First World War. For most of his life my father displayed symptoms of shell shock, nowadays called combat fatigue, which the dictionary describes as a psychoneurotic condition characterized by anxiety, irritability, depression, etc., often occurring after prolonged combat in warfare. When Donna and I visited, we found a surprisingly shrunken figure sitting in the corner of a darkened room, chain-smoking, staring at the damn TV. For as long as two hours he bitched about Gertrude. It was so damn tiresome!

•

Arriving in San Francisco, where we were to see my mother, Donna had to be rushed to the hospital with a ruptured tubular pregnancy and inflammation of the intestines, a life-threatening crisis. She pulled through, and we wound up in Salem, Oregon, where Fanalou grub-staked us while Donna got better and I pumped gas at an all-night service station, shoveled shit on a farm, and delivered telephone books until we had enough money to get back to California. I would look for work in the first place we liked, and that was Santa Cruz. I picked up an assortment of jobs as a hot grabber in a cannery, dumper in a frozen food plant, farm laborer, mushroom cleaner – yes, a mushroom cleaner – and letter-carrier.

I'd kept my vow to steer clear of newspapers and make ends meet as a blue-collar worker, so as to stay pure in the pursuit of the literary life. But after three years of odd jobs and rejected manuscripts and a seemingly broken marriage – Donna and I had agreed to separate; she was working as a receptionist at a tannery – my resolve collapsed and I phoned Hodge.

"How soon can you get back up here," Hodge said. It was as if we'd never said goodbye.

At the moment I was a clerk, selling stamps, writing money orders, and accepting parcels in California in the Santa Cruz post office. I couldn't just pick up and leave.

"I can be there in two weeks," I said.

"Two weeks?" Hodge was impatient. He had a fellow covering city hall whose copy he didn't trust, a classy writer, but he made a lot of it up, getting the paper in hot water.

"Two weeks," I repeated. I had to give notice.

·

Before we'd left Oregon for California, my father died. Funny thing; I broke down and cried on the spot when I got the news, which surprised me, as I had seen little of my dad since my parents divorced. Two decades later when my mother died – she who had played so prominent a role in my life – I was unable to shed any tears.

Uncle Jack, the paper box tycoon who was married to my father's sister, wouldn't help the prodigal nephew with expenses to travel to Boston. He said he did not believe in loaning money to a son to attend his father's funeral. Fanalou, my mother-in-law, advanced the money, though she really didn't have it to spare.

The body was brought back from Galveston where my father had been on a trip selling siding jobs to unsuspecting homeowners, a shady enterprise which required vendors like my dad to keep a step ahead of the sheriff. Death came from a heart attack while he was watching wrestling matches on TV in his hotel room.

"Services Tomorrow For David Levine," said the notice in a Boston newspaper that February of 1958. (Although my father had changed his last name from "Levine" to "Lavine" for family reasons, he remained known to many by the former.) The obituary went on to mention that his age was sixty-three and that he used to live in the Back Bay. "Mr. Levine was a salesman, also known as 'Marty' Levine and was a handball player at the Boston YMCA for many years. He received the Silver Star for gallantry in World War One and served with the 79th Infantry Division in the Argonne."

It listed the survivors, his wife, Gertrude, and me, and three brothers, and three sisters.

The rabbi who spoke in the Jewish chapel in Brookline painted a picture of my father that would have done for a saint. But then, he didn't know my father. The turnout was pathetically meager – my father had been absent from Boston for many years – though one or two old army buddies turned up. Nearly everyone in the room must have sat uncomfortably as the rabbi extolled the deceased. Gertrude rose up, and interrupted, "That's not my husband you're describing. Dave Lavine was not a fine and decent man. He was a sonofabitch but I loved him." The room grew quiet. The rabbi had the good sense to change the subject and lead the mourners in reciting the Kaddish, one of the most ancient of all Jewish prayers glorifying God's name, an entreaty that many Jews believed helped the souls of the dead find lasting peace.

His remains were transported to the Jewish cemetery in a handsome Cadillac. So odd to see such luxury when my father had scoffed at show and pretence! I shivered in a summer-cloth coat during a brief military ceremony in his honor. Then the gravediggers began to dig into the hard, cruel ground. As I was leaving, a representative from the Veterans of Foreign Wars handed me the flag that had covered my father's coffin.

KVIQ

A few months after I'd moved back to Eureka, Donna rejoined me. We were both feeling lonesome, sick of dating, and ready to try again. At the same time I was grateful to Hodge for taking me back and pleased to be doing work for which I was suited, but I was still looking for a way out. The midnight chases in police cars had palled; the rowdiness at council meetings induced torpor.

My humor did not improve with Hodge pressing me every night for a fresh highway fatality or a stickup, even a second-rate burglary.

"This paper's dying on La-*vine*." Hodge tossed his sally when I returned from my rounds empty-handed.

To keep my spirits up, I began taking parts in amateur plays. Around dinnertime I'd scamper down the flight of stairs from the newsroom and find Donna outside waiting with the motor running. We'd race for the theater as I wolfed down her hot supper. The directors ran me through my few lines. Then I'd drive Donna home and race to the city council or school board or sheriff's office or police station, wherever my beat required.

In the end it was Buster DeBrunner who talked me into making a change. Buster, who had been a photographer on the paper, imagined a great future for himself in television and cast his lot with KVIQ, the second station to start up in Eureka. He was urging me to do the same.

"You'd be a natural on the tube," said Buster.

He knew of my eagerness to perform. Indeed, television seemed a likely medium for me; at the same time I had reservations. Most of us in Eureka journalism circles could not accept television as a serious news medium. And Don O'Kane, the publisher of the *Hum-*

boldt Times, had made a realistic, economic case long before when I first went to work for him: if you had a newspaper job, you could always eat. People depended on newspapers; in the Great Depression when one out of every four Americans was unemployed, people still read newspapers. They could not do without the classifieds, the help wanted columns, fire sales, rooms for rent, real estate listings, births, deaths, weddings, the stock market, sports, comics, and so on.

"But that's ancient history," Buster said. "Television's catching on. You want to get in on the ground floor."

The people running KVIQ were looking for a journalist who knew the local scene. When, through Buster acting as honest broker, I expressed interest, they agreed to give me a minute at the close of every broadcast for commentary. When I asked for permission to produce documentaries on controversial issues, they said, "Why not?" The salary was $150 a week, up from $125 at the *Humboldt Times*, and they threw in a Volkswagen van for my personal as well as business use.

Hodge raised no objection, and the next thing I knew I was in television. If the move distressed Hodge, he gave no sign of it.

Although I knew nothing about the technology of TV, Buster assured me I need not worry. He put a 16 mm Bolex movie camera in my hands and said, "Go out and shoot." I shot traffic accidents, fires, school board meetings, police bookings, all the news that was moving. Television meant pictures and I had to have a lot of it to wallpaper a fifteen-minute newscast.

I was a one-man band; reporter, anchor, and cameraman except for times when I was doing interviews. Buster would operate the sound camera. When he was busy shooting commercials, Donna would have to step in.

Despite the circus aspects of my new vocation, in the eyes of my fellow townspeople I was now a celebrity. Not that I knew any more, or had gained any special insights or grown or matured since the first broadcast. I was the same person as I always had been, ate the same food, drank the same beer and whiskey, and yet was transformed into a larger-than-life figure. Within the boundaries of Eureka and Humboldt County I'd become a person of consequence.

The phone began ringing even before I was up in the morning and long after I'd gone to bed at night. Politicians, educators, businessmen and others sought my advice. On at least two occasions I was offered gratuities in return for a favorable mention on the air.

The fact that I'd actually moved into the enemy's camp remained unsettling. I was never quite sure I'd made the right choice; I was abandoning a medium that valued good writing for one that could not have cared less about it, a medium without any sense of history, a medium that exalted the technically adept and placed no value whatsoever on intellectual depth. Pictures and organized noise were what counted most.

The station would do anything for their new boy. A new typewriter? A special camera? You got it! Another phone? Done!

However, when I hired a pilot and helicopter to fly me to a gigantic forest fire in the southern tier of the country, management came down on me.

"Ten thousand acres of virgin timber, lost," I said. "Redwood. Douglas Fir! That's important."

Sam Horel, the frenetic station manager, stood with arms akimbo in my backshop. "No one's questioning your news judgment," he said. "That's why you're here. But there's fire footage on the shelf from a couple of years ago. Use it. No one will ever know the difference. We can't go on spending money on helicopters. Do you have any idea what those birds cost?"

Sam was right; no one knew the difference.

Joe Louis

Sam Horel left sports to our pitchman, but Harry Hubbard was heading out of town one weekend for a confab with fellow hucksters in Los Angeles. So at the last minute, Joe Louis became my interview. As Hodge used to say, Eureka got the names after they hit rock bottom. Joe was in town to referee wrestling matches at the Municipal Auditorium. The penniless Joe, who had been the world's heavyweight champion longer than anyone before him – or, as of this writing, since – and had made more than $5 million as a fighter – maybe $100 million in today's money – was now in the employ of Caesar's Palace in Las Vegas as a glad-hander. The out-of-town gigs brought him a little extra.

Sam set aside a full half-hour for the interview, live in the studio. Although it had been many years since Joe had won the crown, he was still worth thirty minutes in Humboldt County. The problem, of course, was that Joe was not a talker. Whites liked him. He wasn't a braggart, or show-off; he didn't give the white man lip. He acted dignified and self-effacing as befitted a Negro champion of the world, unlike his black predecessor, Jack Johnson, a champ of an earlier day. Johnson enraged white America by flaunting his liaisons with white women, his flashy cars and high living. Johnson's antics sent up a hue and cry for a Great White Hope. Nonetheless, many said, Jack Johnson was the greatest of them all. My father used to think so. Self-effacing, soft-spoken Joe, on the other hand, gave white America no reason for alarm. He knew his place and so was a credit to his race, if a little slow on the uptake. Bill King, the sports editor and my benefactor at the Boston AP, used to say that Joe Louis didn't have enough sense to come in from the rain.

I heard this from Bill when I was sixteen and it was late in the war, late 1944 or early 1945. Joe had volunteered for the Army early in the war. When he was inducted into the segregated military, my number one hero, President Roosevelt, summoned Louis to the White House. Squeezing Joe's biceps for the newsreel cameras, Roosevelt remarked that muscles like Joe's would help us win the war over the fascists. (Joe served as a physical education instructor.)

To appreciate this memory of Joe Louis you have to know that he'd occupied a special niche in my Jewish heart ever since he knocked out the German, Max Schmeling in 1938. I was ten at that time. Max Schmeling had won the first Louis-Schmeling fight by a 12th round knockout two years before. Hitler, Germany's lord and master, hailed Schmeling's victory as proof of the superiority of the Aryan race and the inferiority of the blacks. Before the 1938 rematch, Hitler cabled Schmeling: "TO THE COMING CHAMPION OF THE WORLD, WISHING YOU EVERY SUCCESS. ADOLF HITLER."

When the two gladiators met again in New York, Europe was teetering on the brink of war. A month or two before, Hitler's Nazis had marched into Austria and threatened Czechoslovakia. In November of that year, Hitler's pogrom of Jewish persecution exploded into Kristallnacht, also called the Night of Broken Glass. In organized rampages, thugs were turned loose against Jews and Jewish property in Germany. Ninety-one Jews were killed, hundreds seriously injured, thousands humiliated and terrorized. About 7500 Jewish businesses were gutted and an estimated 177 synagogues burned or otherwise demolished. The police did not interfere.

When Louis and Schmeling went at it for the second time on that June night you could walk the quarter mile of Beals Street, from Harvard Street to Steadman, in Brookline, Massachsetts and not miss a breathless moment of Clem McCarthy's ringside account from Yankee Stadium: "A left to the head, a left to the jaw, a right to the head … right to the body, a left hook to the jaw, and Schmeling is down … the count is … five … six … seven … eight." Louis dispatched Schmeling in two minutes and four seconds in the first round. The fight was over before many people had found their seats, before many more people had turned in on the radio. Cheers rose up from the homes in my Jewish neighborhood. We had won a battle against Hitler.

Although Joe must have been aware of Hitler's contemptuous

attitude toward blacks, on that night he cared only about avenging the beating he took from Schmeling two years before. Schmeling was neither a Nazi nor a racist. But we Americans who rooted for Joe Louis were racists without knowing it. We accepted segregation as the natural order of things. We didn't socialize with Negroes or have them over for dinner. We didn't think it particularly wrong that restaurants and hotels didn't welcome blacks. In World War Two the U.S. Army was segregated. Black units were led by white officers.

Preparing for my interview, I found that Eureka's Carnegie Library had only one book about boxing. It was next to worthless for my purposes. I would have to wing it. Harry Hubbard would have had the dope at his fingertips, and breezed through the half hour. He must have known that Joe was a bomb. Why else would he have fled from so famous a name?

When I got to KVIQ that Saturday afternoon Joe was already waiting for me at the station. Despite the aspect of a monumental ruin, he wore the same non-committal, sober, poker face of a million photographs. He was pushing fifty, meaty, with hands the size of shovels. Surprisingly for such a big man, his step was light.

When we shook hands, I confessed to great gaps of knowledge about him. I'd just gotten the assignment. The library proved useless. The guy who normally did sports, and would have done a perfectly fine job, was out of town. In sum, I apologized but promised to do my level best to make the interview interesting.

"You'll be all right. You just ask the questions," Joe said.

I was puzzled.

"Ask anything you like," he laughed. "I'll take care of it."

Joe did almost all the talking, I mentioned a name, a fight, and Louis talked, talked as he was not supposed to talk, talked with flashes of pride, humor, regret. I don't believe he denigrated any of his opponents or spoke of them unkindly. Billy Conn, the challenger in Louis's worst fight as champ was, he said, the best man he ever faced. He spoke highly, too, of Rocky Marciano who knocked Joe out in October 1951 in the 8th round, putting the finish on Joe's bid for a comeback. He spoke in detail. He'd been embarrassed and humiliated in the first Schmeling fight in 1936, and was set on avenging the defeat. And he'd trained hard, and he and his trainer Jack Blackburn had worked hard on a strategy. And the strategy was to come out swinging, and not give Max a chance to throw his right, which was his exit punch. Joe went in there and with fast punches upset Schmeling and pounded away.

He was undeniably proud of his performance in the second Schmeling fight but I wondered if, aside from the determination to remove the stigma of the earlier defeat, the politics of the times had helped stiffen his resolve as well. He said it probably did, although, strictly speaking, he did not take much interest in politics.

Before Louis and Billy Conn's June 1941 fight at the Polo Grounds, writers said that Conn was a good bet to take the title from Joe because he was different from the other challengers, small, fast, and clever. Louis had replied, "He can run but he can't hide." Joe repeated the famous line on the broadcast. He conceded he was hard-pressed to catch up with Conn as Conn wheeled around Joe in the early rounds. Conn also stood his ground, and traded punches. In the 12th round he nearly knocked Louis down. Conn waded in for the kill with a left hook and a right cross. Louis barely survived the round. In the 13th, Conn made a miscalculation. No longer relying on his speed, he took the fight directly to Joe. This was an unusually bold move, as never before had a challenger switched tactics to trade blow for blow for an entire round with the champ. Joe hit him repeatedly and Conn collapsed. When the two fought again in June of 1946, Joe knocked Conn out in the eight round.

Joe pointed out that he'd defended the title twenty-five times, scoring twenty-one knockouts, and that when he retired in 1949 he was undefeated. But he also made mention of corrupt advisers, women troubles, and income taxes owed the IRS. Desperate for money, Joe returned to the ring. In 1950 he lost to Ezzard Charles, then beat a platoon of unknowns until October 1951 when future champion, Rocky Marciano, KO'd Joe in the 8th round, and finished Joe's bid for a comeback.

Before the half-hour was over I asked Joe what it was like to go to the White House that day in 1942 when he met President Roosevelt, my tone suggesting it must have been incredibly moving and unforgettable. I was a kid then, I said, and like many of my contemporaries wanted Joe Louis to win and go on forever, just as we wanted Franklin Roosevelt to win and go on forever. Louis gave me a blank look. It was as if to say, it was just something that happened. It wasn't anything that he particularly remembered.

Later, when I got back in town from the station I hit the Annex Bar where I knew a lot of the guys had been watching, I came in expecting I don't know what, and got a standing ovation. Everybody said it was the best interview I'd ever done. Nobody had an idea that Joe could, well, talk, and be so articulate.

But I didn't do anything, I protested. It was all Joe's doing. He was the producer and star of the broadcast. The guys laughed, and I just let them.

Nixon

In the fall of 1962, dignitaries were rare occurrences in Eureka. So there was great excitement when Richard Nixon, who was attempting his comeback in California, decided to stop in town for a campaign speech.

I asked Bob Janssen, the Republican county chairman, whether I might interview the former vice president. Bob passed the request on to Herb Klein, the candidate's press secretary. I had my answer in a few days. The candidate would have no objection to an interview, provided I submitted my questions in advance. This miffed me, but I was anxious not to lose the story and so I agreed.

Dogging Nixon at this time was a story involving his younger brother, Donald. Questions were raised about a $205,000 loan that Howard Hughes, the aircraft manufacturer, film producer, and flyer, had made to Donald Nixon in 1956 when Richard Nixon was vice president. For collateral, the younger Nixon had put up a piece of property worth only $13,000. People were asking why Hughes had been so generous to the vice president's brother? Was Richard Nixon directly linked to the deal?

Although Nixon had made no public comment, fending off reporters' questions, he'd yet to be asked about the Hughes loan on camera.

Now, Nixon was coming to town, and I'd have an opportunity to confront him. When I thought of it my heart beat faster. The networks were running something about the governor's race in California virtually every night. We were an NBC affiliate so I queried the network's Los Angeles bureau. Would there be interest in a network spot with Nixon? The reply came back: of course!

It was a memorable visit. The whole town turned out, Democrats as well as Republicans, and even our few fringe groups on the far right and left. Everyone's curiosity – and pride – was aroused.

A platform had been set up in the center of town. Flags were waving. People were jammed into the downtown area. Martial music swelled the emotions. And although I was an unreconstructed Stevenson Democrat, I was caught up in the patriotic fervor. Then a face I'd recognized from news photos came swooping down on me. The eyes were narrow slits. "Mel Lavine: are you Mel Lavine?" I acknowledged I was. "I'm Herb Klein," the man said.

"Oh," I said in an attempt to be cordial. "It's a pleasure to meet you in the flesh." But Mr. Klein was in no mood for pleasantries.

"Those questions you submitted," he said. "They're OK except that one about the Hughes loan. He won't answer it. I can tell you that now, so save your breath. Now, if I were you, I'd ask him about the Communists: that's where the news is."

I suppose I nodded soberly like the Rube he took me for, but I was not really surprised. We separated in the crowd and I made my way to the hotel where the interview with Nixon was to take place.

As I stepped into the room, Buster, my cameraman, was grinning. The film crew hired by Nixon's advertising agency was going to let us use their equipment to shoot the interview. This was no small windfall. We were a small station. And we rode out on our assignments with an antediluvian Auricon movie camera that could only shoot three-minute film clips at a time. We would have to stop an interview when the time ran out, re-load, cue our subject again, and resume shooting. Consequently, we lost not only time but spontaneity, the spark that is the essence of television.

This worried me as I entered the hotel.

So when Buster told me of the ad men's offer, I was grinning, too.

Soon Nixon stepped into the room. He moved lightly, efficiently. A brief handshake, a professional smile. My heart was in my throat when Buster said, "Go!"

I asked all the questions I had planned to, including the ones about the Hughes loan. To hell with Herb Klein. I was a newsman, even if my beat was a provincial, isolated community. It was an exercise in asking the "hard" questions, especially to a famous, powerful person.

I expected Nixon to react in some dark, savage way, perhaps by dressing down Herb Klein. But, no, the candidate answered without a flicker of emotion. Oh, yes, he had heard all about that, but there wasn't a scintilla of truth in any of the allegations of wrongdoing, and for the next minute or two he denigrated the Howard Hughes story.

My heart was beating too hard for me to hear what he was saying. All I could think of was that he was answering the questions, that it was all being recorded on film, and that a great television network was waiting for it.

No one was more keenly aware of the fact than I that this was the first time Nixon had been faced with the Hughes matter on television, and although he denied any wrongdoing, his response was still newsworthy for a broadcasting company. As the substance of TV is not merely what someone says, but the drama, the tension, the look and the sound of how he says it. Often a "no comment" could have more impact than the most concise and well-phrased statement.

We concluded the interview as we had begun it. A handshake, a perfunctory smile, and Nixon was gone. It was after five o'clock. I did my newscast at six. We gathered up our gear – and the precious film – hugged the ad men for their benevolence and sped off in our panel truck for the station atop Humboldt Hill.

I leaped into my crib of an office while Buster dashed into the dark room behind me.

"Tell NBC we've got Nixon responding to the Hughes story!" I cried out to the receptionist and began writing.

A few moments later someone poked his head into the room to say that NBC was making plans to take a minute or so of the film. My heart by now was thundering. My God, my mother would see me on television. My friends, my ... but no time. The clock was moving. I was on deadline, a TV deadline, one that makes a newspaper deadline pedestrian by comparison. And then, as I neared writing the end of my script I heard a fussing, and then a fuming, and then a storming about the dark room. Nothing, I thought. Keep writing. But, no, Buster's voice interrupted me. And he was swearing, swearing incomprehensibly. I tried to ignore him, but his voice rose and he was calling my name.

"For Christ's sake," I snapped. "Will you pipe down? We've got fifteen minutes to go to air and you're ..." But before I could finish I sensed doom. Buster's voice overtook mine. "It's ruined. The f—— film is ruined."

"Ruined?"

"The sound——"

"What about the sound?"

"It's not there!"

"Not there?"

"It's gone – erased, wiped out!"

There was no sound. Not a syllable of that Nixon interview was on the film. We were so close to air that I could only think of the local broadcast I had to do.

How we went on and off the air, I'll never know. But I was determined to report everything Nixon said. And so over film of his triumphal visit I reported it all – everything I could remember about his reply to the Hughes questions.

Of course I lost my chance at a network debut. NBC wasn't interested in a stringer's rehash of a candidate's equivocations.

When we were able to breathe with some regularity again, we sent the film to a lab in San Francisco to find out what went wrong. The report pointed out a number of things could have happened. The film may have been defective, the sound could have been distorted during the interview, something might have gone wrong in the processing.

Not one possibility but many. In the end, my suspicion was – as it remains today – that Herb Klein hoodwinked us into using their wonderful camera, and saw to it that it was loaded with defective film. I was new at the game, but I should have known better. Protecting Nixon from a hostile press was Herb Klein's job.

A Dark Side

I should have been more sophisticated about politics since, during the time that I was anchoring the news on KVIQ, I advised the Democratic state senator from Humboldt County on his public relations. The senator, Carl Christensen, jokingly referred to me as his kitchen cabinet, since I used to enter his big corner house through a back door that led to the kitchen. Here we'd conspire over coffee if it was morning, or something more substantial if it was later in the day. "Will my kitchen cabinet come to order?" the senator would exclaim as I stepped into the room.

I first knew him when he was a superior court judge and thought him a humorless and unforgiving magistrate. But as a political figure, I found him not only approachable but amiable. Often he'd return from Sacramento with entertaining stories. He once recounted a meeting of key Democratic legislators at the behest of Governor Edmund G. (Pat) Brown, the leader of the party. After many views were heard concerning a piece of pending legislation, the governor threw up his hands and said, "I'm not interested in the merits of the case. What I want to know is how am I going to look if I sign the damn thing!"

So much for statesmanship in high places. But I expected better of my state senator when I found him on the phone acting in the most obliging manner to one of the wealthiest and most conservative Republicans in the county.

When the senator hung up, I said, "Why were you so accommodating to him? You know he would like nothing better than for you to lose the next election."

The senator knew all that. He went on, "But I want him to know that he can do business with me, and I will oblige him when it won't cause my Democrats distress."

He added, "If I make him really sore he has the means to run a serious challenger against me and then I damn well might lose the next election."

Carl remained in office for decades. Only age and ill health forced him into retirement.

In return for my help (writing press releases, and helping on speeches) the senator found an ingenious way of compensation or, to speak frankly, of committing bribery. No money ever passed hands: nothing so crass. The body politic works in mysterious ways. I was appointed an adjunct professor of journalism at Humboldt State College in nearby Arcata with a monthly salary of $200. The class entrusted to me was small, eight or nine students meeting twice a week for an hour. Although I'd never taught before I was confident it would be a lark. To my chagrin, I found myself spending hours preparing for classes and grading students' papers. No one supervised me, no one checked in to see if I knew what I was doing. I was left completely alone. Two memorable students, an aging spinster with a crusading heart and a young man of an inquisitive nature, made the hour worthwhile. The others had elected Journalism 101 in the expectation that taking it would be a snap. My finest moment was when a student complained about her C grade. She said the ranking would mar her record, denying her entrance to graduate school. I was, she maintained between sobs, destroying her life. In fact, she was a mediocre student and I stuck to my guns. At the end of the semester I retired from academe (the old lady and the young man deserved better than me), quite happy to continue serving the senator without the rewards of an adjunct professorship.

I had other opportunities to take bribes. A city councilman offered me $500 if I simply would show more of him on television. He made the offer when we stepped into an elevator in city hall. When we go to the second floor of the three-story building, he raised the bribe to $1,000. When we reached the summit the sum rose to $1500. Similarly, a prominent lawyer representing developers of a controversial shopping mall asked me to meet with him in his office in the old bank building a few doors up from the paper. His was a murky monologue but the meaning was clear. In both instances, I fled as if fearing contamination from a disease. True, the senator tendered a bribe, which for a time I accepted. But that was different. I was sympathetic to him on philosophical grounds.

•

Coca-Cola sponsored *News by Six*. As part of the deal I was expected to hold up a bottle, invite viewers to join me in "the pause that refreshes," and begin drinking as we faded to black at the close of every show.

My role as sponsor's pitchman commenced right after my one-minute editorial. My hand shook so I could raise the bottle only a few inches from the news desk. Getting the Coke to my lips was out of the question.

My demeanor was entirely too negative for a "shtick" intended to create a craving for a product.

Buster made obscene gestures in an effort to brighten me up. San Horel, the station manager, planted himself next to the camera, muttering words audible enough for me to hear. "Drink the Coke, schmuck."

Night after night they tried to get me to drink the Coke. I never could. "Drink the Coke, schmuck," Sam and Allen Jones, the assistant station manager, muttered outside camera range trying to loosen me up. It was in vain.

The newscast, however, caught on. Within three months we closed the gap in our competition with KIEM, and within six months forged ahead in the ratings.

We provoked controversy. People were paying attention. A documentary focused on a shady water diversion scheme that a prominent businessman was promoting. An engineer, a one-time communist, led the opposition. I interviewed both men separately on film, and gave their arguments equal time on the broadcast. Incensed that he found himself sharing the limelight with a local radical, the businessman, a super patriot, accused me of being soft on communism.

There was a flurry of hate calls to the station and my house and a bomb threat.

Sam was apoplectic. The businessman was threatening to cancel his advertising with the station unless we retracted the documentary with an apology.

"All you have to say is we intended no harm. You're the scribbler; you can find the right words," he told me.

I refused.

"Hey, this guy spends a ton of money with us and is one of the most powerful men in the county."

"I don't care who he is, or how rich. He's a crook scheming to plunder the public."

"Hey, now, just a minute." Sam was getting irritated.

"Sam, when you hired me you hired a newsman. You wanted me to produce the best news show I was capable of, and I have and so you can't come in here now and tell me to stop the presses. If you want a flack, hire one. If you want a newsman leave me be."

"What is this, an ultimatum?"

"I stand by the story, Sam."

The owner of the station was Carl McConnell, a rangy septuagenarian who spent most of his time looking after investments in cattle and oil in the San Joaquin Valley.

Carl had acquired the station as a lark, not out of cupidity or ego, simply as a curiosity. Television was a hot medium and it fascinated him. No doubt like most businessmen, he had no stomach for public issues that divided the public.

One afternoon he strode into the back shop, and I thought, this is it.

I'd spoken to him once before. It was a moment when I was working furiously to meet my deadline. His towering frame filled the doorway.

"How's it going?" he asked. His smile was open.

"I'm having the time of my life," I replied, not wanting to seem discourteous but also anxious not to miss a beat on the typewriter.

"I hope you'll be happy here."

"Oh, I know I will," I blurted. "Doing what I love, and getting paid for it!"

This time, he paused, but without a smile on his face.

"On this controversy, I want to ask you one question."

"Shoot."

"Are you sure of your facts?"

"I am."

"Thank you," he said and left.

And that was that. I never heard another word on the subject either from him or from Sam.

*

Editorials on controversial subjects were a rarity in Eureka. I deemed it necessary to be cautious in my approach, and sought to explain both sides of an argument, thus assuming the role of analyst rather than polemicist. (I shrank from advocacy journalism except on the most mom and pop, flag-waving, apple pie topics.)

Covertly, I tried to advance a liberal point of view, but, because of my muted – really cowardly – manner, people understood me in their own way; they heard only what they wanted to hear.

I admired the anchors of the day – Chet Huntley and David Brinkley on NBC and Walter Cronkite on CBS – but my chief influence was Edward R. Murrow. As a youngster of twelve and thirteen, I had listened to his broadcasts of the Nazi Blitz from London and the European Theatre in World War Two. Murrow set an ethical standard for broadcast journalism with his documentaries discrediting the red-baiting Senator Joseph McCarthy and exposing the exploitation of migrant workers in the 1950s. He reached a larger public with his "Person to Person" conversations with famous people in their homes. I strove to emulate his dramatic style, a style more in keeping with covering wars, death camps, and grave matters of state than with reporting the agenda of the Eureka school board or city council.

But Eurekans tuned in. Looking back I can see why our conservative rival was appalled and indignant. The station ran announcements on their air and ads in the papers and on billboards urging people to turn to KIEM for their news because it was Humboldt County's only "believable" newscast. Nonetheless, our ratings rose.

The competition between KVIQ and KIEM got red hot on election night. In anticipation, Sam and Allan posted a dozen or so people in key precincts to keep tabs on the local races. Nonetheless, our rival posted bigger numbers. During a commercial break Sam came over to me at the anchor desk to complain, "Why are their figures better than ours?" (By "better" he meant bigger.) "Why are we lagging behind in the count? What do they know that we don't?"

I shrugged. Our numbers were coming directly from our own people at the precincts and courthouse. We had no choice but to believe they were accurate. Sam shook his head.

When next I was on the air and read the numbers off the blackboard, our returns were gaining on KIEM's. Soon we were posting bigger or "better" numbers than they.

Anxious to keep the momentum going, Sam broke in on me on camera, waving a piece of AP copy under my nose. "Hey, look at this!" he said. "What do you make of it?"

The wire service was reporting the results of a congressional race in Oklahoma.

"What do you make of this? It's a surprise, is it not? Pretty significant, huh?"

"Significant?"

"Sure."

"In Oklahoma?"

Friends watching at home said I had an incredulous stare. They were beside themselves, collapsing in gales of laughter.

But I'd been forewarned about the business. One of my first broadcasts ended in a fiasco. The film came up upside down; the sound track quacked like Donald Duck. Once we were off the air I stormed into the control room, demanding an explanation from the young engineer I found ensnared in a pool of film.

"For this I left newspaper work?" I said. "So this is television, the wave of the future? Well, what are you going to do about it? What have you got to say for yourself?"

"Mel," he shrugged, barely cracking a smile. "Take it easy. This is show business."

•

The station manager, Sam Horel, and his second in command, Alan Jones, sang my praises as they raised the rates for advertisers and raised them a second and a third time during the course of the glorious year that I delivered the evening news and commentary five days a week.

"They're begging us to take their money," Sam chortled.

Alan, a would-be song and dance man, broke into a jig.

"Watch our thunder," he said.

"We got the shtick," quipped Sam, an Episcopalian who reveled in the Yiddishisms of the industry.

"*News by Six*, that's the shtick," shot back Alan, a Roman Catholic. He also served as Sam's straight man.

"With Mel Lavine as the gontser macher," crowed Sam.

One morning, Alan, wearing a big smile, led me into Sam's office. Sam, too, was wearing a big smile, and rubbing his hands together. The atmosphere was charged. Something extraordinary was going on.

"We've just sold a block of time, thirty minutes, for a news special, a first for KVIQ," said Sam.

"Actually a documentary," said Alan.

"On a development in a redwood forest south of Eureka."

"A kind of Disneyland! Can you imagine!" said Alan.

"Of course, on a smaller scale," said Sam.

"Oh, sure," said Alan. "I didn't mean to imply it's on so grand a scale."

"But big. And dammit, what this county needs, a bonanza nonetheless for this depressed neck of the woods."

"And guess who the developers want for the reporter of the documentary?" asked Alan.

"He means it could have gone to KIEM," said Sam.

"None other than ..." Alan gestured towards me.

Sam was looking sober. "The deal is a tribute to you, big guy. People trust you."

"The most trusted man in Humboldt County," chimed in Alan.

"See what we've done for you," said Sam.

"Hey, the big guy's good," said Alan.

"He still doesn't drink the Coke," said Sam.

"Schmuck," said Alan wagging a finger.

"You've come a long way, baby," said Sam.

"Ain't we the cat's pajamas?" said Alan as he and Sam broke into a dance routine.

While the two shuffled in a crazy pattern of steps, I tried to sort things out in my mind. The documentary they were touting was no documentary at all, rather it was a thirty-minute paid commercial produced under the imprimatur of news with me playing news director and anchor, impersonating myself.

"I'm a newsman, not a con man," I protested. "You put me up to something like this and I'd lose my credibility, the very thing you were so proud of a minute ago. I mean, how could I face the mayor, the cops, the other newsmen in town? I'd be a laughingstock, and so would the station."

"You think you're better than Chet Huntley?"

Sam was being a prick. Though the *Huntley-Brinkley Report* was the biggest newscast on the air, that very week Huntley was featured in a testimonial in *Life* in praise of a chain of pancake restaurants. I had been appalled when I came upon the advertisement. Sam must have seen the same two-page spread and experienced an epiphany: the news as a limitless revenue-producing cash crop.

"I don't know anything about New York but I know how it is here," I replied. "I have no place to hide. He's got a network to protect him. I have to get along with everyone here. All I got is my credibility."

Now it was Alan's turn to weigh in. He countered, "You don't care about the station?"

"Come off it."

"Where's your loyalty?"

"I'm loyal," I insisted.

"We made you a name, made you someone who counts for something in this town, and this is how you thank us?"

It was Alan talking and it was bullshit again. And I said so.

"Hold on guys," I rallied and reminded them, however immodestly, that long before Messrs. Horel and Jones invaded my life I had made something of a name for myself on the *Humboldt Times*, a nomination for an AP prize for an earthquake story, and an award from the California Teachers Association for a series on education. "If I had not been 'a name,' to quote my betters, you never would have given me this friggin' job."

"Hey, Sam, why is he getting so hot under the collar?"

"The big guy can't take a joke."

"It was a joke, big guy. Now this ain't no joke. Do you know how much we're getting for the hour? Can I tell him, Sam? Close to seven thousand five hundred dollars. Do you know what seven thousand five hundred dollars means to a station of our size? What we can do with it? The things we can plan? And in news, too?"

Sam said, "I told you it was big. It opens up a whole new territory for us."

"Sleep on it, big guy," said Alan.

I began shaking my head and started to speak but Sam stopped me, raising a hand. "Sleep on it. We'll talk later. But you ought to know this, whatever your personal feelings, and I really respect them, I'm asking you to set them aside, this once. Not for our sake, but for the station's, for everyone's future."

Sam and Alan may have acted like clowns but I sensed they were in earnest. And I wanted to appease them, but my thoughts were focused on Hodge back at the *Humboldt Times*; the dull but decent Newt Stewart, my competition at KIEM; Mack, the grumpy but gutsy radio reporter who drove me nuts with his conspiracy theories; Guy Fowler, an old drunk who wrote the best newspaper English in northern California; and a procession of elders stretching back to my office boy days at the Boston AP and the high principles of my first editor, Red McCann, up in Maine.

"I'm not a saint, God knows," I agonized with Donna over the weekend. "I'd take the dive so long as I could get away with it."

"But you can't. And you wouldn't even if you could," she said.

"I'm not sure," I said, thinking of the attention I reveled in and that I'd be giving up for … what, a pompous show of self-righteousness?

Then the phone rang. It was Sam.

"Well?" Sam said. It was all he said.

Grappling for words was heavy lifting. I didn't offer him any.

After a moment, he said, "You're an asshole," and hung up.

On Monday, when I returned to work, I fully expected to a find a new face in my stead and my few possessions gathered up and set aside for the miscreant. But business went on as usual; neither Sam nor Alan spoke any unkind words, nor did Sally Kravitz, the station secretary, provide any meaningful looks.

I took up my place in the back room as usual, skimmed the wires and the morning papers, worked the phones, and rolled out in my VW bus to begin another day in the field. I shot my stories, wrote them up, went on the air, (still, however, not drinking the Coke) and nothing happened.

It was the same the next day.

And the day after.

Nothing ever happened.

But as the perspicacious Donna prompted, the handwriting was on the wall. It was not too early to start looking for another job.

There was an opening for a newscaster in desert-dry Fresno, a place that provided negligible journalistic development but no doubt would be good for my asthma. I prepared a reel of my newscasts and sent it to the station manager.

A few days later he wrote back saying that my looks and delivery were not what they had in mind for the grape and cotton growers of the San Joaquin Valley. (Presumably, the loggers and fishermen of the North Coast were a hardier breed.) However, were I willing to lower my sights, they would be happy to consider me for a writer's position.

Well, screw them, I thought. The notion of being a ghost, writing up the news for someone else to deliver, was preposterous, maybe illegal, and certainly unethical.

Then I remembered. A bit earlier a letter had come across my desk from NBC News reminding newsmen in the affiliated stations that the deadline for applying for an RCA/NBC Fellowship to the Graduate School of Journalism at Columbia University was at hand.

I'd been out of school for thirteen years, and at thirty-four was much too old for college life; I felt ill equipped for the challenge.

So I put it aside. This was nothing for me. Then after being rejected at Fresno, I thought, what the hell, why not? I wrote my alma mater, the University of Maine, and requested my college grades. To my astonishment I'd done well enough (B average) to meet Columbia's academic requirements for admission.

I dithered until my wife drew me up short with the revelation that the deadline for posting the application was but a few days away.

The stumbling block was an essay, in 1500 words or more, on

the daunting subject, "Why I Chose a Career in Journalism." It was made clear in the bold print that the essay would weigh heavily in the jury's deliberations.

"My God," I said. "I don't know what to write. What do you say to a bunch of academics and professional journalists sitting in judgment? How do you win their approval?" I plainly didn't know.

"There's Jimmy Householder," said my practical wife. Jimmy Householder, then nearing fifty, was a professor of mathematics at the state college and a close friend. He was an old hand at helping students apply for advanced degrees and scholarship money.

I got him on the phone. "What do I say to these characters? This isn't a news story I'm doing. I'm trying to win their favorable consideration."

"Well," said Jimmy, "you've got to hit 'em where their conscience lives."

He explained in the dry, nasal cadences of his native Southwest.

"They're professionals, or consider themselves professionals. That means they have ideals, a philosophy to profess. This is where you come in."

"You are addressing a select body of professionals, the gate-keepers to big-time journalism. So, hit 'em where their ideals are, where they profess to principles a lot higher than the common run of mankind. And good luck!"

When I sat down to write the essay, the words flew off my keyboard. I said something about the sanctity of the First Amendment and the Bill of Rights to be sure; something about championing the underdog and befriending society's victims; something about the crusading spirit, especially where corrupt politicians, businessmen, and labor leaders were concerned. Something, too, about the journalist's unique perspective for observing the workings of a great democracy, however flawed. And I added yet another thought: I equated journalism with the ministry, asserting it served no less a need and was no less of a calling. Hell, I even titled my essay, "A Holy Calling."

Weeks passed without a word. I'd long forgotten the whole business when I answered the phone in the city hall pressroom. On the other end, a voice said: "Mel Lavine?" Then he introduced himself.

It was an unfamiliar name. "This is Milton Brown." Then he added, "NBC News, New York. Con-*grat-u-lations!*"

I raced home, and tore up the stairs. "Donna!" I screamed in a voice that could have been mistaken for an unspeakable calamity. "We're going to New York!"

Two weeks later, in the midst of packing for our trip, we were interrupted by another call from New York.

This time there was a problem that had to be cleared up before I could be admitted to the journalism school.

"Problem?" I said.

"Well, yes," said the admissions officer. "It's about your check."

"My check?"

"Yes, your twenty dollars to cover the filing fee."

"Yes?"

"Well, you see, the registrar's office informs us that it's no good."

"No good?"

"Insufficient funds, Mr. Lavine."

"You mean my check bounced?"

"I'm afraid so. You can't be admitted to the class until the check clears."

We'd always lived on the edge, writing checks when our balance was low. But people in town knew us. This time our laissez-faire ways caught up with us and threatened to cut short a promising career.

"It was an oversight, I assure you. I'll take care of it right away."

"Thank you, Mr. Lavine. We didn't think there would be a problem."

·

I carried my pride in the successful year at Channel 6 to New York. It was while we were living there that I learned the unsweetened truth. My New York years would have me writing and producing for television behind the camera, not in front of it; I gave up hope of ever landing an on-air job at the network. One day, when I was bragging to New York friends about my Eureka days, my wife lifted the scales from my eyes. As a matter of fact, she said, I induced torpor among viewers. In a word, many found me boring. I was shocked but she went on. People would come up to her in the grocery store and on the street. Although most complimentary about the quality of the news, they nonetheless complained about the newscast.

"Your husband puts me to sleep," they said. "Your husband talks like a metronome."

Columbia

In New York, we moved to an apartment listed at the university's housing office. It was in a nondescript building on Manhattan's West Side close by Broadway. The street – 107th – was bleak, sunken in heavy shadows, the setting relieved to a degree by a rose window in a Catholic church and a florist shop on the corner. The rent was outrageous, but everything else we'd seen was even more costly. There was a bright side. The apartment was only a ten or fifteen-minute walk to Columbia. Above all, according to the housing counselor at the university, we would be subletting a sixth-floor apartment from a lady on the point of leaving town. The flat would be ours for as long as we wanted it.

What we moved into was an apartment filled with overstuffed furniture from the 1920s and 30s. The lady herself was a dowdy, dumpy, elderly person of dark complexion caked with white makeup. Her hair was dyed a freakish red.

She told us she was leaving immediately for Florida to live with a son. Days, weeks followed. Our landlady continued to live with us.

Then the day came when we saw her off. She stepped into the elevator carrying a suitcase and clad in the same black coat she always wore.

"Goodbye," she said.

"Godspeed," we waved.

But a strange thing happened. Some days later we discovered food we hadn't purchased stowed in the refrigerator; we found evidence of an unknown person making use of the bathtub. At night, especially late at night, we heard ghostly moans originating from a second bedroom, the same room our landlady had made such a fuss over locking before bidding us farewell.

It was plain the old lady had never left. The son in Florida was a fake. But we couldn't just pick up and move. I was struggling at the journalism school to keep up with young men and women ten years my junior. Donna was out job-hunting. Our living allowance of $2100 barely covered the rent for an academic year, let alone groceries. For two months we stayed on in the 107th Street flat husbanding our money until there was enough to put down for the security and extra month's rent that New York landlords exacted from new tenants.

In the end, we confronted the old woman. She'd rented the flat to us under false pretenses; she'd promised to be gone, moving to Florida; in fact, taking advantage of us as greenhorns, she'd never had any intention of leaving. We asked for our money back.

She sputtered in a rage, assailing us as thieves with the intention of robbing her blind, and invoked the name of her late husband's cousin, a powerful judge and her protector. The judge would hear of our felony and show us no mercy.

On a stormy November we hand-carried our belongings to a walkup studio in a brownstone six or seven blocks away near Riverside Drive. We were toting books up the steps when the old woman, clad in her familiar black coat, startled us by her presence. In her tow was a young cop.

"There they are, arrest them! The pair of them – they've run off without paying the rent."

The officer looked uncomfortable, especially so when we said, "We still rent that apartment," and brandished the receipt. The cop turned on his heel and vanished. Even after we closed the front door, the old woman continued to remonstrate in frustration.

•

In my first days at journalism school, I called one of my benefactors at NBC, Milton Brown. I wanted him to arrange a tour of the network. This was the same Milton Brown who had called me in Eureka with the news that I'd won the RCA/NBC Fellowship, a grant awarded to a working newsman in the NBC system.

As Milt showed Donna and me around the network, I hoped we'd meet the legendary pair, Chet Huntley and David Brinkley. Were they ever to materialize I was prepared to introduce myself as their

Eureka lead-in. (The local newscast on the other station in town led into Cronkite.)

But the two failed to materialize.

As Milt led us through the newsroom we passed a row of clocks marking the hour in London, Moscow, Paris, New York, Chicago, Los Angeles, Hong Kong, and Tokyo, cities where NBC maintained bureaus. A legend across a wall proclaimed NBC to be the largest broadcast news organization in the world. I confess to a tingle of pride when we came upon a map of the world with each of these locations illuminated.

It was a joyous thing picturing myself as a working newsman in this environment, working the phones, skimming the wires, clattering out copy on a typewriter, running off with camera crews to city hall, the White House, Timbuktu. And eventually, who could say, maybe I'd be posted in a bureau overseas. Was it not only a matter of time?

Just off the newsroom we set foot in a finely appointed carpeted area, which Milt identified as the executive suite.

Without rising, Julian Goodman, an NBC vice president, took my hand and said, "I want you to know we didn't pick your name out of a hat."

So that was something. I was on my way back from exile in backwaters like Eureka and entering the world of big time journalism.

•

Midway into the fall semester I spent a little time as an intern with NBC, first in the fall in New York and months later in Washington. In New York, I drew Gabe Pressman, WNBC's premier street reporter, as my mentor.

Gabe, a dark, short, frenetic man with darting, coal-black eyes, extended a perfunctory greeting.

"You should have been here yesterday," he said. "Not much going on today."

It was a sparkling morning in late November, a season when New York looked its best. Gabe's four-man film crew – cameraman, assistant cameraman, soundman, and electrician – followed in a second car. We drove through thick traffic in midtown to the Queensborough Bridge and then on to the heavily traveled Long Island Expressway.

"We're doing what I call a sob sister piece, a feature," Gabe said. "It's not for tonight. Chances are we'll get an early goodnight."

Gabe fidgeted with the radio, looking for news about President Kennedy's trip to Dallas. People were apprehensive. The week before, Adlai Stevenson, JFK's UN ambassador, was attacked in the Texas city by a mob of conservative women. One dowager wielding an umbrella actually struck him on the head.

Stevenson, I'd seen in the papers, had urged the president to put off the Dallas trip because of what he described as an explosive political climate in the city.

The radio was saying the president's visit was going very well, that he was being met by enthusiastic crowds, and that he and Mrs. Kennedy were delighted with the warm reception.

I had seen Kennedy in the flesh just the week before, at a convention of labor leaders at the Americana Hotel on Seventh Avenue. He was as handsome as a movie star, as stalwart as a fullback, as golden as one would imagine a Greek god of old.

Initially, I'd been turned away from the hall. The police refused to honor my graduate school press credentials. A fellow student, Ralph Blumenthal, who was to become a reporter for the *New York Times*, suggested we march past security "as if we belonged there and had every right to be in the auditorium." He was a street smart New Yorker.

"No," I said. "We'll sweet talk our way in."

I was thinking back to the Humboldt County sheriff's office where you didn't stomp in demanding information on last night's shootout in Willow Creek. Rather you sauntered in, inquired of the sheriff's wife's health, the price of beef (the sheriff owned a ranch), Eureka High's football prospects, and so on. Somewhere along the line you'd bring up the shootout – easy, of course, as if it were the last thing on your mind. And at length, when the sheriff got around to it, you started scribbling.

"OK," said Ralph, skeptical of my strategy.

"Quite a turnout," I said to the policeman with kindly eyes.

"Yeah."

"I bet you've seen them all, presidents, I mean."

"Oh, I've seen a few."

"I've never seen anything like this," I said, speaking of the huge crowds. "I'm not from these parts."

"You don't say."

"Eureka, Humboldt County. California. The redwoods."

"I've heard of them. What are you doing around here?"

"I'm a student. Journalism. Columbia. Sent over here with my classmate to cover the president's speech." I whipped out my J school press card, with name and photo and ID number. "We got to get in. It's for a class assignment."

"Sorry, Mack."

"But I got a press pass."

"Only press with White House credentials can be admitted. Orders."

Ralph tugged at my arm. "It's getting late," he said.

We joined a line of union people.

"You don't say anything," he said.

"OK."

We marched right in. No one raised a voice or hand to stop us.

•

"So far so good," said Gabe, fidgeting with the radio as the car moved with the traffic. He hadn't liked the things he'd been hearing about Texas. "Just a gut feeling, you know," he said. Gabe was a reporter driven by instinct.

When we pulled up at the location for the Long Island shoot, the crew lumbered forth with camera, lights, tripod, sound equipment, and the like. Gabe got out to chat up a farmer and his wife, down on their luck, whom he planned to interview.

Several times he called over to me.

"Hear anything?" I shook my head. I was still tuned into the car's radio.

And then an announcer broke in and said shots had been fired. Gabe heard the bulletin and came running.

The shots were fired at the president, this was certain, but what was not certain was whether the president had been hit. Then there was word; yes, the president was wounded. "Repeat, President Kennedy has been wounded. There's been an attempt on the president's life. He is being rushed to a hospital ..."

"They'll want us back in town," said Gabe, starting the ignition.

Some minutes passed. Suddenly, the radio began playing heavy classical music. Gabe said, "It's serious. He may even be dead. Why else would they put that stuff on the air? They're telling us something, preparing us for the news."

As we made our way through the canyons of Lower Manhattan and Wall Street we could see the news of the president's death rapidly traveling, as if along a human grapevine, from one shocked citizen to another.

Back in Rockefeller Center, I followed Gabe into the NBC newsroom, awash in white shirts and faces stunned by the tragedy. He spoke for a moment with a pacing executive and then rushed down to the street with the crew at his heels.

"How do you feel?" he said, importuning homeward bound commuters. "You've heard the news. The president's been assassinated. How do you feel?"

How do you feel?

I was appalled, thinking sardonically, that's a great reporter? That's advancing the story? Why, it was pure sob sister stuff.

Looking back after all those years I can see where Gabe's approach made some sense. He knew instinctively that TV was, at its core, theatre, an ideal conduit for conveying emotions, feelings.

The critics were always getting it wrong when it came to television news because they were always confusing it with print, which was – and is, admittedly – a better conveyer of ideas as well as information.

"How do you feel?" was the right question for television on the night of November 22, 1963.

•

Television news came of age, so to speak, with its coverage of the Kennedy assassination.

Speaking to my Columbia class some weeks after the Dallas shooting, Tom Wicker, who covered the assassination for the *New York Times*, said he could not have written his story without the help of television. In the confusion that followed the firing of the shots,

Wicker had stepped into a cocktail lounge in search of a telephone. From the phone booth where he reached his editors in New York, he found himself staring at three television sets, each turned to one of the major networks. The story was unfolding before his eyes.

With the ability to switch to locations throughout the city, television kept track of the bewildering events, a feat no earthbound print reporter could have hoped to match. Without ever stirring from his place, Wicker filed his story, drawing upon the flow of information that filled the screens. Ironically, as Wicker himself pointed out, his editors could have filed much the same story from the *Times* newsroom on 43rd Street.

•

As part of my time at Columbia, I also interned in Washington, D.C. During my week there, I saw Pierre Salinger again for the first time since our raucous night in Eureka ten years before. In the interval he'd made a name for himself as President Kennedy's press secretary. Five months after Kennedy's assassination, in the spring of 1964, he was working at the White House in the same job for President Johnson. After attending one of his press briefings with Bob Gorulski, the NBC correspondent, Bob led me up to the platform, saying, "This fellow says he knows you from California, Pierre."

I approached with trepidation. By way of greeting, Pierre said frigidly, "You son of a bitch."

Some weeks later I heard that Governor Edmund G. (Pat) Brown of California had appointed Pierre to fill Claire Engle's senate seat when the northern California Democrat died. In the fall election Pierre would face the actor George Murphy, a Republican.

Enter Tom Knight, a Jacques Tati character, well meaning but chaotic, who taught photography at Humboldt State. Hodge used to hire him from time to time to work with me and other reporters on Sunday features. Tom was the perpetual student, inquiring, baffled, intrigued, indignant, and innocent.

A month or so before Californians chose between Pierre and Murphy, Tom phoned me in New York from Arcata. He was working for Murphy, and needed a favor. There was a rumor that Pierre had been arrested in Eureka, while he was still on the *Chronicle*, for drunken and disorderly conduct. My name had come up. What did I know about the incident? The police wouldn't talk. He was leaning on me for the sake of old times.

"Listen, Tom," I said, struggling for the words and full of sleep; it was ten or eleven in California but the middle of the night in New York. "I deny that such a thing ever happened. Should you circulate such a libel, I will personally fly back to Humboldt County on the first plane and kick your ass all over the state."

I never heard any more about it, and hoped that I'd spared Pierre an embarrassment; Murphy won the election anyway.

•

In the spring, close to graduation, we were required to turn in a lengthy article based on interviews with authoritative figures. The paper would weigh heavily in an evaluation of our performance. Inasmuch as I was the broadcast fellow in the class, I took for my topic TV and Politics.

My adviser, Penn Kimball, suggested several people for me to interview; chief among them were Louis Cowan, a former president of CBS television, and James A. Farley, President Roosevelt's postmaster general and his campaign chairman in the triumphant elections of 1932 and 1936. Farley was a master political strategist in the heyday of radio. The old pol should have some interesting things to say about the tube. Penn thought Cowan's perspective on television could be especially helpful as well, given his own rise and fall at CBS.

I'd set out for Cowan's house armed with facts. Before ascending to the network presidency, Cowan had invented *The $64,000 Question*, one of the popular quiz shows of the 1950s. When investigators found that this show, as well as other quiz shows, were rigged, CBS insisted on his resignation in an effort to appease a furious public and Congress. Cowan, however, had always maintained that the deception took place under his successor, after Cowan became head of the network.

The questions were fixed in my mind: in view of the history of the manipulation of television in the hands of dishonest producers, do you view TV's growing influence in politics with misgivings? Your critics say either your subordinates had rigged the shows under your very nose, in which case you were guilty of gross incompetence, or you were somehow involved. What do you say?

The moment I stepped into his luxurious Park Avenue apartment, Cowan took me by surprise.

"Tell me about yourself," he said, leading me into his study. "I want to know to whom I'm talking."

As I took a seat I stumbled through a recitation. The news-making questions died on my lips.

"I'm not clear about that," he'd interrupt. "Would you mind going back to where you went to college? The University of Maine? I don't believe I've ever met anyone who went to the University of Maine. Well, why would you go there? I wish you would answer more fully. And about your parents? What kind of people were they?"

I was thoroughly cowed. His lordly manner reminded me of my Uncle Harry, an equally dour, intimidating person, who relished putting the children through inquisitions at family gatherings.

"Well, what did you learn this week at school?" he'd say with a broad wink at other family members. "Have they taught you how to compute the Pythagorean theorem yet? Well, why not? What are they waiting for? As a taxpayer and property owner, I have a right to demand some answers." Again, the broad wink, followed by family laughter.

I left with nothing, really, save for a few well worn kudos Cowan bestowed on TV's coverage of Martin Luther King, Jr.'s March on Washington the year before. "How sensitive the camera work! How dignified the presentation!" No doubt, he'd sized me up as a neophyte, and, sensing my hesitation to raise embarrassing questions, silenced me with beatitudes, again in a manner reminiscent of Uncle Harry's.

•

Jim Farley was a name I'd known since childhood. The bluff Irishman was always in the news, the president's man, the political mastermind.

Though I was but eleven or twelve at the time, I remembered being saddened when Farley split with Roosevelt in 1940 over the issue of a third term. (Farley himself nursed presidential ambitions.) After the break, to my dismay, Farley joined FDR's critics.

I found Farley at seventy-six still hale when I stepped into the Manhattan office he occupied as president of Coca-Cola International. The walls were filled with signed pictures of prominent politicians, Republicans as well as Democrats; happily, I discovered, FDR was among them.

Gingerly, I asked him about Roosevelt. Did he have any regrets about the breakup with the president? He shook his head. He'd resigned from the administration on principle. No president was entitled to a third term. He thought so then, and thought so now.

About television? I asked. Has it changed the dynamics of elections? Again, he shook his head.

Citing the Roosevelt landslides in the depression years of the 1930s, he said voters were motivated by fear, not hope. Today, in general, people vote against someone or something rather than for. Although he claimed no special knowledge about television, he believed the principle held true with new technology.

Under the impression that the interview was over, I rose, thanking him for his time. But he protested. We chatted for another twenty minutes about New Deal and New Frontier politics and the new president, LBJ.

My paper mirrored Farley's views and prejudices. "You need to read more about politics. You're too easily impressed," read Penn Kimball's verdict.

My hero-worshipping cost me a C.

•

Towards the end of the second semester, I was elected president of the Class of 1964. I can't account for it, except that at thirty-six, I was one of the oldest students, ten or more years older than most of my classmates. They may have believed that my age put me in a stage in life where one was in need of consolation. In any event, Richard Baker, then the acting dean, summoned the newly chosen officers to a meeting. As we gathered around, he wanted our input. Now that the school year was virtually behind us, what did we think of the year just past? Were there changes we would propose? In other words, what could be done to make things better for the classes coming after us?

I was well prepared, inasmuch as I'd long wanted to talk about a need for a course on ethics. Back in Humboldt County, my fellow newshounds and I had bemoaned the by and large lack of journalistic ethics and standards; our provincial press functioned as a mouthpiece for the lumber companies and major advertisers. Now, enrolled in a graduate school that prepared people to become professionals, I had looked vainly for direction on how to deal with conflicts of conscience.

From time to time, professors stressed the importance of fairness and even-handedness, of a sympathy for the underdog, and a healthy skepticism in general. But my major was radio and TV. The advisor, William Wood, rarely if ever raised the subject of ethics. He was preoccupied with the technical aspects of broadcast journalism.

When I argued for a period to be set aside for ethical concerns, thereby keeping faith with my Eureka brethren, I was shouted down, not least of all by the dean himself. Above all, he admonished, the purpose of graduate school was to enable students to find employment. Ethics, standards of professional behavior, one picked up that sort of thing on the job. The academic year was brief, less than nine months, leaving no time for homilies. The only reason the school existed was to fill the ranks of the profession with its graduates.

Stimulated by the dean's remarks, the others called for instruction – at the minimum – for a course on how to get jobs: how to handle interviews, how to cut through the red tape, how to connect with the right people.

Paul D. Zimmerman – later a book and movie critic for *Newsweek* and still later a screenwriter – scoffed at my notions. The others clamored in disapproval as well. My title of class president was not to be taken seriously.

Graf

Just before commencement, I went back to NBC, this time on the advice of my media-wise advisor. "What you want to do," Penn Kimball said, "is offer your benefactors first refusal. As a courtesy, you're giving them the first opportunity to hire or not to hire you."

When he returned my call, Milt Brown told me to see the director of local news. There was nothing to be gained by another visit to the executive suite.

"You've come at a good time," said Dick Kutzleb, the head of news for WNBC-TV. At six feet six, the rangy ex-paratrooper of World War Two eclipsed my own six feet four. With the political conventions, the campaign, fall elections, the war in Vietnam, and the unrest in American cities, there was a good chance he'd be hiring extra people.

He phoned a week later.

"They're down a writer on the *Today* graveyard shift. I told them you could plug the hole. I talked you up. Now don't let me down."

•

"So you're this year's blue ribbon winner from the boonies. So, you're what's considered the best of the bumper crop. Well, welcome to Siberia. And, be advised: we like our copy to snap, crackle, and pop."

Thus, Dick Graf, the burly news editor of the *Today Show*, busy paring his nails, welcomed me to the overnight.

After a pause, he set down his clippers and led me to the desk where I'd be working. He pointed out a pile of wire copy and morning editions.

"We keep the copy tight, twenty, thirty seconds, no frills. Words of one syllable preferred. Our millionaire newsreader, Frank Blair, has to read them. He has an IQ on par with a paramecium."

"A what?"

"A paramecium," he said, as if it were an everyday word.

It was two o'clock in the morning, the RCA building silent as a tomb. One's footsteps made a terrible clatter. The only hint of life was in the newsroom where the teleprinters thumped.

The writers straggled in. Introductions took the form of a nod or wave and a touch of gallows humor.

"What are you in for? Who's got it in for you?" they said.

From the start, Graf was my nemesis.

"Too long," he piped up, handing my story back to me. "Too much explanation. We want it quick and dirty. Snap, crackle, pop!"

He bullied the other workers but complained more loudly when rewriting me and causing me to wonder each shift whether I was going to last the night.

One day I made straight for the wire room. Perhaps there was a story, a sidebar, something I could write that would redeem myself in Graf's eyes, but he barred my way.

"You're not ready for the network," he said. "You're a busher like all the others they send me. No one in his right mind would volunteer for this work."

I offered to resign on the spot.

"I won't hear of such talk," Graf replied. "The short and the long of it is I'm stuck with you. I just want you to know that you're not a one-man band around here, whatever you were in Eureka. You don't go waltzing into the wire room or film editing or any place without my OK. You don't make a move on this watch unless I authorize it. Is that clear? You got it straight? It goes for you; it goes for everyone on this show!"

Later, I would overhear him muttering on the phone, "Jesus, Mary and Joseph, why is it I always wind up with the rubes?"

●

At the very beginning, I had a problem.

I turned to Graf. How does one write for someone else? Does one mimic them? Imagine the pattern of their speech and then replicate it? I'd never done such a thing. In truth, I thought the practice corrupt and amazed that it existed.

Graf shrugged. "Write it any way you like." Frank Blair, the newsreader, was a human metronome.

"But, isn't it – ?"

"Isn't it what?" he snapped.

"Isn't it dishonest? Ghostwriting the news?"

"It's news, it's not the Gettysburg Address. It doesn't make a whole lot of difference who writes it. The facts are the same. It's not an editorial. The stuff's on the wires, in the papers, it's already been through the mill.

"We package the news. That's what we do, that's who we are, packagers; we make nice, neat packages of the news and send it into the wild blue yonder. We add a fancy line or two of our own – the pride of authorship – that's the pink ribbon."

•

Jocular one moment, bullying the next, sometimes volcanic, Graf was someone to try one's soul. In the middle of the night there was no one to rein him in. The newsroom was his fiefdom.

While we were busy grinding out the news of the day, Graf often busied himself with the crossword puzzle.

Looking up, he'd say, "Hey, get this! A way of getting around coastal towns? Anyone? The word is ferries. I knew they were well organized but I didn't know they had a navy!"

And, a moment later: "Hey, a colloquialism for birds that don't fly? Answer: jailbirds. Easy. But do you know the only geese that can't fly? Give up? Portuguese!"

One night, setting down his pipe and rising up from his desk, he announced there was a traitor in our midst.

He ignored Len Luddington, an old AP writer, and Jim Boozer, a burned-out radio writer, and me, and stood, arms akimbo, over Lamar Falkner, a frail, young Mississippian.

I liked Lamar, a cousin of William Faulkner, the novelist. Lamar was friendly and ironic. On my first day on the overnight, he'd sought to calm my nervousness.

"No great secret to this lobster trick, Mel. You just write till you get tired," he had said.

I'd pored over Lamar's copy a few times in an effort to detect family tracings of genius. A nebulous pursuit. There was little room for creativity in the sort of stories we turned out. They were written more or less by rote, something like painting by the numbers.

Now we learned that Lamar had had the temerity to look for another NBC job in an attempt to steal away from the overnight. But he'd underestimated Graf, who'd got wind of the traitorous behavior from friends who were – as Graf put it – "up and down the building."

Like a drill sergeant, Graf marched Lamar into a darkened office, switched on the lights, and slammed the door. His thundering voice seeped under the closed door.

He was putting the younger man on notice: if ever he tried to pull another fast one, Graf would see to it that Lamar never worked in the industry again.

"Do I make myself clear?" Graf thundered, clearly implying that he would so blacken Lamar's name that no producer would dare touch him.

"You can count on it, put it in the bank," said Graf. "I'll break you. So help me, you'll never work in this industry again."

When they emerged, Lamar looked ghostly. His lower lip quivered. Graf was beaming, not least because the rest of us had gotten the message.

.

In preparing the news for the top of each hour and at the half hours, we relied almost entirely on the wires and the New York morning papers (the *Times*, *Herald-Tribune*, and *Daily News*, mainly). We hardly ever made a phone call and never left the building.

As Lamar said: we simply wrote until we got tired.

Yet at the end of the week a scrambling took place over who took which newsmaker to what fictitious lunch in order to claim the $25 expense allowance that was available to us graveyard workers. The deliberations put everyone, including Graf, in a good mood.

"You couldn't have taken the police commissioner to lunch because I did," said one of the writers.

"How could you have? I've got the receipt," said another.

"Not fair. I've already listed Murphy on my voucher. You take the sanitation commissioner to lunch. Here, I'll give you my Sardi's receipts."

I refrained from putting in any vouchers. None of us ever stirred from our desks during the long night. It may have been all right for these older hands to commit petty larceny, but it would have been foolhardy for someone on the threshold of a network career.

A few Fridays had passed before Len Luddington, the senior writer on our small staff and a shameless Graf suckup, took me aside and said, "You're not putting in your expenses." His voice was troubled.

"I have no business doing it," I said. "I'd only get myself in hot water."

"You're screwing it up for the rest of us. Someone in accounting will start sniffing around and asking questions. 'How come all these guys put in for expenses but this new fellow doesn't?' It's got to be all for one and one for all."

"I don't dare," I said flatly.

"You're going to get the rest of us in trouble," he said.

"I don't mean to."

"But that's the way it'll work out."

"You need not worry about receipts," Graf interjected. "Here's a fistful of 'em. Four Seasons, Pearl's, the Palace, the Waldorf. Didn't I hear that you took Dr. Kissinger to 21? Valuable background for your ten second lead-in on the Middle East."

I'd never taken a dime I had not honestly come by; now I was being corrupted, and, in all places, at the center of my chosen profession, television journalism.

·

As I said, Graf mocked, humiliated, and bullied us all. So I did a cowardly thing. If I couldn't escape him, maybe I could make an ally of him. In hindsight, it was a foolish thing to do. I'd seen Luddington brown-nosing his way into Graf's favor only to be slapped down. Graf loved flattery but his moods were mercurial.

The idea to win Graf's favor came from my mother, from her writing, "Melvin, you are in a city of coreligionists and, more to the point, employed in a business led by coreligionists. So appeal to them on a fraternal basis. Everybody does it, especially when you're new to a city as you are to New York. It's expected. It's nothing to be ashamed of. Do not be put off by their titles or airs. They're just like you, no better ..."

Thus, one morning, after hearing Graf talking to his mother – he talked to her and his wife nightly, his speech, as always, enlivened with Yiddish words – I made up my mind to cast an ethnic net. I marked time until we were off the air and then made mention of Jewish holidays and letting fall a word or two of Yiddish.

"Do you still fast on Yom Kippur? Take the day off? Did you grow up orthodox or conservative in Brooklyn? Reform?"

"What? What is this? What are you raving about? Huh?"

"I'm just asking questions."

"If you're wondering if I'm Jewish, I'm not. Is that what you're fishing for?"

"I'm sorry, Dick. Meant no offense," I offered.

"Jesus H. Christ, what did I do to deserve this?"

.

I laid low writing all through the summer of the presidential campaign and Lyndon Johnson's landslide in the fall. But we rarely remarked about the stories we were dealing with. Our interest picked up when someone came in reporting a sound eight hours of sleep. Then we pressed for details. How did you contend with the noise from the street? The neighbors? The phone? The barking dog?

The only other stirring moment was when a desk assistant bounded in every night from a run to the Stage delicatessen laden with beer and a feast of delectables.

I ate ravenously and after work made short order of more beer and chips in Hurley's. On arriving home, I wiped yet another plate clean before falling into bed, still in want of absolution.

Donna and I were still living in the walkup studio on the Upper West Side. It was a rear apartment looking out on small yards and other buildings. From a distance its black hulk reminded me of a freighter tied up in a busy port.

We both liked the polyglot nature of the neighborhood, the many races represented, the traders, artisans, and artists who made their homes there.

Nonetheless, it seemed as though the entire neighborhood was in a conspiracy to keep me awake during the day by means of trucks, automobiles, horns, radios and TVs, garbage collections, telephones, sirens, cats, dogs, kids, airplanes, motorcycles …

Donna shut the windows, drew the shades, took the phone off the hook, and rebuffed visitors. Sleep, however, remained fitful.

She'd rouse me at midnight. I'd shower in a stupor, throw on some clothes, down a hasty breakfast, and make my way to the IRT at 103rd and Broadway, a haven for the down-and-out at that hour. One trod gingerly. The subway would reek from human waste and degradation. Many nights I was the only passenger on the platform.

I'd climb out of the subway at 50th and Seventh Avenue and drop in at an all-night Rexalls for a fortifying milk shake and a word with Abie, the counterman.

My Eureka years were an endless source of fascination to Abie, a shapeless tower of flesh and spindly arms and a weary, mournful face. He looked as if he had never slept.

He'd often say, "One of these days me and the missus will take a trip out there and see them big redwoods of yours." They'd interested him all his life. "Seen pictures where you can drive the car right through 'em, is that right?"

And then the refrain: Why, he always wondered, would a nice guy like me ever leave a paradise like the California redwoods for the muck of New York?

And he'd shake his head.

Abie and I became friendly by virtue of sharing confidences about our tyrannical bosses. His was Jake the Gonif.

Whenever I'd be contemplating a showdown with Graf, he'd say, "It won't get you no place. Look what I got to put up with, with Jake the Gonif. The abuse he hands out. As long as you got to work for a living, you got to grin and bear it. That's what I say."

In time, Graf's tyrannical nights and the sleepless, stupefying days brought me to the edge of a nervous breakdown.

"Your husband's flirting with disaster as long as he stays on that overnight shift," the doctor told my wife upon checking my vital signs. I was tipping the scales at 230, up from 190 before I left Eureka. My blood pressure hovered ominously at 220 over 190. The doc attributed my perilous state to stress, lack of sleep and exercise, and an unhealthy diet. I'd been on the overnight for eighteen months.

"Put it in writing, Doc," I said. It was the million-dollar wound, not bad enough to kill but bad enough to get me off the graveyard shift.

•

I began knocking on doors selling myself to other producers of local news. At length I succeeded in landing an audition for a job as a street reporter on radio. It wasn't TV, my preference, but at least a step in the right direction.

So for an entire day I covered the city. And I was happy again. People who'd chanced to hear my reporting said, yes, you performed marvelously.

However, a vice president, a slight, dapper fellow, had the last word. He demurred.

"You're too much of a stylist," he pronounced, concluding, "One David Brinkley is enough for any network."

In effect, the personal touch, which had worked so well in my news delivery in Eureka, did not win favor in New York. But I would still do for a ghost.

Many times I thought of quitting and returning to California but I hesitated. People back in Eureka would snicker, "He didn't have the shoulders." And so I remained in New York, a news writer, and a ghost, putting words into the mouths of others.

But my health rebounded. I was working in the sunlight again.

Stuart Schulberg
and the Today Show

In the spring of 1973, after eight years in local news, I went from covering potholes, tenement fires, and school bonds to writing about great happenings in this country and abroad. What persuaded Stuart Schulberg, the executive producer of the *Today Show*, to take me on was the fact that I'd come to New York from the grass roots. This was a plus in Stuart's mind. Until then, I'd thought Eureka was something to gloss over, even apologize for.

But by 1973 it was "grass-roots" time in America.

"Keep hammering away with your experience in Eureka," counseled my *Today Show* friends, Chris Brown and John Dunn. Chris was a *Today* writer and John the *Today* editor.

"Keep reminding Stuart of your roots," my friends persisted. "Forget you were ever born in Boston and raised in Brookline, Massachusetts. Remember, Eureka is your hometown now."

All this tutoring was in anticipation of my third and decisive interview with Stuart.

"I've been doing some calculating," I told my friends. "The truth is I've only lived in Eureka, figuring all the times I got up and took off – I was always trying to leave – no more than five or six years."

"Just don't tell Stuart," they counseled.

"You might as well know, too, that I don't know a great deal about film." Although videotape would soon replace it, we were still shooting everything on film in those days at WNBC.

"Just don't tell Stuart."

On the day of the interview I happened to run into John Dunn in the hallway outside the *Today* offices. He took hold of my shoulders and shook. "Remember, Eureka!" he pressed.

Stuart Schulberg, fiftyish, with high color and a goatee, was sitting in a cramped, narrow room with his legs propped up on a kidney-shaped desk. As he spoke, he sipped from a Styrofoam cup. (Later, I would learn that the cup was always filled with either Scotch or vodka.)

He was Hollywood royalty. Stuart's late father, Benjamin Percival (B.P.) Schulberg, had been one of a handful of men who ran Hollywood in the 1920s and 1930s. In his heyday, as production chief of Paramount Studios, B.P. was the peer of such tycoons as Irving Thalberg, L.B. Mayer, and Samuel Goldwyn.

Stuart's brother, Budd, was the successful novelist and screenwriter (*What Makes Sammy Run?* and *On the Waterfront.*) Their mother, Adeline Schulberg, ran noted talent and literary agencies.

I'd been cautioned about Stuart's drinking. If you had serious business with him, you were well advised to catch him before he hurried off to lunch. (On this particular day, it was ten o'clock and he was perfectly lucid.)

"You've got quite a fan club," he began, lighting a cigarette and waving me to a seat. "Wherever I turn I hear your name." I took this to mean that Chris Brown and John Dunn lobbied shamelessly on my behalf.

He drew deeply and said, "You really are from Eureka?"

"I really am."

"I don't believe I've ever been to Eureka. You grow redwoods up there?"

"Oldest, tallest living things on earth." I replied. Sensing his interest I sketched the terrain: incessant precipitation and fog, a boiling and jagged coast, a country of logging camps, ranches, sheep men, cattlemen, fishermen. And I added a word or two about riotous Two Street, the town's skid row.

"Unless I miss my guess, you're just what this show needs," said Stuart.

And so I was hired. On my first morning in the studio, I was taken aside by Joe Gottlieb, a senior staffer. He pointed out a spot at some distance from the set where Frank McGee and Barbara Walters hosted the broadcast.

"This is where the writer stands."

"Seen and not heard?"

He nodded. "Above all, you don't speak to the cast unless they speak to you." By "cast" he meant the people who performed on the air. But he might just as well have meant "caste" in terms of social status. He was advising me that the divide between on-air performers on the one hand and researchers, writers, and producers on the other was indeed wide.

I protested. "But I'm the writer. That's my script they're reading. My words. What if it's important? What if a story changes? A guest turns out to be hard of hearing?"

"Important?" he replied testily. "What could be more important than keeping Barbara Walters happy?"

From the moment I'd set foot on the premises until the day Frank McGee died, the staff was torn in its sympathies between the pair. "You couldn't be coming at a worse time with things as bad as they are between Barbara and Frank," said Joe Gottlieb. "Sooner or later you'll have to choose sides."

Joe was an unabashed fan of Barbara Walters. A short, stocky man of sixty, he talked of her as a father might of a favorite child.

"She's frantic for freshness," he said. "If one word were to describe her, I would say it was immaculate, immaculate to a fault. She chooses her own colors and clothes. She has impeccable taste."

Her morning routine, Joe went on, rarely varied: for the first fifteen or twenty minutes she closeted herself in her dressing room. This was the time she devoted to her personal needs. Bobbie Armstrong, Barbara's hairdresser, washed and rinsed her hair. Then, as Barbara sat under the dryer and Bobbie attended her nails or pressed a skirt or blouse, she skimmed the morning's script. If something struck her as amiss she cried for Stuart or the writer and, as the case might be, the person in question came running.

"Incidentally," he asked, "whose side are you on?"

"Pardon?"

"Are you a Walters man or a McGee man?"

"I take it you're a Barbara person?" I said.

"You're not kidding. If you're smart, you will be, too."

He took a breath.

"I've been in this business a long time. I've been a press agent, a copywriter in advertising. I've been associated with productions of Broadway shows, off-Broadway shows, movies, radio programs, lecture tours, public relations, you name it. I've flacked for them all, Mike Wallace, Johnny Carson, Phil Donahue, you name 'em. But, believe me, Barbara Walters is the best, the best in the world. As for Frank McGee, he couldn't carry her microphone."

Barbara Walters came into sight. At that moment, even her public would have had difficulty identifying her and they would have been amazed upon realizing that the woman crossing the room was she. She was wearing no makeup. Her hair was covered by a scarf. She looked positively plain, almost unrecognizable, on her arrival at the NBC studios.

She swept by without saying hello or good morning. Her attention was elsewhere. She seemed to walk right through you rather than right past you.

A few minutes later, Bobbie Armstrong came looking for Joe. When he returned, he was in despair.

Barbara hated Joe's script and wanted changes. She thought he'd made her come across as naïve.

"Naïve? It's the last thing I'd think about Barbara Walters. Inconsistent, that's the word for her," said Joe. "She loved my script last week, adored it, couldn't praise it enough, and now?"

He began typing, muttering under his breath, "Sometimes, Barbara, you try my patience."

This morning, she was pressing Stuart for her due, that is, to let her take charge of an interview that she and Frank were doing together. Besides introducing the guest, she also wanted to ask the first and last questions; this insistence was a sticking point since these, too, were prerogatives reserved to Frank as principal host of the program.

Stuart, sighing heavily, made all this known to both Joe and me as he stepped into the green room.

"It's impossible, of course; you know how Frank's contract reads," he said. Stuart had complimented Barbara for showing initiative in landing the interview; however, he might also have pointed out that the newsmaker may have agreed to appear because it was the *Today Show*. But, Stuart said, he had refrained from "getting into this fine point."

He paced. "I told her I'd do what I could, speak to Frank, try to get him to relent. But you know Frank. It's mission impossible."

Down the hallway floated a man's voice, cheerful and salty. It was Frank McGee, a sturdy figure in his early fifties with white-blond hair and a handsome, square face. He was trading good-humored insults with a stagehand before disappearing into a dressing room.

Stuart sprawled into a chair and took a reflective sip of Scotch.

"I'll do what I can. Perhaps I should call him first, see what mood he's in." But his hand lay heavy on the receiver.

Frank McGee
and Barbara Walters

Frank McGee was born in 1922. The son of an oil field worker in Norman, Oklahoma, he was drawn early in life to the populist beliefs of his native Midwest. A fiery temper got him in trouble with a history teacher with whom he argued about the Civil War. He was given a failing grade. Lacking a half-point to graduate, Frank left high school without a diploma.

He sat out World War Two as an enlisted man in stupefying boredom in the Aleutians. His temper got him in trouble again. Following a row with an officer, Frank was busted from sergeant to private.

On his return to civilian life, he reenrolled at the University of California at Berkeley on the GI Bill. But a dispute with an instructor led to the loss of his grant. He never graduated. For a brief period Frank wrote scripts in Hollywood for the popular TV series *Dragnet*, starring Jack Webb, in the 1950s. But, as he told a friend, he soon burned out, and gave it up.

He found his niche in television news in the 1950s, first in his native Oklahoma and then in Alabama during the Montgomery bus boycott. His view of life as a conflict between good and evil, and right and wrong, was perfectly attuned to the epic struggle over civil rights. His candid reporting caught the attention of NBC. By the time he was named the principal co-host of the *Today Show* in 1972, Frank was already one of the brightest stars in broadcast journalism.

•

Barbara Walters was born in Boston in 1929, and, like Stuart, was the child of a father in show business. Lou Walters was a nightclub impresario, known for his extravagant floorshows and beautiful girls.

Barbara attended Sarah Lawrence College in New York where she nurtured aspirations for careers both on the stage and in literature. After graduation, through a friend of her father's, she went to work in publicity, promotion, and advertising at WNBC-TV. Barbara did a stint as a network producer, and then moved to CBS where she worked for five years as a writer on its morning show, in competition with *Today*. After the show folded, Barbara joined a public relations firm. Her mentor there was William Safire, later a conservative columnist for the *New York Times*.

In 1961 she joined the *Today Show* as a writer and segment producer. Before long she began appearing on the air. A scoop that drew raves from her producers was an interview with Jacqueline Kennedy on the First Lady's tour of France.

By 1970 and a television personality, Barbara published, *How to Talk with Practically Anybody About Practically Anything* – reportedly a ghostwritten best seller. Barbara is said to have rejected the first manuscript because she found it too literate. People who knew her would know that she could not have written it. In the end, the manuscript was re-written in a simpler style before she found it acceptable for publication.

When I joined the show in the spring of 1973, Barbara was in a second marriage, the mother of an adopted daughter, and the supporter of her parents and a retarded sister. By now, her father, Lou Walters, was ailing and broke.

•

Frank claimed to be appreciative of Barbara's enterprise, but he didn't conceal his disapproval of her Park Avenue lifestyle and what he saw as her fawning over Broadway, Hollywood, and Washington personalities. He didn't think her a serious journalist; she hadn't earned the credentials to be on a program like *Today*. Off-camera, the two rarely spoke.

There was reason for McGee to be resentful of Barbara. During a Middle East crisis, Barbara pursued Anwar Sadat, the president of Egypt, and Menachin Begin, the prime minister of Israel. She shut-

tled tirelessly between Cairo and Israel before Sadat and Begin succumbed and agreed to talk to her on camera in separate interviews.

Barbara's coup infuriated McGee. He thought her questions soft
and self-serving, yielding no news, and to no purpose other than
promoting Barbara's career.

She further upset McGee again with an interview with President
Nixon. Douglas Sinsel, Barbara's field producer, recalled a Nixon
aide reminding the president of other appointments. Anxious to
keep Nixon talking, Barbara said if he could manage to give them
more time, they would have enough footage to devote the entire two
hours of the broadcast to the president. In so many words, Nixon
told his aide to get lost.

"McGee hated this," says Sinsel. Frank believed (as did Stuart
Schulberg) that Barbara was being exploited by Nixon, Henry Kissinger, and other high officials.

Nixon once referred to her as his favorite journalist. This made
Frank, who shunned personal ties to politicians, nearly apoplectic.
In his view, it was Barbara's weakness as an interviewer rather than
her strength that led Nixon and Kissinger to grant the interviews.

With Barbara's adoration of celebrities in mind, Frank once said,
"When I die I want to be remembered for the things I didn't do."

Like Frank, Stuart believed that the news was merely a means
to an end with Barbara, a vehicle to draw the attention she craved.
He was given to complain about her late nights in the company of
the rich and famous, which led her to neglect her homework for the
broadcast.

Once, Barbara interviewed Moshe Dayan, the Israeli defense min-
ister and war hero, at great length but failed to raise the issue of the
Palestinians. Finally, Stuart broke in on her earpiece and told her,
"The Palestinians, ask him about the Palestinians!"

That evening Barbara won praise for her diligence in raising the
Palestinian issue from no less a critic than Ad Schulberg, Stuart's
perceptive mother. "Why, she's marvelous, that girl; what a clever
journalist," she said. "Imagine, her pressing Dayan about the Palestinians." Stuart was rendered helpless, muttering in frustration to
himself.

One day, Frank came to Stuart with a demand: Barbara must no longer do Washington interviews. She was professionally inept. Her interviews with statesmen, government officials, and important politicians embarrassed the show. Henceforth, she should be restricted to figures in the entertainment world and show biz gossip where her real talent lay.

Once again, Stuart found himself in the middle, as a former colleague put it, "a lion tamer in a cage with these two monsters, Barbara Walters and Frank McGee."

McGee was a daunting figure when aroused. Stuart agonized. Nonetheless, he was going to leave Barbara alone. He refused to budge. In spite of her shortcomings, he was not going to make any changes; this would only make matters worse. While Stuart accepted much of McGee's criticism as valid, he nonetheless admired Barbara's on-camera skills and would not hesitate putting her on the air in an emergency. He also admired her "spunk." Some of her interviews were indeed memorable.

In an interview with Mamie Eisenhower, she'd brought up the rumors of her drinking. Was Mrs. Eisenhower aware of the rumors? Yes, she knew of the rumors, but what led to them was an inner ear problem, not alcohol, answered the president's widow.

And when speaking with Lady Bird Johnson, Barbara asked about rumors of her husband's womanizing. As I remember it, the former first lady replied, "Why, Barbara, Lyndon just loved people, all people."

Was Lady Bird jealous of her late husband's reputation as a ladies' man? Barbara pressed. Unblinkingly, Mrs. Johnson said no.

Frank continued to demand that Stuart downgrade Barbara's role on the show, but Stuart refused to give ground. Then Frank threatened to go over the producer's head.

"I'm the newsman on this show," said Frank defiantly.

He took his protest to the president of NBC News, Richard Wald, but he got nowhere. In so many words, Wald, according to Sinsel, told Frank that "if Barbara gets the interviews, she may also do them."

In my heart, I was a McGee man. I'd seen him long before I ever set foot in the *Today Show* offices. I'd watched him on the march to Selma with Martin Luther King, Jr. and remembered his interview with Spiro Agnew when Nixon's vice president was heaping scorn on the press and Frank, who remained composed, more than held his ground. And I remembered Frank's commentary on space explorations, making the business intelligible by the use of homely metaphors, and translating bureaucratic gobbledygook into plain English. He also had the ability to sum up succinctly a complicated story in the closing seconds of a broadcast. I remembered him covering political conventions, election nights, and presidential debates, and of his looking for answers in an effort to unravel the causes of an energy crisis that convulsed the country in the 1970s.

As for Barbara, I more or less shared the disdain for her mawkish behavior with presidents, royalty, and show business celebrities; I thought it tacky, smarmy, and, along with other male staffers, wondered wickedly how she'd gotten so far.

My first *Today* script found favor with Stuart. But early the next morning, Bobbie, Barbara's hairdresser, came in a rush down the hall. She was looking for me.

Barbara was sitting under the dryer when I entered her dressing room. She smiled prettily. In her lap was the script.

"It's fine," she said of my lead. "But if you and I are going to get on, let me give you some advice."

She gave me a penetrating look.

"I'm not an actress. I'm a journalist. I don't like it when people put words in my mouth. I welcome background material and suggested questions, but it makes me uncomfortable to find everything all laid out in front of me. All right?"

"All right," I said, though what I really wanted to say was, "Then, what's the point of having writers on the show?"

As I was taking my leave she said, "Welcome. I look forward to working with you."

Despite her admonition, Barbara followed the script – lead-in and questions –virtually to the letter.

Over time I saw sides of Barbara that disabused me of so simplistic a picture. She was talented, intelligent, and a good writer. I also found her to be a caring person where I often found Frank McGee distant and guarded.

When my wife was going to have heart surgery, Barbara, unsolicited, came by my office and said, "I heard about Donna. Please, let me help. I can get her the best surgeon in New York."

When her own secretary became gravely ill with cancer, Barbara sent her to her own doctors and saw to it that the young woman was provided with the best medical care available during her illness.

And she was an indefatigable worker, staying with a story through the long hours of a news emergency.

"What can I do?" she called one late October night in 1973. I was busy making over the show for the morning. The Yom Kippur War had just broken out. Egypt and Syria had launched an attack against Israel on the holiest day of the Jewish year.

She pitched right in, running off with camera crews to interview this newsmaker and that and rounding up major figures for live morning interviews in the studio.

She was indefatigable.

.

And my opinion of Barbara remained conflicted. Over time, I found Barbara often dependent upon the opinion of others. She would come away from interviews convinced she'd done a terrible job. How was I? she'd ask. Once, when I insisted she'd done just fine, she pressed, Was I too tough? No, you weren't too tough, I replied. Then she'd be convinced she'd been too soft, not tough enough.

When we were taping a show at Pearl Harbor, she complained about my script, insisting it would not work. But once we'd finished recording, she thanked me profusely. "You were right and I was wrong," she said. Could I ever forgive her?

In New Hampshire, however, I faced a more daunting Barbara. I'd gone ahead a few days in advance to arrange interviews and plan location shots in Gilmanton where the late Grace Metalious had lived and where she wrote her famous novel, *Peyton Place*. A huge best seller, it led to two movies and a popular television series.

The book created an uproar in Gilmanton when it came out in 1956. Metalious's fellow townspeople felt betrayed. In their eyes, the author spread family secrets, defamed decent people, held the community up to mockery for the sake of profit and fame. Now, twenty years later, our mandate from Stuart Schulberg was to discover what the town was like today. How did it look back on its most famous resident? With anger, shame, pride? Perhaps no one gave a hoot any longer? Perhaps the novel's fame had led to Peyton Place bookstores, boutiques, cafes, and the like? It all made for soap opera as television news.

When I started asking around, people would talk to me – but only off the record. Few had a good word for old Grace. No less a luminary than the Speaker of the New Hampshire Legislature, a Gilmanton resident, stifled me at the start. He wouldn't mind talking politics, the state of the economy, the energy crisis, you name it, but he'd be damned to talk about "that slut," the author of *Peyton Place*.

I faced the prospect of a tempestuous star swooping down on a mere writer with untold consequences for his career should one of television's most formidable interviewers find no one worth talking to.

People must have taken pity on me for I began hearing the name Sybil Bryant; she was represented as the late author's chief accuser and tormentor. Sybil was the authority on Grace Metalious. If Sybil would open up, Barbara would have more than enough dirt to make her happy.

"What I want you to know is we're not a prejudiced community, and we don't go in for book burning," said Sybil Bryant on greeting me at her rug shop on the edge of town. She was a tall and energetic matron with an open, let's-call-a-spade-a-spade manner.

"But Grace's book is full of malicious gossip that hurt a lot of decent people."

Of Grace, she said, "A drinker, a God-awful mother and an unfaithful wife. I could forgive her a lot, even the awful tales she told about us, but not for the way she neglected her kids, their going around in rags, hungry; break your heart. I'd like a nickel for every time the women around here, including myself, took those kids in and fed them a hot meal."

As she fixed me coffee and a plate of oatmeal cookies, she said, "I'm not going on that TV, now let's get that clear."

It was a bleak afternoon, the windows icing up, the temperature hovering around 10 degrees. "I've got nothin' against it, mind you. Watch the *Today Show* every morning. I'm a great fan of Barbara Walters, too. I respect her; she's done a lot for the image of women in this country. But I'm not going to let you get my picture. I'll be happy to welcome her to Gilmanton, just as I'm happy to greet you."

As I sipped coffee, conscious of Barbara's lengthening shadow, I spoke admiringly of the community cemetery where men who fought in the Revolution were buried, as well as the graves of early settlers; and of the 1774 Meeting House, the Latin Academy, the unadorned, dignified churches, the spacious homes and lawns. It was all good story material, good pictures.

"There's lots to talk about from the standpoint of history here," she said.

I proposed a deal. "Tell us what you know about Grace – just what you're comfortable with – and then tell Barbara about the town, its history, whatever you think would interest people."

"Well," she said. "But there isn't a whole lot I could say about Grace that would be fit for a family program."

"Whatever you care to say," I said.

"If you'll let me talk some about the history, and the plans our veterans have for the Fourth of July, and the new grange hall, well I might be willing. So long as it's not all about Grace."

·

The next morning, stepping gingerly over crunchy snow and ice, I led a petite Barbara clad in a pinkish winter coat and gleaming pink boots from our hotel in Manchester to our Hertz rental. As we drove from the parking lot, she let it be known that she was not happy with the script. "It's too literary," she said flipping the pages. "I don't think you have a story."

She went on. "Brusque, abrasive, doesn't suffer fools gladly – this is what people expect of me! Honestly, I don't see why we need all these literary allusions."

"We're doing a book."

"But that's not our story."

I have this fatal ability of seeing another's point of view, especially when it's someone who could have an effect on my career. I swallowed hard.

"Well," I said. "You are probably right, Barbara, we don't need all those allusions." And I repeated it quite firmly, "Yes, we don't need them." I didn't actually know at this point whether we needed them or not, so shattered was my state of mind.

For the next minute or so, it remained an effort to keep my attention focused on traffic.

"But you don't agree with me entirely," said Barbara.

"Well, no, not exactly. You see ..." My voice died on me.

"Oh, speak. I can't stand it when you're like this!" she cried. "I want to know what you really think. We're in this together. We both want a story out of this."

"Yes, of course," I murmured and nodded my head. At the same time I tried, as only a coward would, with grimaces and sighs but not with the English language to express rage over the way Barbara was persecuting me.

I glanced up to take note of the approach of an oil truck. Snow mixed with rain was falling, making the unfamiliar road hazardous. As the oiler swept across the dividing line and rumbled past, I strove to remain resolute, though it struck me that Barbara's life lay in my hands. I could end it and my own life, too, of course, on a turn of the wheel.

She may have read my mind.

"I *do* think the script is very nice," said Barbara in a softened tone. But she wanted more: the crime rate, the number of divorces, out-of-wedlock pregnancies, abortions, runaways, school dropouts.

"The crime rate in Gilmanton?"

"Be it ever so humble," said Barbara archly.

By the time we drew up at Sybil Bryant's ruggery, a hut on a rising by the road, Barbara said, "I believe we're going to make a bit of news in Gilmanton."

"What do you mean?"

"There's not a single copy of *Peyton Place* in the town library."

"How do you know that?"

"I asked."

For the past forty-eight hours I'd gone around Gilmanton looking for an angle and never once thought of checking the public library. Barbara, lately arrived, had picked up the phone and scooped me.

"And now the news," said Barbara.

"What do you mean?"

"We're going to donate a copy of the book to the library."

"What a great idea," I said dryly.

"I'll present it to your friend on camera."

"On camera? Of course."

I'd brought the novel along for an entirely routine purpose. Barbara would read a few descriptive passages of the town. Then the camera crew would cover the text with shots of the actual locations. Compared with my idea, hers was as vivid as live TV!

Due to a mild turn in the weather, we decided to shoot the interview outside Sybil's shop. Her ruggery and low-lying, snow-covered mountains in the distance provided just the right backgrounds.

Once the camera was whirring, Sybil, prompted by Barbara, recited a litany of grievances against Grace Metalious as mother, neighbor, and author.

But, despite all that, said Barbara, would not Sybil agree that Grace was the most famous person ever to live in Gilmanton, a writer whose work had been read by millions around the world?

Many prominent people have lived in Gilmanton, including some distinguished people, too, said Sybil. But, if Barbara wanted to frame the questions in terms of name recognition, why, yes, Sybil would have to agree.

And, yet, despite the renown of the author, Barbara went on, not a single copy of this famous author's most famous work is to be found in the library of the town where she once lived and where she wrote? Wouldn't even you say that is carrying a grudge a little too far? Twenty years later?

The big-boned countrywoman, in mackinaw, corduroy trousers, and overshoes, collected herself. The library budget, said Sybil, is a hundred dollars a year, the money spent on acquiring books for children. The library is really for young people.

And in all this time, asked Barbara, no one has donated a copy of *Peyton Place?*

SYBIL: Afraid not.

BARBARA: But if someone were to do so, would it be accepted?

SYBIL: Why, I think so.

Barbara rummaged inside her satchel. The cameraman covered her movements as she came up with the book.

BARBARA: Let me be the first to do so.

SYBIL (*befuddled, as the camera zoomed in on her*): Why, thank you, Barbara.

BARBARA (*not yet finished*): If I come back next year or the year after, will the book still be in the library? I have your promise?

SYBIL: Oh, yes, Barbara. We're not book burners. We've never gone in for censorship. It's just that what little money we can spare for books goes for the children, as it should be. And we hope you will come back. There's a whole lot more to Gilmanton than Grace Metalious and her trash novel.

BARBARA: Well, then, why don't you go right ahead and tell us. Mel says the town played a very important role during the Revolution....

Before taking our leave, Barbara spent a few minutes picking through a pile of throw rugs in a corner of Sybil's shop. She settled on a soft fabric with patriotic colors, counted out three one hundred dollar bills, and left the proprietress with nothing but words of gratitude on her astonished lips.

As we sped off, Barbara, waving goodbye, said she didn't know what she was going to do with the rug. She had no use for it, and didn't want it in her own house. Perhaps she'd give it to someone. "But," she explained. "I thought we should do something for your friend." Barbara was feeling a lot better about the trip. "I think the story is coming closer."

•

I don't know, can't remember – which came first – Frank's illness or Frank's office romance.

During Frank's absences, veteran correspondents like Edwin Newman and Garrick Utley, and comers like young Jim Hartz, sat in as co-hosts of *Today* with Barbara. The more Frank McGee was absent the more *Today* became Barbara's own show.

If I'd had my wits about me, I would have sensed that something was wrong with Frank. One day he took me by surprise by asking about my health. "You've lost a lot of weight," he remarked. "Are you all right?"

As it happened, I'd taken up jogging with just such a goal – to shed extra pounds – in mind. He seemed unconvinced. "You should see a doctor, just to be on the safe side." I laughed, but now I recall hearing genuine alarm in his voice.

I should have suspected something on the morning when a back specialist was a guest on the show. He could not fail to notice the pain McGee suffered as he walked across the set and cautiously sank into his chair.

"I believe I can help that man," the orthopedic surgeon said.

As soon as we were off the air, I broached the matter with McGee.

'Frank," I said. "This guy, the back doctor. He believes he can help you."

Frank moved away.

"Frank," I pressed. "This guy's an expert, a top specialist. He's waiting for you in the green room.

Frank fixed me with a bottomless gaze. "Nobody can help me," he said, and turned toward the elevators.

Stuart Schulberg conveyed a sense of urgency about Frank when I was flying up to Boston to do a piece on the John F. Kennedy Library. McGee was to join me the next day.

"Get through the parts you're shooting with Frank as soon as you can, so he doesn't have to spend the night in a hotel," urged Stuart. Frank wanted to wake up in his own bed in the morning.

I never got to spend much time with Frank – he died about a year after I joined *Today* – but we did share a bit of travel. During the Watergate crisis, on a flight back to New York from Washington, I learned he was not much of a reader. Comparing the nefarious Nixon to a predecessor of the stature of Lincoln, I made mention of the Lincoln portrayed lovingly in Carl Sandburg's works. Frank had never heard of Sandburg's Lincoln; nor, he said, did he spend much time with books. Save for a popular version of philosophy by Ariel and Will Durant, he read little if any serious literature. Fortunately, he was in television, a medium that puts a premium on dash and aggressiveness, a field where journalists can succeed without shouldering a knowledge of the past.

Late one night in Hurley's, an NBC hangout at the corner of 49th Street and Sixth Avenue, I spotted Frank sitting in a booth by himself. He looked oddly flushed as if with a fever and had trouble holding his drink. The place was full, smoky and noisy; everyone was aware of Frank's presence but, as was the case with correspondents of Frank's eminence, no one made so bold as to trespass on his privacy. After a time, I felt compelled to approach the booth. Did he want company? Was he feeling all right? He shook his head, and waved me off.

It was not until a few months later, when Frank died, that we learned that he had been suffering from bone cancer.

Most of us were taken by surprise. We knew he'd been in and out of hospitals several times but none, at least in my circle, was aware of the fatal nature of his illness. He simply went into the hospital one more time and was pronounced dead of pneumonia 48 hours later.

·

Frank proved surprising even after his unexpected death. By no means were affairs unusual in this period of the *Today Show*. It was well known that Stuart Schulberg and one of his staffers were romantically linked while Stuart was still married. In what Stuart himself described to friends as a very emotional scene, he tearfully informed management of the relationship, and offered to resign if it caused embarrassment. The offer was refused, and Stuart retained his post. (Eventually, Stuart got a divorce and the couple were married.)

Stuart's was a name unknown to the public, his affair of interest only to people at NBC. Frank, however, was in the public eye, a respected correspondent, known to millions. In his case, word in the press of an extra-marital affair could adversely affect the show's ratings. Thus, when Frank left his wife to live with a vivacious black staffer, Stuart was beside himself with worry he later told me. In the early 1970s, interracial couples were still widely rejected by both blacks and whites. Even more troublesome was the fact that *Today*'s audience was overwhelmingly white and middle class, and socially conservative. Were Frank's affair to become public, Stuart, or so he feared, would get the blame. Management would hold him responsible. A producer's job included keeping unfavorable publicity out of the press. When he picked up the tabloids, he was full of trepidation for fear of seeing an item about Frank and Mayme.

During the period Frank was enamored of the production assistant, Stuart paced more than was his custom. To those close to him, he would ask, "Who could be trusted on the tabloids to keep the story out of print? Who needed fixing?" As it happened, news of Frank McGee's secret life went unreported until after the correspondent was dead.

Most of us were stunned, and had difficulty understanding why Frank would put his reputation – to say nothing of the show's valuable name – at such risk.

One of Frank's few close friends was a *Today* staffer who, on occasion, had visited Frank at his Westchester home. He drew an appalling picture of Frank's home life. Night after night, he said, Frank and his wife sat at the kitchen table drinking themselves into a stupor, all the lights in the house ablaze. The McGees rarely went to restaurants, or socialized, or visited the theatre. They lived as virtual recluses.

After McGee's death, Frank Field, a science reporter, gave as good an explanation as any for Frank's behavior. With time running out, said Field, McGee no longer cared what people thought. He was intent on grasping whatever happiness he could from life, whether it would be for a year or for only the months that were left to him.

·

The mourners made their way into the Ethical Cultural Society, a nondenominational meeting house, on Manhattan's West Side. McGee's family, his wife, children, and their spouses, were prominently in attendance. People looked for Frank's young lover but she was nowhere in sight. Notables abounded: Walter Cronkite, Eric Sevareid, and Harry Reasoner from CBS; David Brinkley, John Chancellor, and Sander Vanocur from NBC; Frank Reynolds, ABC; the presidents of two of the three major networks and heads of all three news divisions; "name" actors from Broadway and Hollywood; Frank's admirers in business and the professions; and clerks and secretaries, blue collar types, and others of the lower classes. Stuart presided, a compact man on a great stage, saying, "Enough of death. We've had enough of dying." In the past year the broadcasting community had mourned the passing of Chet Huntley.

A hush fell over the throng as Barbara, one of several speakers, mounted the dais. People exchanged knowing smiles. In her eulogy, she heaped praises upon Frank for his journalistic integrity and courage. Ever vigilant in the pursuit of truth. Unflinching in his commitment to the highest ideals of the profession. Then she described their own "unique" relationship as one marked by mutual esteem and affection.

"Such chutzpah!" was one wag's post-mortem.

As the parade of eulogists droned on, the gossip focused on a more immediate and worrisome matter: the outcome of the spirited competition for Frank's chair.

"Have you heard anything about a new co-host?"

"Not a word."

"I hear it's Ed Newman."

"Not a chance."

"Why not?"

"Stuart doesn't think two Jews doing the show is a great idea."

"Oh, but Newman's great."

"I agree. But that's the word."

"Then it's Utley?"

"Garrick Utley?"

"He's good, too."

"Yeah, but Barbara doesn't like him."

"What's the rap?"

"Boring. She's holding out for young Jim Hartz, the fellow they brought in from Tulsa to do the local news."

"He's not even dry behind the ears."

"Yeah, but he's somebody she can control."

"Garrick Utley's terrific. Brilliant on foreign news."

"Barbara agrees he's brilliant but dull. D-u-l-l, the four-letter word in TV from which there is no reprieve."

"You got that right, pal."

"So it's Hartz?"

"Yep, everybody's second choice, I hear, except for Barbara's."

"Who does Stuart want?"

"Does it matter? Barbara's in the driver's seat now."

The gossipmongers acknowledged there were hazards for Barbara in bringing in the boyish Jim Hartz who was many years her junior. The disparity in ages invited an unfavorable comparison. (While there were mainly exceptions for men, the public was not apt to forgive a woman for looking her age.)

Nonetheless, the important thing now for Barbara, everyone said, was for her to emerge from Frank's shadow. By promoting Jim Hartz she was giving evidence of her determination to become a star in her own right.

I made my way through the departing crowd with Joe Gottlieb, Barbara's biggest fan on the *Today* staff. "Wasn't she terrific?" he said, his eyes shining with a fatherly light. "She pulled it off. What a performance!"

As for the contest for Frank's chair, Joe said, "I hope it's Hartz. She'll eat him up."

Chief Bicentennial Writer

Not long after Jim Hartz succeeded to Frank McGee's chair, Carolyn Churchill, Stuart's secretary, swept into my office. "Stop whatever you are doing," she said, "and go in to see Stuart." When I paused to tidy my hair and tie, she cried, "He wants you now, right away!"

I rather admired Churchill, partly for her looks, partly for her determination to perpetuate her good name. Though she did not claim a blood tie to England's great wartime prime minister, she professed an abiding, spiritual kinship with him. To any future spouse, she let it be known: you may take me for a wife, but you cannot take from me my good name. A Churchill I was born, a Churchill I shall die.

When I rushed into his office, Stuart waved me to a chair. He now ruled from Frank McGee's old office, a spacious seventh-floor room in the RCA Building looking over the skating rink in Rockefeller Plaza. At a network where even a small office window was a sign of status – for example, when I moved up to the *Today Show*, former colleagues on the local news would stop by and say, "You have a window? You?" – Frank enjoyed the ultimate of perks: not merely a picture window, but a private toilet and shower.

Stuart had stolen the march on Barbara, who had also coveted Frank's office. Within hours of Frank's death, after everyone had left for the night, he simply took possession with his files, trophies, cassettes, books, and pictures.

As consolation, Barbara was given Stuart's office. Though modest in size, it was still larger than the one she'd formerly occupied.

Between pausing to sip from a Styrofoam cup camouflaging his drink and puffing on an ever-present cigarette, he began to confide in me certain matters affecting the show.

First, he said, Frank McGee's long absences due to his terrible illness had wreaked havoc on the ratings. Since his death the loss in audience continued.

Now, for the first time in the five years that he had been the executive producer of the *Today Show*, Stuart was under more fire than ever from the fifth floor (where the news division heads were quartered) to come up with an attention-grabbing strategy "to keep viewers in the tent."

"Can you beat that?" he said. "After all I've done keeping peace in the family. When you think how things were between Frank and Barbara, it's a wonder we ever got on the air. You know, they barely spoke a word to one another off-camera. And now none of that's important. None of those great shows I put on in spite of Frank and Barbara's willfulness. It's 'what have you done for me lately?'"

As for Stuart's predicament, he didn't have to spell it out. If he didn't increase the ratings he was headed for one of those rooms where the network dispatched their old elephants. I had seen those offices for failed producers, filled with lost and bewildered men, their hands sunk in their pockets, staring all day at telephones that never rang. Stuart was determined not to be one of them.

He offered me a drink. I shook my head. It was not yet ten in the morning.

Just as I began wondering if he was ever going to tell me why he'd asked to see me, he began pacing. (It's said Stuart picked up the habit from his father, B.P., also a prodigious drinker, who reputedly did his best work while pacing the floor of his Hollywood office.)

"It'll soon be the spring of 1975," said Stuart. "The nation will be preparing to mark the 200th year of its independence. The fifth floor is hounding me to death about it: seize the moment, give us a great show."

Well, he'd come up with a plan. It was, he said, "bold and ingenious."

We were going to do a program from one of the fifty states every Friday. We'll kick off in Washington on the Fourth of July and windup in Philadelphia on July fourth, 1976, a year later – all told fifty-two programs. A production on this scale had never been done before. Imagine, we'll be making television history, even as we're rediscovering America.

And this was where I came in. With my small-town Eureka roots, I was, Stuart judged, an ideal choice for chief writer of the bicentennial series.

Although I accepted on the spot, Stuart urged me to take a few days to consider the matter carefully before making a firm commitment. "Sleep on it. You'll be away from home for weeks, the hours will be long, the travel relentless; the road can be a very lonely place."

Why wait? I asked myself. I'd be marching in lockstep with Edward R. Murrow and Ernie Pyle! It was the journalistic opportunity of a lifetime.

"If you come aboard, there'll be a bonus in it for you," said Stuart. "In recognition of the sacrifices you'd be making."

"I'm not in it for the money," I protested.

Chief Bicentennial Writer. The title swelled my head. Had I known that I was being offered the job only after other staffers had turned it down, I might have given the matter more sober thought. But I was naïve and unsuspecting of Stuart's machinations.

Stuart's choice of a producer for the bicentennial unit was a middle-aged hippie who fancied himself a filmmaker. I'd known Vernon Hixson in local news and wondered what in the world possessed Stuart to put him in charge. People who knew Vernon thought him amiable and witty, but were not impressed with his producing abilities.

Stuart spoke admiringly of Vernon's "way with film." He did play the part of a filmmaker by going about in beret, beads, stop-watch hanging from his neck, sneakers, safari jacket, and blue jeans, propounding views on the arts picked up from the avant-garde media of the day.

Stuart may not have been as sold on Hixson as he pretended. He gave the number two slot, that of associate producer, to an employee with no producing credits but one who was a fierce Schulberg loyalist. William Cosmos could be relied upon to act the part of Stuart's watchdog.

From the start Hixson and Cosmos were rivals for Stuart's favor.

In charge of the business side of our unit – that is, the one who wrote the checks, scheduled trips, booked hotels, and so on – was a pasty-complexioned stub of a man with a fringe of yellow hair ringing a bald head. Howard Malley, about thirty-five, would soon become better known to some of us as "the Clucker" because of his inordinate appetite for the fried chicken served up at drive-ins. We were all to eat at many a drive-in.

I suspect Stuart was drawn to the Clucker because his tastes in television fare matched the sampling surveys of mass audiences. He would thus serve as a guide, help us keep one foot on the ground.

•

Throughout the year, shows were subject to change due to logistics, clashing personalities, and politics.

My log chronicles the "Sturm und Drang" on the eve of the first broadcast.

6/10/75:

Hixson comes rushing into my room saying Stuart wants a black face for the July Fourth kickoff program in D.C. Some way to say black without saying black; that is, acknowledging the fact that Washington has the largest per capita number of blacks of any American city but, keeping in mind, that *Today*'s audience is predominately white, middle-American white.

I am pondering the possibilities of the new turn in strategy as I follow Vernon past the warren of writers' quarters into Stuart's office. Bill Cosmos and Howard Malley, the Clucker, are already settled comfortably in easy chairs deliberating with Stuart.

"There is a consensus building for a black actor to help carry the show," says Stuart, acknowledging us. "Imagine, a black actor reading 'The Emancipation Proclamation' from the steps of the Lincoln Memorial. Stunning!"

The Clucker throws his head back, imitating the clucks of a chicken. It is his way of showing enthusiasm for an idea.

Stuart is beaming his approval. "But we must take pains in getting the right person," he says. "We don't want an agitator. This is a birthday party. We don't want anybody mad at us. There are 364 other days in the year for their stirring up controversy."

Addressing me, Hixson interpolates as he sinks into a leather armchair, "Go find us an all-American black whose soul is white."

6/15/75:

Headline: We've got our black actor. He's Billy Dee Williams. Everybody's ecstatic. Stuart leaks news to the press.

6/17/75:

Bulletin: Our first major crisis. Williams's agent says his client has changed his mind and won't do the spot, flatly refuses. Says he'd be "Tom-ing" it; in sum, Lincoln may be a god to whites but he's just another honky to blacks.

Stuart, summoning the high command to his office, is furious. Calls blacks "ingrates" and worse, then simmers down to contemplate a course of action. He is much too agitated, however, and is soon shouting, "They can't do this to me! I promised to deliver Billy Dee Williams to the American people!"

Hixson is speculating aloud, "Maybe we should drop the idea of a 'shvartse' and assign the Lincoln reading to Jim Hartz?"

"Jim Hartz?" says Stuart, his voice trembling. "Jim Hartz reading Lincoln?"

The matter is quickly dropped.

Pacing, Stuart exhorts me to find another black.

6/19/75:

The agent is on the line with a new name and suggestion: Arthur Burkhardt, a fine though not famous black actor, reading Frederick Douglass, the 19th-century abolitionist and black Lincoln.

Stuart reconvenes his white citizens' council. All eyes shift towards the Clucker, "the common man." He confesses he's never heard of the actor or Frederick Douglass.

"That's neither here nor there," snaps Stuart.

"Frederick Douglass," Hixson says, "was the Malcolm X of his day. A troublemaker."

"Oh," says the Clucker in a low moan.

"But that's all right," avers Stuart. "So long as we reserve the right to edit or change what we don't like. And the spot doesn't have to be longer than, say, three minutes."

The Clucker nods. A cloud passes from his eyes.

"Now show some spunk," Stuart says to me as I part from my colleagues.

A quarter of an hour later Hixson comes jogging into my cubicle.

Have I called Arthur Burkhardt's agent? Has he talked to Arthur Burkhardt? Is everything all right?

"It's OK," I say hanging up from the call. "Burkhardt's looking forward to his three minutes of fame on *Today*."

Hixson goes dancing down the hall.

Cosmos pokes his head in my door. He's complaining about Hixson, saying, if he, Cosmos, seems overbearing at times, I should try to understand. "There's a power vacuum in the bicentennial unit. Somebody has to fill the void, make decisions."

6/22/75:

Arthur Burkhardt's script arrives. Stuart and Vernon find it inflammatory. It's a mini-version of the oration Frederick Douglass delivered in Rochester, New York, on July 4, 1853.

Sampler:

"What, to the American slave, is your Fourth of July? I answer, a day that reveals to him, more than all other days of the year, the gross injustice and cruelty to which he is the constant victim. To him your celebration is a sham; your boasted liberty an unholy license, your national greatness, swelling vanity, your sounds of rejoicing are empty and heartless ..."

Stuart thunders, "We're not going to stir up a hornet's nest on our inaugural program. Let the blacks rave any other day. But not on this one. This is a birthday party and you should so inform them."

He strikes one offensive passage after another.

"Oh, you should listen to this," he says.

Then, "Oh, my God," he cries out, as if wounded.

I say, "Frederick Douglass was speaking 125 years ago. The speech is a classic, part of history."

Stuart replies, "People don't hear disclaimers. Put this on the air and they'll say, 'There they go again, those nigger-loving eastern liberals, stirring up trouble!' Nothing is going to interfere with our birthday party."

In the end, Arthur Burkhardt's script is a blackened ruin.

Later, when I tell Arthur Burkhardt's representative of the alterations in the script, he sounds distant.

Vernon drops in.

"Was he angry?"

"Tense," I say.

A snicker. "That the whites still rule?"

"Something like that."

6/23/75:

Arthur Burkhardt is insisting on retaining one of the sections Stuart has killed.

Stuart skims the passage:

"Is it not astonishing that, while we are ploughing, planting, and reaping, using all kinds of mechanical tools, erecting houses, constructing bridges, building ships, working in metals or brass, iron, copper, silver and gold; that while we are reading, writing, and ciphering, acting as clerks, merchants, and secretaries, having among us lawyers, doctors, ministers, poets, authors, editors, orators, and teachers; that while we are engaged in all manner of enterprises common to other men, digging gold in California, capturing the whale in the Pacific, feeding sheep and cattle on the hillside, living, moving, acting, planning, living in families as husbands, wives, and children, above all, confessing and worshipping the Christian's God and looking hopefully for life and immorality beyond the grave, yet we are called upon to prove that we are men!"

Stuart's unmoved. "If they don't want to go to a birthday party then the hell with them. This is our program, not theirs, and if they can't accommodate us this one time, then we're under no obligation to let them walk all over us. God help me, they're not going to mess up our bicentennial salute on the Fourth of July."

I convey my regrets to Arthur Burkhardt's agent, saying, "Personally, I agree with Arthur. But I am merely an instrument, the messenger. This is not my idea and I want you both to know that."

The agent, who is also black, is in a hurry to hang up, shake me off, shake us all off. He terminates the call so abruptly that I interpret his message to be that the media, while masquerading as liberal, is at heart racist. How could he feel differently after witnessing the emasculation of Frederick Douglass?

But I am getting ahead of myself. As a political maneuver Stuart thought we should make contact with the organization that Congress created to promote the bicentennial year. So I headed off to Washington.

The offices of the American Revolution Bicentennial Administration occupied seven floors in a new building in downtown Washington. Only a handful of staffers were at work in the midst of rows upon rows of empty offices. The people bent over tasks represented the vanguard of the manswarm that in a few weeks would fill the rooms and corridors and lobbies. But on a breezy, sun-lit late winter morning in 1975, business moved at a snail's pace.

I'd made my way there in the company of Molly Sharpe, the *Today Show*'s liaison to the high and mighty in Washington. A spirited Brit of middle age, Molly booked interviews with government officials for the show when they were needed.

We were on a delicate mission: to book Barbara Walter's estranged beau, John Warner, later a U.S. Senator but then ARBA administrator, for *Today*'s inaugural bicentennial broadcast. The situation was complicated by the fact that Warner and Barbara were feuding; according to Molly, a Barbara confidante, the TV star had grown tired of Warner; jilted, his pride injured, Warner was in a pent-up fury. It was Molly herself who had introduced them, having known Warner since he was a law student from a genteel but impecunious Virginia family. A vigorous young man with great ambitions, he captured the heart of one of the Mellon girls and married into one of America's richest families. The marriage, which produced children, foundered and ended in divorce; Warner received a handsome settlement that permitted him to continue to lead a privileged life-style.

"Barbara was smitten," said Molly as we rode across town for our appointment.

"He typified a breed of male that was new and exciting to her, someone out of fairytale America," said Molly. For all her sophistication, Barbara's horizon was bounded by the people who patronized her father's famous nightclubs, Jewish comedians, actors, and movie people. Warner represented another world, that of a country squire riding to the hounds, playing polo, sailing a yacht, moving in the circles of America's oldest and richest families.

"Why did she drop him?" I asked.

"At the heart of it is their careers. John's ambitious and fancies a run for public office. Marrying Barbara would be an asset for a politician. For Barbara, marrying John would bring no profit. She's attracted to him, of course, and his polo-playing, riding-to-the-hounds style of life, but her career's gotten bigger than ever, much bigger than his; there's no stopping her. She could never marry John Warner."

"Why not?" I persisted.

"John's a charmer and very sweet and he is very, very rich. But he's not very bright. Barbara can't live with a man she doesn't respect."

When we arrived, a tall, soft-spoken receptionist with a motherly face led us into the administrator's conference room. In the large, airy quarters we immediately came across a beautifully crafted model of a man-of-war. The woman identified it as one of the administrator's fondest souvenirs from his days as Secretary of the Navy in the Nixon administration.

Warner strode into the room, greeting Molly effusively and cordially welcoming me.

He established himself at the head of a glistening conference table and drew out a pipe, which he began filling with tobacco. Molly and I took seats at the far end. He wanted us closer. We moved but he shook his head. He was not satisfied until Molly and I occupied seats next to him. Then he lit his pipe and began puffing contentedly.

Pointing wistfully at the model of the sailing ship, he remarked how he missed the sea and his old watch at the Navy department.

"I am a man of action, not one for the committee room," he said. "But if this is how my country deems I can best serve the national interest, then so be it." He settled back in his chair, crossed his long legs, and puffed with great authority.

He put our minds to rest. He was quite agreeable to making an appearance on the *Today Show* but first he wanted "a meeting of the minds." As if on cue, a slight man of forty with dyed, blondish hair slipped into the room.

"Herb's job," said Warner by way of introducing Herb Hetu, "is to keep me honest, straight with the facts. Herb's worked up a scenario for this broadcast."

The aide handed him a slip of paper. After taking a moment to study it, Warner said, "Well, now the first question you want to ask me is, 'What do I see as the chief goals for Americans in this bicentennial year?' I realize it's a broad question; I see it as a warm-up question, but we've got some good answers.

"Next I want you to go for the jugular. I mean go for the knockout and say, 'Hey, there's a big hue and cry in the land that the Bicentennial Committee is favoring corporate interests, and putting the seal of acceptance on a raft of shoddy goods and rip-offs.'

"Well, now we've got 'em in the palm of our hands; Herb and I have the statistics, we've done our homework, which we'll recite chapter and verse, to give the lie to these assertions. You see, we won't fudge; we'll take the hot ones, indeed we welcome them. You watch our thunder. We'll tell it like it is." Molly and I dared not look at one another during Warner's remarkable monologue. He turned in his chair, tapping a pencil on his yellow legal pad.

"All right, let's see. Now I think we might get some mileage if we face our critics directly and not try to hedge it. People have wondered – there's no point in denying this – people have wondered ... are you writing this down?"

"Yes," we said.

"People are wondering why don't we have a single wedding cake. A single pavilion. A single city, that is, for the Bicentennial. So let's just ask the question, get it out in the open. And we're ready for it. The answer is simple: we tried that. We gave it all we had in 1876, in Philadelphia, when we celebrated our first Bicentennial, and it wasn't very successful."

"Centennial," Molly corrected.

"Centennial," Warner nodded. "1876. There was no energy crisis then, no Vietnam, and it still didn't work," he went on. "And do you know why? Because we got a lot of other cities sore at us. They thought the centennial should be celebrated in their backyard. So we don't want to go through that trauma again."

The administrator, focusing on a faraway point outside his window, said, "At this point, we can get to the question, 'What do you think of what NBC is doing, what the *Today Show* is doing?' and I'll come in with both barrels. I think what you folks are doing is simply extraordinary and I'll shout it from the rooftops, you can be sure of that. Wait, I see an analogy here, that what you folks at NBC are doing is what we here at ARBA are preaching to the whole country: getting involved, that's what NBC is doing, telling the story of people's involvement and getting involved themselves. It's simply marvelous."

Warner paused to give Molly, Herb Hetu, and me time to get it all down.

When he resumed, he said, "The next question, and maybe the last question, I'm not sure, is 'What is the president doing?' And the answer, of course, is 'a great deal.' Now you may want to take a clip out of the news stories when the president greeted us last week. It played on all the networks. I know it was on NBC."

There was an awkward pause. Then Herb Hetu spoke up. "That's kind of old news, isn't it?"

"Yes, but it's awfully good film," Warner replied. "The president really cracked up when I said to him, 'Mr. President, here is your Continental Army.' So I think if you wheel through those clips you're sure to find it. Now, I don't want to tell you your business but I respectfully urge your considering it."

While we were jotting down his last words he asked if we'd be filming the reception.

NBC was hosting a bicentennial gala at the Statler-Hilton the next night. All of official Washington, from the president on down, had been invited.

"We'll show some of the party on the *Today Show* next morning to plug the upcoming series," I said.

Warner surprised us by scowling. "I think that's wrong," he declared, waving a finger, "and I want to stop you right there. Now you can't call it a party. People are out of work. This country's in a recession. If we go on the air with film of a party, you know what the folks back home will think? They'll think, 'See, there they are in Washington, all on a spree with our money!' Why, you can't do that. We'd never sell the bicentennial."

"No," he continued, his eyes darkening. "We've got to call it a reception, and let me add a further word of caution. There will be many bicentennial functions which you and other TV crews will be covering and that's only as it should be, but remember this is a people's bicentennial and the pictures should be chaste. Smiles and handshakes, harmless chit chat. But no alcohol. You show your Mr. Congressman, your United States Senator, your Mr. Vice President, your Mr. President with a drink in his hands and the folks back home'll see red. Americans don't take too kindly to drinking where their politicians are concerned."

Warner turned to Herb Hetu. "Is there anything else? Have we touched all the bases?"

Nodding, the aide said he couldn't think of anything.

"Now, she will interview me, of course?" Warner said addressing Molly.

"Well," said Molly stiffening. "Nobody speaks for Barbara."

"Well, I realize that's your business and I'm not really probing," he muttered, biting the stem of his pipe. There was none of the swagger of a moment ago.

"You'll see her at the gathering," said Molly.

"I don't know," said Warner lamely. "The president's addressing the nation on Indochina. I may be needed. One never knows."

In a burst of congeniality, he went on, "Now, I can't let you walk off the way you are," and produced two bicentennial insignias from a pocket. He pinned one on Molly and handed me the other.

"Don't be such a stranger the next time," he said, placing an arm around her as he escorted his visitors into the hallway.

•

On March 6, 1975, despite the presidential address, virtually all of government turned out to celebrate NBC's forthcoming bicentennial programs. Two thousand people filled the huge, ornate ballroom of the Statler-Hilton.

It was a sumptuous affair. Costly and exquisite delicacies were piled on a seemingly endless buffet: choice cheeses, fruits, hors d'oeuvres, ices. A battalion of waiters rushed to and fro with rare and expensive wines. Chefs carved huge joints of meat according to the taste and preference of each guest. The glitter of jewels reflected and augmented the glitter of the chandeliers. An orchestra played incessantly, though there was no dancing save for the dances of power that whirled around the chief company officers, dances of power makers and their minions ablaze with glory fever. It was a spectacle that most of us see only in movies.

Everybody was expecting the party to be something less than the sensation it was. That's because the president was going on the air with a major statement at a nationally televised news conference on the deteriorating situation in Cambodia. The reaction around the network was one of alarm. As it happened, almost no one stayed away.

Indeed, that gay, graying cavalier, Vice President Rockefeller, and his wife, Happy, made their entrance at 7:30 on the dot. It was the moment President Ford had chosen to deliver his speech. In the Rockefellers' wake, the great world followed. What crisis in Indochina? one felt compelled to ask. What presidential pronouncement? Secretary of State Kissinger himself would have attended were it not for the fact that he happened to be in the Middle East.

John Warner moved amid the acres of opulence. One could not help but note the change from the overbearing director of ARBA to the self-effacing bureaucrat jockeying for position, or perhaps survival. He was but one of scores of satellites circling the great planets, the centers of power, looking for sustenance and light.

Stuart, too, was a disconsolate figure, making frequent trips to the bar. One heard through the grapevine that the nabobs had received him coolly.

At first I'd avoided the reception line but then thought better of it. There was this business of my grass roots. Hadn't I come to *Today* by way of Eureka, a small, lumbering community? Surely the men who commanded the network had seen my name in the press blurbs. Surely they'd bid me welcome.

My heart thundering, I found myself holding the hand of the Chairman of the Board of the National Broadcasting Company.

"I'm the chief writer for the *Today* bicentennial series," I started, but as soon as I spoke, he tapped me on the shoulder.

"Now that will do," he said. "We have to keep the line moving."

I protested. The Chairman wagged a finger then grasped for the next hand.

It was apparent nothing was more important than keeping the line moving.

Nonetheless, I took heart that the company officers were paying deference to Barbara, surprisingly petite in contrast to the larger image she cast on TV, and resplendent in a red gown. Good old Barbara was a force in the power game.

•

The Washington establishment could ignore the speech but I could not. Should Ford drop a bombshell I'd have to make changes in the script for the next morning, drastic ones perhaps. I faced the likelihood of working through the night.

I was on my way to the foyer (where the network had thoughtfully installed a TV) when I was met by a swelling crowd. So great was the crush that I was swept back inside the ballroom. A great cheer went up. My first thought was that the president had made some momentous announcement, some new revelation about Indochina.

I tugged at someone's arm. "What's he said?" I cried.

"What's who said?" came the reply.

"Ford, the President."

"Ford?"

Another cheer went up.

"Who are they cheering?"

"Anna Moffo. Who do you think, dummy?"

The hurrahs were for the Metropolitan Opera star and bride of Robert Sarnoff, chairman of the Board of RCA, the parent company that owned NBC. Some were unkind enough to say that this was the real reason behind the party: a chance for Sarnoff to show off his new wife.

Again I noted with pleasure how the officials in the reception line bowed and scraped. What humility the arrival of a Rockefeller or Sarnoff doth breathe into the corporate soul!

Meanwhile, President Ford did indeed make news. In his TV appearance, the president warned that "time is running out" for Congress to provide additional military aid to Cambodia and prevent a "massacre" should Phnom Penh fall to the Communists. But, as we have seen, many, if not most, lawmakers were otherwise engaged, paying no attention to the president.

Back in New York, Stuart wanted us to think big as we deliberated and planned for the inaugural Washington broadcast on July 4.

"Towards the end of this hapless day," I wrote in my log some days in advance of the first bicentennial broadcast, "Stuart learns that the president has declined our invitation to take part in the Washington program; he's not willing to amble across Lafayette Park from the White House to bid Barbara and Jim Hartz Godspeed …"

The log continues:

It's Stuart's surmise – he's playing his Mussolini role as I am taking my seat – that the president wants a war with the *Today Show*.

"He's blaming me for the party," Stuart is declaring, "holding me responsible for upstaging his Vietnam speech with the gala, as if I'd taken all of Washington hostage to spite him. So we can be damned; he's not going to lift a finger to help us."

Pausing to sip from his ever-present Styrofoam cup, he lapses into reflection:

"You know what I think? I think somebody, maybe Kissinger, whispered in his ear that he can do himself a lot of good by taking on the media, especially when his own ratings have nowhere to go but up."

He goes on: "It's not an auspicious picture; opening in Washington for a year-long run of bicentennial salutes without a presidential blessing."

We are all intent on looking down at our heels thinking of something grandiose to say.

Hixson is the first to speak.

"Well," he says, "if that's the way he's going to behave we'll strike the White House location."

Stony silence.

"I mean, we don't have to be in Lafayette Park."

"But," I say, "we've got to show the White House in our opening shots."

"No, we don't," shouts Hixson. "And that's precisely my point. If Ford's not going to be a part of our show it'll be gratuitous."

"For heaven's sake, Vern" – I'm shouting as well – "the White House is the oldest and most popular building in Washington. Why, not to show it, that would be wrong."

Clamor.

"Vern's right but not for the reasons he states," says Bill Cosmos, the associate producer.

The Clucker is pleading for more information so he can get "the right fix on how this will all play" with the viewers.

I am saying, "What do you have against the White House?"

"I got nothing against the White House," replies Hixson. "But I got plenty against the imperial presidency and that's what we're doing, pandering to this dangerous concept. It led us into Vietnam, Watergate …"

"The White House did that?"

"The imperial presidency did."

Cosmos, ever conscious of budget costs, is raising his voice, and saying again, "Vern's got a point but not for the reasons he's stated. Whenever you broadcast outside you're talking mobile units and they're expensive. As an alternative we should consider the studios of the NBC Washington affiliate. It's cheaper. It'll keep …"

Stuart drowns out Cosmos. "No, hell, no!" he says pounding his desk.

I happen to catch sight of Hixson. His eyes are dancing.

"No," the executive producer goes on, "this show has got to be outside. It can't be in a studio. On this we mustn't save money. We must look expensive."

"To this end," he continues, "we're taking our cues from the garment industry. They don't spare the horses for the new season. Later, after they've captured the market, they cut corners with cheaper materials, flood the market, but the price stays high, goes higher, in fact!"

He falls silent, pondering a new idea. "The Lee mansion in Virginia," he says. "Great view of Washington. Most people have never seen the capital from there. We turn the camera around and Barbara does a quick tour. Two locations – maybe more – for the same price. I think it's a fabulous idea."

A few minutes later, Hixson and Cosmos are engaging in a shouting match outside my office. Hixson, betraying his insecurity, is insisting upon Cosmos and the Clucker scouting the Lee mansion location with him.

"It's your name not mine that's going to be on the credits," Cosmos rebels. "The decision has to be yours. Are you the producer or not?"

Hixson: "Yes, and as the producer I'm ordering you –"

Cosmos: "You can't delegate responsibility for a decision of this magnitude."

Hixson prevails.

Cosmos drops in on me before heading out for LaGuardia, full of concern for my well-being. A program a week, each from a different state of the union.

"But, really," he wonders, his voice dropping to the bottom line, "if you take a day off on the road would you still charge us for the weekends?"

"Fuck off," I reply.

6/25/75:

The Lee mansion won't do. The noise level is horrendous. Jets fly over every few minutes. Stuart wonders why none of us bright boys ever thought of that.

We're back to Lafayette Park, site of the imperial presidency.

Stuart's a realist at heart. Granted, he says as Hixson, Cosmos, the Clucker, and I re-assemble in his office, the president is in a snit and won't walk into frame and wish us well. Maybe we're asking too much of him.

"So what," wonders Stuart, "if all we ask of him is to wave from the south portico? He won't have to leave the White House. It's a great picture opportunity. I hope he's smart enough to take advantage of it."

Washington, D.C., 7/2/75:

Crisis of the cruelest kind. Stuart doesn't like my script. So Hixson says, as we check out location shots in steamy Lafayette Park.

"Do you want it straight?" he asks, then answers. "Of course, you do."

A shocking moment made humiliating by the presence of our researchers, Karen and Marjorie.

"No style, just another *Today Show* script, not a bicentennial script, words wrong ..." Hixson's quoting Stuart.

"And you?" I say. "What's your opinion?" Hixson OK'd the script.

"I told Stuart I disagree. On the contrary, I think it's a good, fine script."

Stuart is coming down tomorrow. Meantime, I have a cramp in my leg and a numbness in the thigh. Hixson likens it to his heart attack. When I put in a call to Dr. Sklaroff in New York, he says it's a nerve end, and to forget it.

I sleep badly, dreaming. I'm back in Eureka, churning out copy but nothing is happening. My fingers work the keyboard but nothing moves. Twenty minutes to deadline, and I know I'll not make it. Hodge, the fedora set at a rakish angle, is anguished.

The publisher is hustled up the stairs to the newsroom to witness my firing. Because of his station in life he has to sign the legal documents separating me from the paper. As he draws out his pen, he's supposed to be Don O'Kane, the actual publisher, but he's really Red McCann, my first editor, from the *Tribune* in Sanford, Maine.

"Knew it'd happen," snickers Red, picking his yellow teeth. "I warned him, told him to get out of the business, find a rich Jewish girl and marry her. Grown man, nearly fifty, my age when I ran the *Tribune*; watching him stuck in a writer's block like this, why, it's grotesque."

When next I look Hodge has vanished. Probably fired, too. There's so much I want to apologize for. Occupying the managing editor's chair is Joshua Eppinger III, late executive editor of the *San Francisco Examiner*.

"So, you got it, too," I taunt him, Eppinger, who had given me the sack after a week's trial.

He scowls, "I say fire the kid. He's had every opportunity to show his stuff."

Hodge reappears, clapping, "The kid's all right, give him a break," lines he keeps repeating while my own hands remain stuck in cement.

Washington D.C., 7/3/75:

I confront Stuart saying I understand my script pissed him off. He falls apart like a jigsaw puzzle, protests he'd never say such a thing, not his language, never stoops to express himself in street language.

"I don't want anything between us," I say.

He replies, gesturing, that this was, of course, without question, the way he wants it, too.

But I don't press any further. The questions remain stuck in my throat: "Hixson says you found the script pedestrian? Is that true? What do you really think about the script?"

·

Long before the sun ever rose on the morning of the broadcast Stuart was still hoping to lure President Ford to the cameras. Inside the trailer that served us as a command post on the park grounds he kept badgering Molly Sharpe to keep after the White House. At length, Stuart became convinced that Ford was not going to stir, but would, as he put it, just "sulk in his tent."

Hartz read Lincoln passably. Barbara led viewers through revolutionary history and art. On film, Jim discovered hidden treasures deep inside the Capitol. Barbara talked with a White House Fellow who'd worked for Secretary of State Henry Kissinger and Vice President Nelson Rockefeller. Gene Shalit introduced the Singing Master's Assistants, a not-very-good a cappella ensemble singing songs of an early America; but they were young and eager and, above all, cheap.

As soon as he arrived on the set for his interview, John Warner insisted on changing places with Barbara Walters. The camera angle from where she sat, he maintained, would be good for him, show off his best side. Barbara resisted the move. Stuart broke in ordering Warner back into his assigned chair. Warner retreated. In the idiom of the day, the interview that followed was "dead on arrival," listless questions followed by listless answers. No spat. Too bad!

It wasn't an auspicious start to so ambitious a series. No doubt a flick of the presidential pinky would have helped. In the segment featuring a black actor that seemed to matter so much to us a few months before, we substituted the mayor of Washington and his wife.

Walter E. Washington was the first elected mayor of Washington,

D.C. in over 100 years. He was chosen under a new Home Rule Charter signed into law by President Nixon two years before, in 1973.

It was a good news hook, but the mayor turned out to be a poor speaker, self-effacing to a fault. His wife, loud, pushy, and giving the world to understand she'd married beneath her station, upstaged him.

I grieved for our lost actors and for the passion of Frederick Douglass. And I think Stuart grieved, too, but was damned to admit it.

•

Before we set out for the hinterland, Stuart reminded us that our mandate was nothing less than the re-discovery of America. This meant re-enforcing the stereotypical. When we were in Oklahoma, our shots were to "say" oil, Indians, Will Rogers. In Iowa, it was to be corn, hogs, and Meredith Wilson, the native son who wrote *The Music Man*. And when on the point of leaving for Montana, we needed big sky, cowboys and cowboy songs.

When the four of us – Hartz, Hixson, the Clucker, and I – stepped into the lobby of the Trail Head Lodge in Great Falls, our cowboy singer, a nervous young man, was waiting. His name was Joel.

The songs that rose up from Joel's guitar shattered our expectations; he gave us rock 'n' roll, country western, blue grass, but not cowboy.

Hixson turned to the Clucker. Our Everyman rolled his head in agony.

"Cowboy songs?" Joel said. He didn't know any.

"You're playing c-country music," said Hixson, who stammered when aroused. "You were b-booked to sing c-cowboy songs."

"They asked about western music. Nobody said anything about cowboy songs."

"It's all right," said Hixson. "Not your fault, a misunderstanding."

"Yes, sometimes these things happen," said the Clucker.

"We'd be perfectly happy," said Hixson, "with a couple of evergreens like 'Home on the Range,' and 'Get Along Little Doggie.'"

"'Home on the Range??' 'Get Along Little Doggie?'" Joel was stumped.

"H-how could somebody living in M-Montana not know – or ever hear of – 'Home on the Range.' It's not p-possible, is it?"

"I'm not a cowboy," our hapless friend replied. He was an air controller. Born and bred in Chicago.

Sheet music, we said. We'll get our hands on some sheet music.

Again, a blank look. Joel didn't know how to read music. He played by ear.

"M-my mother's mother played the piano by ear," reflected Hixson. "You only had to hum a tune once and she'd play it as if she'd known it all her life."

So we decided to see if Joel had Vernon's grandmother's gift.

The Clucker began humming.

"Now, listen closely," said Hixson.

The Clucker began to sing, "Oh, give me a home, where the buffalo roam ..."

"Where the deer and the antelope p-play," chimed in Hixson.

Joel struggled. One or two notes picked true but the rest sounded flat.

We called saloons, ranches, radio station, newspapers, high schools, churches, the grange, and so on. What we wanted was someone who could pick and sing true-blue cowboy songs.

Next morning the lobby of the Trail Head filled up with men in tall hats bearing guitars and banjos. In truth it was an unlikely collection of computer programmers, electronic technicians, TV repairmen, mechanics, and car salesmen. You name it. But not a cowboy in the lot. Worse, all the music was country, blue grass, rock 'n' roll.

As prospect after prospect fell away we began to look with favor on a railroad man who had shown up to audition. There wasn't a pure, plain, plaintive ballad of the Old West in his repertoire. But he had a pleasant voice and he picked beautifully.

We were, however, holding out for the real thing, but as the sun was sinking into the hills, our spirits were sinking with it. Then a leathery fellow, his face poetically glowing with the romance of the mythical West, shouldered his way into the Trail Head.

"I was bringing in the wheat but as soon as I got word that you fellers were looking for a cowboy singer my feet turned toward town."

Eureka, we thought. The Marlboro Man!

"Of course, I know them ditties," he said. "Why else would I have bothered to get here?"

He picked up his guitar, strummed for a while and then began singing. Our hearts froze. Something was terribly wrong. It was his voice, falsetto, soprano even.

"My G-God," said Hixson, stammering after we thanked the farmer for his trouble. "What'll we do?" Hixson was flailing the way Stuart did in a crisis.

"You can't put him on the air," said the Clucker.

"Whose p-putting him on the air?"

Jim Hartz said, "We've got the railroad man, remember?"

"The railroad m-man?" Hixson looked uncertain.

"Yes, sure, the wiry little guy with the pretty voice."

"B-but he doesn't know any cowboy s-songs."

"I say let's call Stuart and throw ourselves on his mercy," said the Clucker.

"Easy for you, Cluck," said Hixson. "I'm facing the ruin of a career."

One of the great things about journalism is that sooner or later you have to go with what you've got.

So we hustled the railroad man up to Hixson's suite. Over many cups of coffee we rehearsed "Home on the Range" and "Get Along Little Doggie."

At the crack of dawn we jumped into our station wagon and raced out to meet the technical crew at Hangman's Bluff. With a deep gorge for background and the sun's rays providing ideal lighting, the railroad man warbled the songs he had just been taught with profound authenticity for the camera.

Then it was a matter of getting the tape aboard a flight to New York.

Next morning the phone rang. Hixson picked it up warily.

"A blockbuster," cried Stuart. "What did I tell you? Nothing like a real cowboy!"

•

Early in my job as chief bicentennial writer, I took a call from Andrew M. Genzoli, local historian and farm page editor for the

Humboldt Times in Eureka, the place of my former stint in daily print journalism. A tireless booster, Andy wanted us to include Humboldt County in our California coverage. I wanted to accommodate him, but I needed a peg if I was going to sell Stuart on a trip to a remote corner of the state.

"What do you have in mind?" I said. "The redwoods? Oldest and tallest trees on the planet, but that's not really news."

He agreed. "No," he said. "What I'm proposing for your show is the world's greatest producer of butter fat, an old cow by the name of Berna, owned by Mrs. Mary Coppini of Ferndale. You ought to come out and do an interview."

"With Mrs. Coppini?"

"Naw," Andy teased. "With Berna."

When I went in to tell Stuart about my discovery, he raised his Styrofoam cup.

"Go do it!" he said. "Don't put it off." It was the sort of offbeat story he loved and encouraged us to look for on our travels.

•

"You've picked a winner," said a dairy farmer on the outskirts of Ferndale, giving us directions. "The Coppinis are right proud of Berna." He chuckled. "But we all are. The damn cow's put us on the map. Ha, we don't care how we get there, so long as we're there."

The farmer lingered, holding us.

"You don't suppose *she*'s coming out here, too, do you?"

"Who?" I said.

"She, the proud one, the famous one."

He was referring, of course, to Barbara Walters.

"I was just wondering, with all the excitement about you all coming out to these parts, whether Barbara was going to do the honors herself. Barbara and Berna." The thought, the juxtaposition, caused him to laugh.

"Sorry," he said. "No offense."

A few minutes later we pulled up at a sprawling old farmhouse with an open porch where an old woman sat waiting.

Mrs. Coppini had been expecting Barbara Walters, too. Her first words were, "Where's Barbara? I was expecting Barbara. I wanted her to meet Berna."

I tried to explain. Barbara doesn't make it on every trip, especially during the bicentennial. She's needed in New York. Somebody has to keep an eye on the national and international picture.

Mrs. Coppini shook her gray head, then rose up from her chair and led us inside. Pictures and awards of past champion Coppini cows were everywhere.

"But where's Berna?" I said.

"We're coming to it," replied Mrs. Coppini.

We approached a living room wall filled with prizes attesting Berna's productive prowess.

"She's never been spoiled," said Mrs. Coppini. "That's how I know she's been able to do so well, and she carries her load, does her job. Otherwise, I couldn't keep her. That's the way my husband and I ran this place, the animals had to do their share, carry their load, or we just couldn't afford to keep them, that's all. And you see, she's what's good about that."

"What's even more remarkable, she's seventeen years old. This would be over a hundred for a human being, and Berna is still producing twenty-five pounds of rich milk every single day, the richest milk in the world in terms of butter fat."

"How do you explain the phenomenon that's Berna?" asked the reporter, Paul Cunningham.

"Explain?" asked Mrs. Coppini.

"What kind of person, character, is she?"

"Well," said Mrs. Coppini with a show of maternal feeling, "how do you explain genius?"

"A genius, you say?"

"Absolutely," said the proud lady. "And you can write it down!"

An hour or so later, once the crew had set up the camera and lights in the milking barn, Mrs. Coppini demonstrated the miracle that was Berna.

Reagan

Stuart rated the Berna spot as the hit of the California show, despite the fact that we'd concentrated most of our energies on the San Francisco segment. Our San Francisco footage fell far short of expectations.

My script called for Jim Hartz to appear on camera riding a cable car and saying, "Good morning, this is *Today* in California. And this is Jim Hartz at Powell and Market Streets, one of the busiest corners in San Francisco." Then with Jim aboard, the car would begin its rollicking ascent up a mighty hill.

I hadn't reckoned on Hixson. He – the frenzied artist – sat in the electronic van directing the shots. "No, that wasn't quite right," he'd say. "The zoom was too fast or maybe too slow?" Or, "Jim's delivery sounded funny. Let him do it again."

He never could make up his mind. He turned to the Clucker. "What did you think, Howie?" Or, suddenly, "Did some sonofabitch say, 'Fuck you?' Did I overhear that on the audio? Howie, help me out."

Out on the street the gripman driving Jim's cable car fumed. "Don't you guys know what you're doing?"

A white-haired matron whose car was stalled in the traffic shook a gloved fist. "Go home where you belong!" she cried, addressing Jim Hartz. "You're supposed to wake us up every morning but you put everybody to sleep."

The swelling crowd began to grumble, "Get your show on the road."

I was growing restive for another reason. Ronald Reagan, the much-talked about contender that year for the Republican presidential nomination, had agreed to an interview. He had just stepped down after two terms as governor of California. Maybe Reagan, prodded by Jim, would declare his candidacy on our air. If so, the *Today Show* would score a scoop, and merit mention in the newspapers and on television the next day.

There was a problem, though, and it was not about politics; it was logistics. Reagan had been a popular California governor, elected twice, but he was not a popular figure in San Francisco, a liberal outpost going back to New Deal days and probably as far back as the city's start in the free-wheeling Gold Rush.

With Reagan's interview and possible proclamation in mind, we picked out towering Telegraph Hill with its teetering homes and myriad of spectacular angles over the city below, far enough above the rabble to make it safe for the conservative ex-governor. Or as safe as we could make it, given the fact we had to have open spaces on which to spread our electronic impedimenta.

I waited until noon before entering the van, tapping Hixson on his back and reminding him of our one o'clock appointment with Reagan.

"Don't push me," he said.

"I'm reminding you."

Hixson was obsessed with shooting a group of street musicians. "Camera two, wide shot. Camera one, slow zoom to saxophone."

"If we're going to do Reagan we have to start moving out now. Given the congestion, the trek up to Telegraph Hill will be slow and tortuous," I said, but he paid me no attention.

As soon as I stepped out of the vehicle I was assailed by a dark woman with sharp features.

"Yoo hoo," she waved. "Has Warren showed up?" It was Claire Harrington. She was with a corpulent male whom she introduced as Hobbs.

A few hours earlier, the same Claire Harrington had woken me from a sound sleep.

"I have tragic news," she had said. "I don't know how to tell you."

My first thought was: who is this nut and what is she talking about?

"Francis is not going to make it to San Francisco," she went on. Then I realized Francis was Francis Ford Coppola, the movie director, and my caller, Claire Harrington, was his press agent.

Things were in an awful mess in Australia where he was making a big movie. He couldn't get away.

The script I'd written called for the director of the *Godfather* movies to lead us on a tour through North Beach, the city's Italian and Bohemian quarter where Coppola had once lived.

"Do you want to hear the cablegram I sent off to him?" said Claire. "It's nasty, very nasty."

"Not really," I said.

She rang off but was back on the line fifteen minutes later to say that Coppola would make the shoot after all. Indeed, he was leaving Australia immediately and would catch up with us before the week was out.

He'd taken ill, "la tourista," she explained; he was too sick to remain in faraway Australia but not too sick to do the *Today Show* gig in North Beach.

"A case of an ill wind doing us some good," she cracked as she hung up.

Then she rang a third time. Coppola was not coming. Repeat: he was truly sick with "la tourista" and flying directly to his Tahoe home.

"Believe me, the man is in terrible shape."

The director, however, had picked his replacement. He was Warren Hinckle III, the onetime editor of *Ramparts* and *Scanlon's* magazines, and Coppola's choice to edit a new magazine that the filmmaker was starting up in San Francisco.

Now, in person, Claire Harrington sought to save the day for Coppola's surrogate. Hinckle's tour, she pledged, would be deliciously irreverent; and it would be a San Francisco view, not confined to North Beach.

And I could relax. Warren was on his way. He'd left New York hours ago on a red eye flight.

"Speaking of your client," I interrupted.

"Oh, he'll show, there's no doubt of that," Claire said.

"Any moment," said Hobbs.

"He will have been up all night," said Claire.

"Flew the red eye," said Hobbs.

"Well," Claire said thoughtfully. "He may need some libation."

"Warren is fond of refreshments," noted Hobbs.

"Yes. You might take note of that. He's fond of bars, striking up chance acquaintances. He's known to forget his appointments for the day."

"But he won't forget yours," said Hobbs.

Claire spotted him. At thirty-six, Hinckle was a plump, Dickensian figure, wearing a dramatic patch over the left eye, a velvet jacket and fancy-laced shoes. He was a fashion plate circa London 1890. He was also a bit tanked.

"I say," he said. "Do I have a moment? We're not quite ready, are we? May I get a six-pack?"

Claire looked at him sharply.

"On my honor, dear, I'll bring it out here."

"Now, remember," cried the motherly Claire. "Only a six-pack and you'll drink it out here."

He crossed himself in mock solemnity, then plunged into the crowd.

Hixson was pushing his way through the crowds crying wildly for me.

He seized my arm. "You know what? You're ab-absolutely right. It's time, but – " And he stopped short as he took in the madhouse scene that we owed, at least in part, to him.

"No way in hell we can wriggle the van loose and be up on Telegraph Hill in t-twenty minutes."

There was a desperate pause.

"You got to head him off. Keep him calm. Tell him there's been a delay, technical troubles. He'll understand, he's been in this business."

"OK. When do you expect to be up there?"

Silence.

"Ball park?"

Hixson ran a hand through his wild hair and shrugged. He didn't have the foggiest. He was still shooting his darling street musicians.

"What do you propose to do about Hinckle?"

"Hinckle?" said Hixson. He'd almost forgotten. "Oh, we'll worry about him later."

As I made my way through mobs of San Franciscans in search of a cab I was painfully aware of my wilted appearance. Tomorrow, I pledged. Good grooming starts tomorrow. In the meantime Ronald Reagan lay straight ahead. I fretted, how would Reagan receive me if he took me for a wild-haired hippie?

Let me be perfectly clear. That summer I thought Ronald Reagan was a mental lightweight, an undistinguished ex-movie actor, a right-wing fanatic, an itch on the body politic. I didn't think he stood a chance of taking the nomination away from President Ford. Or ever becoming president. The man was, well, just not a contender. But nonetheless, he was news, a figure to reckon with in American politics, especially with a presidential election year just ahead.

I finally caught a cab. "Step on it," I told the driver after glancing at my watch.

"Hey, I'm doing the best I can. Where's the fire?"

I told him.

"Yeah?"

"I've got to get there before he does."

"Yeah?"

"Protocol. California governor. Maybe president."

"Oh, he's easy to spot."

"Yeah?"

"Big ears. That's what you look for. That's how we know when he's in town. I bet that's him in the limo up ahead." He said it so matter-of-factly, I thought he might just be right.

"You think so?" He was talking about the second car ahead of us.

"Well, Reagan usually rides around in limos. That one's going our way. Your appointment is around now. It figures, don't it? And there's a guy in the back seat. I bet it's him. It's him, all right. Just look at them ears. Jughead ears."

"I hope you're right."

"I'm right, I tell you."

The line of traffic coiled around the summit of Telegraph Hill and the view of the city was breathtaking. We had been right to schedule the interview here.

The place was abuzz with people, but they were the right kind of people for our purposes, tourists, middle-class, middle-aged and senior folk. Reagan was already working the crowd, signing autographs, posing for pictures, when I got out. He was a big man of sixty-four in glowing health. Fullbacks, as Theodore White had said, made the best presidential prospects; meaty men with the stamina to withstand the tumult of a national campaign. On the face of it, Reagan fit the bill. People gravitated toward him. He had the charisma, or whatever it was, that made for political success.

"May I shake your hand?" people said, coming up to him. "I'm Joe Davis, from Bakersfield," one said.

"May I get a shot of you with my wife?" asked another.

"Is that a movie camera?" Reagan laughed.

"It sure is."

Reagan threw an arm around the man's wife, and quipped, "You're in the movies with Ronald Reagan." Then he asked for the camera and began shooting the couple. "Now," he said, "you're in a movie directed by Ronald Reagan." He was like a kid having the time of his life.

"Governor," I said, introducing myself, and then told him of the delay. "Technical problems."

Reluctantly, he pulled himself away from his admirers. He looked at me askance, disturbed by my message and no doubt my wilted appearance, too.

"Hopefully, it won't be long, and we'll be setting up for your interview with Jim Hartz very soon."

In an effort to keep his mind off the hour, I drew on heated issues, such as the strike of San Francisco patrolmen which left San Francisco's 700,000 citizens virtually unprotected.

Reagan would give them no quarter, ordering the patrolmen back to their beats. What about those who would fail to comply? He'd fire them. No excuses. No exceptions. But what if it meant firing all of the strikers? He shrugged. So be it. He'd fill up the ranks with volunteers.

"Really?"

"Absolutely."

Though I had no way of knowing at the time, it was a harbinger of how he would deal with the first labor crisis of his presidency. When the air controllers walked off the job, he fired them.

"Would you say all that on the air, sir? That you'd fire the lot of them if need be?"

"Why, certainly," Reagan replied with a touch of exasperation. Hadn't he already answered the question?

Reagan's stand on the strike was sure to make the papers. Would Hixson not hurry?

I hit another hot button, and for the first time heard the expression "welfare queens," an unfair Reagan generalization of women on welfare spending their government checks on luxuries rather than on the necessities of life.

The environment was another topic.

Environmental laws, he said, were ludicrous. Talk of air pollution, for example. Most of it comes from trees. Yes, he insisted, trees create pollution, poison the air. But you don't hear any of that in the press.

Bureaucrats propose and dispose. The poor citizen can't make a move without their say-so.

If he had his way, he'd dismantle the kit and caboodle of liberal government: welfare, housing, energy, education, transportation, save for those areas prescribed in the Constitution. The country would be better off left to the wisdom of corporations and the market place.

Charity begins at home, he argued. What did people do before the Depression and the New Deal? Well, there was old-fashioned charity. Ever hear of noblesse oblige? Before FDR, people of means looked out for the less fortunate, the hungry, the aged, the orphans. The system worked. All that was a far cry from today's world where government ran everything and bureaucrats were all-powerful.

I found his grip on statistics that he used to buttress his rhetoric impressive. But at the same time, I had the uneasy feeling the data had been memorized, that he was drawing form a memory bank; the B-actor of old running through his lines.

A critical hour or more passed before I caught sight of Karen Callahan, our researcher, jumping from a cab and sprinting toward me.

"May we talk?" she said breathlessly.

"Television," I said throwing up my hands and leaving Reagan with an aide who, I was certain, doubled as bodyguard.

Karen delivered the news I'd feared most of all. The mobile unit, our control room on wheels, could not possibly move through the clogged streets until after the rush hour. Damn shame, but it meant Reagan would have to come to the downtown location if there was going to be any interview at all.

"And we do him on a street corner?"

Karen made a face.

"At Powell and O'Farrell, maybe the busiest intersection in San Francisco?"

"Yes."

"Like a man-in-the-street inquiring reporter? A bang-bang interview with a guy who just might say he's going to challenge a sitting president of his own party?"

"We have no choice," said Karen.

"But downtown San Francisco, that's enemy territory for Ronald Reagan. Doesn't Hixson know it? He's settling for a sidewalk interview instead of Telegraph Hill?" I indicated the Olympian setting with a sweep of my arm. "We'll get nothing down there. All for the sake of a corny cable car opening, a shrill jazz band, and a few arty downtown shots, he's going to trash an interview, forfeit a possible headline, with a former governor of California who may be the next president of the United States?"

"Yes, yes," said Karen.

"Governor," I said approaching Reagan. "The mobile unit we've been waiting for isn't going to make it up here, after all. They want us to go down there instead." I told him of the great size of the truck and the difficulty it would have fighting traffic across town and then making its way up the hill.

Reagan consulted his watch, and then turned to the young, muscular aide accompanying him.

He wondered whether a Sacramento appointment could be put off for the day. When told it would not create a problem, he nonetheless hesitated.

"Powell and O'Farrell? As you well know, San Francisco's not my town."

"I know, sir."

He was shaking his head. We might just as well have been turning him over to the Bolsheviks in Red Square. But in the end, he nodded.

Karen and I climbed into his limo where the mood was leaden, attempts at conversation stillborn. As we made our descent, words stuck in mid-air, as if cleaved by a butcher and hung to dry. The absence of patrolmen on the street due to the police strike increased a sense of foreboding.

Karen sat on a jump seat directly across from me. Taking note of my frenzied look she spread her hands apart as if to say, "Mel, there's nothing more we can do."

Reagan's chauffeur maneuvered the limo into a fire zone, a block or two from the location. As we climbed out, we assured Reagan that the wait would be a short one. We left him fidgeting with the locks on the doors, making sure they were working properly.

A few minutes later, I nearly collided with Hixson.

"Vernon, he's here. Reagan. Around the corner. We have to get him in and out as fast as possible."

He looked at me as if I were mad.

"It could get dangerous out here. The sooner we do Reagan, the better for all concerned. He's anxious as hell to get going." Hixson took no heed. He was frazzled, screaming at techs to correct a real or imagined problem.

I rocked the shoulders of the stuporous producer. "Reagan's here, around the corner."

The fog lifted from his eyes. "Things are just crazy." He put a hand to his brow. "I mean crazy, man."

On my way back to Reagan, I was wishing it was all a bad dream, that I'd wake up and find that none of this had really happened.

So far no one had taken notice of the limo, let alone of Reagan. Homeward bound commuters slid past in an oblivious rush. But just in case he might be discovered, he sank back, averting his gaze from the street. In his penned-up state Reagan could have been taken for a suspect in police custody.

I slipped inside. It would be a little while longer, I reported.

"With luck we'll get you in and out of here in five, ten minutes. With luck."

Then it struck me that Reagan should be sitting next to someone closer in rank, that indeed protocol called for Jim Hartz, *Today*'s co-anchor, to lighten his mood and chat up the former governor rather than an inconsequential writer. Jim was an amiable fellow and glib talker; if anyone could help ease Reagan's torment it was Jim.

When I left again, announcing I'd only be a minute or so, but that I'd be bringing the *Today* co-host back with me, Reagan's look was one of immense desolation.

To my amazement, I found Hartz still re-doing takes with the Powell Street Jazz Band!

Warren Hinckle suddenly emerged from the noise and confusion. He and his associates had been conspiring about a list of questions for Reagan, all loaded. Hinckle would ask the ex-governor such and such and Reagan, the dunce, would say such and such. And then Hinckle would plant the haymaker.

"What do you think of the shtick?" he demanded.

"Not much," I said shaking my head.

Hinckle flew into a rage, first over my refusal to take him seriously and then over Stuart Schulberg, *Today*'s executive producer.

"What's this business about Stuart calling me a wild-eyed agitator, and not allowing me to espouse my beliefs?" he cried. He was swinging his fat arms preposterously.

Hixson must have been admonished by Stuart to keep Hinckle on a single track, that being away from politics and toward the postcard imagery of San Francisco. I had to smile. Hinckle didn't look like a bomb-thrower but he was enough of an egoist to screw things up.

"Why, the last time I was on the *Today Show* Stuart swarmed all over me, telling me how great I was, what a great future I could have on TV. Now, what's the matter here?"

"You're not doing Reagan," I said.

He drew close to my face. "Ho, ho," he winked. "I have the *Today Show* just where I want it."

"No, you haven't," I said. "The *Today Show*'s been around long before Warren Hinckle and will be around long after him."

"He's had enough to drink," Claire Harrington despaired as Hinckle drifted off. "If he keeps this up, we're lost. Where's Reagan?"

"What do you mean?" The question startled me.

"Well, you're here. But you were gone for awhile. Wouldn't you have been where he was?"

Hobbs tugged at my elbow. "You've got to bring Hinckle into the interview with Reagan."

"No," I said flatly.

"God," said Claire. "We thought you were on our side."

"I'm on nobody's side."

And then I heard myself saying, "I'm on the side of the news."

When I caught up with Jim, he was finally done taping the Powell Street Jazz Band.

As we set out for Reagan, it struck me as fortunate that the blond, boyish Jim Hartz still remained (unlike Barbara) all but unrecognizable to the public. As I led him through the streets, no one took particular notice of him. One or two people may have stared. He may have looked vaguely familiar. Oh, the *Today Show*, yes, they may have been thinking: he's that nice boy on the *Today Show*; yes, we see him every morning with our breakfast, yes. But then they'd wonder, where was she, Barbara? Without Barbara, attention wavered. It was she who electrified a crowd.

Hartz and Reagan greeted one another amiably, and were carrying on like old friends when I left them safely secured in the limo.

On stepping inside the mobile unit, I told Hixson, "Jim's in the car with Reagan, stroking like crazy. That's what he needs, someone like Jim, a star to sit with to take his mind off the hour. But we don't have a whole lot of time before Reagan gets fed up and pulls out."

"Jim's in the car? With Reagan? I need him right now." He said a sequence of shots of Jim with the street musicians had yet to be taped.

"You're kidding," I said.

"Don't argue with me about television priorities," he screamed.

"When are we going to do Reagan?"

"How do I know?" said Hixson.

"I've got to tell him something."

"The situation is out of hand."

"I'll tell him five minutes."

"Tell him whatever you like. I need Jim."

When I got back to the car, Reagan was rubbing his nose, a sign, I'd been told, of distress. I sent Jim back to Hixson and took his place in the limo. A quarter of an hour passed in oppressive silence. Then I mumbled a few incoherent words and slipped away for yet another attempt to persuade Hixson to give Reagan priority.

By now it was past five o'clock, and downtown San Francisco was at flood stage in rush hour traffic. Hixson saw me coming. It was all right now, he was bellowing through cupped hands. I could let Reagan out of his cage.

Quite frankly, I wasn't sure whether we'd ever see the limo again, and I said as much to the Clucker whom I had commandeered to accompany me. When we turned the corner, we were thrilled to find the car still there.

"They're ready for us," I told Reagan. "Right now," I said breathlessly. He nodded gravely, and reached for the door. When he stepped out, he stood for a moment, drew in the button of his suit jacket, and assumed a stance that reminded me of a prize fighter at the opening bell.

The aide who had been sitting with the chauffeur also got out.

"You fellows lead, we'll follow," said Reagan.

The sight of four men bent on a mission of some urgency drew people's attention.

Reagan was recognized. But to my surprise, people were friendly. Once again passersby squealed and clapped. A man came forward to ask for an autograph. Reagan obliged. Another wanted to take Reagan's picture. He acquiesced. A moment later, Reagan startled me by borrowing the camera to shoot a few frames of the tourist and his wife.

But as we approached the location where Hixson and the camera crew had been languishing all day, I glimpsed glum aspects, and caught disapproving shouts of Reagan's name.

Vainly, I looked for the cop we'd hired to provide security. He was a rangy, bronze-skinned lawman in sunglasses. I spotted him darting about the edges of the crowd, absolutely useless.

As Reagan drew closer to the camera, people chanted, "Fascist! Warmonger! Patsy of big business!"

San Francisco, my fair city, had turned ugly on me.

A smart-ass kid slipped past and stood next to Reagan. I pulled him away. He only wanted to mug.

Another kid loped through. I turned him back as well.

The heckling grew louder.

"Fascist pig! Fascist pig!"

Reagan's face tightened.

The Clucker and I exchanged panicked looks.

Reagan's burly aide moved to shield his superior from harm, but the ex-governor ordered him back.

"I'll deal with these people," Reagan said.

He advanced toward his tormentors, fists clenched, knuckles bony white.

It was the movie scene he'd never played, the *High Noon* no one had ever cast him in, given his status as a B actor. But friends and fellow lefties, here was a Ronald Reagan, in living color, worthy of our attention.

I waited for the metallic blast, saying to myself, so this is how my life ends, as a casualty of the First Amendment? At the NBC memorial (surely, the network will sponsor a memorial) someone would be likely to blab, "Greater love hath no man than this, that he lay down his life for the First Amendment." How does that grab you for a line on a tombstone? I asked myself in a fit of hysterics.

But nothing happened. The moment when gunfire might have rung out, or stones hurled – that moment flickered and died. The mob had flinched, or so it seemed. Or maybe, after venting pent-up frustrations with the former governor, the hecklers tired and simply turned their backs on him and drifted away.

The fading light, as well as anxiety that the clamor would erupt again, impelled us to make haste with the interview. Still, Hixson kept breaking in, fretting over the lighting or a camera zoom or angle, asking Jim and the governor to repeat the same question and revisit the same ground, upsetting the rhythm, the flow, the spontaneity of a good exchange. We wound up with a stew of pieties and banalities, no headlines, no news, not even a sound bite worthy of the designation.

None of us breathed easy again until Reagan was comfortably settled in his limo and lost in traffic. Only then were we able to turn our attention to the irrepressible Warren Hinkley III. Later, when I duly informed my liberal friends of my afternoon with Reagan, I said they could rest easy. "The man is living in the nineteenth century. He isn't going anywhere."

Stuart's Folly

At the end of a taxing week, I picked up the phone and called Stuart. Looking for a bit of the balm in Giliad, I asked him about the promised bonus. How much would it be? When could I expect it?

"Bonus?" said Stuart dismissively. "What bonus?" He claimed to have no knowledge of a promised bonus. When I pressed, he broke off the conversation, said he was preoccupied with more important matters, and rang off.

•

His behavior was not characteristic and it was the first hint – now that I look back – of the trouble he was in.

A few months later, on December 17, 1975 – by this time I'd been with the bicentennial unit for almost a year – I sent Stuart a note from Indianapolis asking to be taken off the assignment. In the message I said that I was worn out, and wanted "to come in from the cold." By now I was by no means the only writer doing bicentennial shows; others were going out as well.

He acquiesced and I was able to quit the unit and come home, though there were a few times when I was dispatched into the field when Hixson found himself short a "scribbler," as he would put it.

•

Soon after I'd returned to New York, Stuart asked me to lunch at his favorite restaurant, the Promenade in Rockefeller Center. As always, the headwaiter made a fuss over the *Today Show* producer and had saved a table for him.

Although I knew Stuart drank steadily through the day (the Styrofoam cup was truly forever at hand), this was the first time I believe I ever witnessed the copious amounts of alcohol he consumed at the noon hour; a couple of martinis before ordering lunch, a bottle of wine with a rich plate of food, dessert plus another drink or two. Since I have never been able to drink and work at the same time, I abstained. He shrugged. He was more than happy to drink alone.

He seemed surprised to learn things had often been in disarray on the road and that Hixson had not turned out better as a producer. Perhaps, he said, he'd made a mistake about Hixson. He lamented that the bicentennial series had not done what he had hoped in helping revive the show since Frank McGee's death. Jim Hartz, with his sunny, casual outlook, had made life better for everyone on the show, not least of all for Barbara Walters. But the ratings were not good, indeed were in decline. Management was disturbed and he found himself under terrific pressure to improve the popularity of the broadcast.

That said, he hoped that I'd had fun on the assignment, that it had not all been grief and frustration. And I assured him I had, mentioning my own discovery of America in the heartland of the Midwest, in the Rocky Mountain and southern states, and most spectacularly in Alaska.

On a flight to the North Slope on the Arctic Circle, we had passed over an infinite glacial landscape that put one in mind of how the world must have looked on the day of creation. We had flown over a mountain pass where a polar bear rose up angrily as our Lear Jet dipped down for a better look at the mother and her brood.

By way of comparison, I said, there was the port of Valdez, a wild place in the throes of the oil boom. On a particularly shining morning, we had encountered a procession of black prostitutes clad in evening dresses, tip-toeing ever so gingerly across the mud flats toward a row of huts filled with hotly eager working men. Leading the way, at the head of the procession, was their rakish pimp.

"Minus the hassle, it really was a dream assignment," I said.

Stuart smiled faintly. He was too preoccupied with his own thoughts to be his ebullient self.

●

The duo of Jim Hartz and Barbara Walters was a mismatch. The rivalry between Frank McGee and Walters that once had sparked

Today was gone. Now Barbara dominated the broadcast, overwhelming the easygoing Hartz whom executives denigrated as "too laid back" and "too local."

Except for a sortie or two to a Las Vegas casino or an Iowa pig farm, Barbara had remained aloof from the bicentennial broadcasts. Most every weekday she did the show from New York and, when warranted, from Washington, interviewing big names in politics and other fields, often alone, thereby bolstering her credentials as a serious journalist. The bicentennial series hurt Jim's career, since it took him away from the screen and newsworthy interviews. He didn't get much from it, save for a few of those bicentennial Fridays.

The concept mandated that we broadcast the entire two hours of *Today* from a different state in the union, every Friday, for fifty weeks – fifty-two when one added the kickoff in Washington and the finale in Philadelphia a year later. Thus, on the handful of Fridays when we broadcast from glamorous locations like California, Hawaii, Las Vegas, Florida, or New York, the shows did well. But for the most part, we originated from places with less box office appeal. Fridays became Black Fridays for many viewers who looked elsewhere for their morning fixes.

Early in 1976, Stuart's situation was complicated by the entry of a new competitor in the early morning field. *Good Morning, America*, ABC's answer to the long-reigning *Today Show*, was making its debut. GMA, as it came to be known in the trade, represented the first real competition the *Today Show* had ever had. (CBS had long aired a morning news show but even with such hosts as Walter Cronkite, it failed to challenge seriously *Today*'s pre-eminence.)

•

By April of 1976, when the bicentennial salutes were nearly over, Barbara made her move. She demanded a starring role on the NBC *Nightly News* beside John Chancellor. Reportedly, the network did not resist her demands for more money, publicity, and a list of perquisites. But NBC balked at giving her (and probably any woman then) equal footing with Chancellor. According to published accounts, Chancellor exercised a veto in his contract to keep her off the show. In the end, she stunned the world of journalism by signing a million dollar contract with ABC News. Overnight, she became the highest paid journalist in the country and the first woman to co-anchor (with Harry Reasoner) a network's evening news. She would go on to greater renown and earn millions in the years ahead.

By the time the bicentennial shows had run their course, Jim Hartz was fast on his way out of the network, replaced by Tom Brokaw, and Stuart Schulberg's career as executive producer of the *Today Show* was at an end. He wasn't fired from the network, but he was removed – summarily – from the show.

Douglas Sinsel, Stuart's chief lieutenant and a close friend, told me recently, "Stuart was fired. It was pretty brutal. He didn't want to go. One day he was the executive producer for the *Today Show* and the next day he was transferred." Stuart was given documentaries to produce (at least one, dealing with violence in America, scored high in the ratings). But his heart remained with *Today*.

"After Stuart left the broadcast, he'd still call in early in the morning, as if he had something to contribute," said Sinsel. "We'd be on the air, and Stuart would call the control room and object to something he saw on the screen at home and say, 'You can't do this or you can't do that.' He couldn't let go. The new producer, Paul Friedman, was polite, but ignored him." Sinsel knew Stuart was drinking because he could "hear the ice cubes in his glass in the background." And this at seven o'clock in the morning.

Eventually, the network had no more work for Stuart, but offered to keep him on as a consultant as a pitiable $25,000 a year, less than a fourth of what he had earned. Friends in influential positions at the network pleaded for a better deal for him. Stuart ended up getting $75,000.

But by now his health was deteriorating rapidly. One day he was bound for a trip to Haiti, his favorite haven, a refuge that never failed to revive his spirits in the past. (In addition to enjoying the people and the island of which he was fond, he was a serious collector of Haitian art.) But at the last minute, before leaving for the airport, he put off the trip.

The next day he phoned Sinsel, who was surprised to hear from him.

"Where are you?" said Sinsel.

"I'm still in New York."

"I thought you were in Haiti."

"I cancelled the trip. I'm sick. Picked up some bug and feel like shit."

"The next thing I knew he was in the hospital," Sinsel told me. Stuart's kidneys were collapsing. "In one day his liver, kidneys and other organs failed as he was literally being eaten up with cancer."

●

A memorial for Stuart was held at the Ethical Culture Society on the West Side, the institution where Stuart had presided at the memorial for Frank McGee five years before. Later, a celebration in Stuart's memory took place at his favorite Promenade Café. Besides friends and colleagues, network executives turned out for the function. Douglas Sinsel, Stuart's longtime friend and associate, recalled that Sidney Bechet music was played that day, a reminder that jazz was one of Stuart's enthusiasms and that, as a younger man, he had studied with Bechet, the late master of the saxophone and clarinet.

One learned, too – such is the nature of funerals, wakes, and memorials – that, as a child, Stuart was a great mimic and talker. "Mark Twain in knee pants," his older brother Budd has described him. Loquacious, a born story-teller, never boring.

His dream as a kid was to become a newspaperman and to write like Heywood Broun, the liberal, iconoclastic journalist who helped found the Newspaper Guild.

As it happened, Stuart did stints as a movie and Broadway producer, but found his niche in television, where he profited from his father's example.

As a Hollywood producer, B.P. Schulberg dutifully delivered the low budget, so-called B-pictures the studio demanded. But every so often, he redeemed some of the capital he'd piled up with the front office in order to make films that won the respect of critics.

One of his most acclaimed films was *Wings*, produced in 1927 with Clara Bow (in which Gary Cooper made his debut), the first movie to win an Academy Award as best picture. Its combat flying sequences rank among the best in Hollywood history, according to the critic Leonard Maltin.

Two years later, B.P. brought *The Way of All Flesh*, based on the

Samuel Butler novel, to the screen. The German who starred, Emile Jannings, won the first Academy Award for acting.

Morning after morning on *Today*, Stuart produced the kind of show management expected – lively but non-controversial programs aimed at reaching the widest possible audience. But every now and then he'd digress from the formula and risk addressing issues he cared deeply about: poverty, racial justice, the environment, or sometimes just a new idea that was in the wind. He befriended shunned artists like the folk singer Pete Seeger, who was convicted of contempt of Congress in 1961 for refusing to cooperate with the House Committee on Un-American Activities. Although the conviction was overruled on appeal the following year, for several years afterwards the networks refused to allow him to make television appearances. Seeger was still a controversial figure in the early 1970s, active in such causes as anti-nuclear protests and removing pollution from nation's rivers and streams, notably the Hudson River, when Stuart featured him on the *Today Show*.

Unlike most of his contemporaries in commercial television, Stuart was a producer who went after stories because they fascinated him, not necessarily because they were what the public would buy. They were stories he thought the public ought to be aware of, and know something about. To Stuart, books were news (he taught me that), as were plays, paintings, dance, sculpture, jazz, sports, and nature.

The *Today* producers who followed in Stuart's wake were more interested in television. They were doing stories that audiences liked, that focus groups had targeted, stories that could be translated into ratings. It was a totally different approach, and a different kind of journalism than the one Stuart was best suited for.

A veteran staffer remembers walking into the office of Stuart's successor often, and finding Paul Friedman preoccupied with viewer surveys, as well as rising and falling numbers, as he programmed future shows. One was not likely ever to see Stuart so absorbed.

Of course, Stuart could ignore all that because *Today* had no real competition when he was its producer. ABC's *Good Morning, America* was just getting started in Stuart's final days on *Today*. But for someone like Stuart – close in spirit to his crusading idol, Heywood

Broun, putting on pieces only to pander to the public's fancy was not journalism.

Stuart was only fifty-six when he died in October of 1979, three years after being kicked off the *Today Show* on which he'd been executive producer for seven and a half years.

Before coming to the *Today Show*, Stuart had won recognition for his documentaries. But it was *Today* that he regarded as his greatest success. In the beginning, as Jonathan Schulberg, one of Stuart's four children, recalls, his father was terribly excited with the new job.

"Imagine," Stuart had exclaimed. "Two hours of network TV, five days a week. What a canvas!"

•

I happened to run into Tom Brokaw on the day NBC named him the new co-host of *Today* after Barbara's departure for ABC. When I congratulated Tom on his promotion – he was working as the network's White House correspondent – he said he'd actually been offered the job before, when Frank McGee died, but had declined the offer.

How was he able to resist such an opportunity?

It would have been a perilous move, he said. As long as Barbara dominated the show, he would have been stepping into a lion's cage. He was afraid of being eaten alive.

I thought to myself, this guy will go far in television.

•

Under Paul Friedman, a bright, brash Princetonian, *Today* became light and trendy. I missed Stuart's social conscience and his enthusiasm for covering not only the news but also the arts, as well as cultures other than our own. With Friedman, market surveys and demographics determined pretty much what went on the air: news as defined by consensus, public opinion polling.

Paul happened to be away when Elvis Presley died in 1977. The people in charge gave the story nine and a half minutes, the entire opening segment. I thought it excessive, but not Paul. On his return he gave us holy hell for not spending more time on Presley, for blowing what he believed was the story of the year, if not the decade. He would have devoted the entire two hours of *Today* to Presley.

Paul brought in Michael Krauss, formerly of *Good Morning, America*, to help us compete against the ABC rival, then surging in the ratings.

Snapping his fingers, Michael, a frenetic producer of no journalistic standing, would cry out during a screening, "Where's the shtick? Give me the shtick."

Every piece had to have a gimmick, a comic bit.

Once, when I questioned the amount of airtime Michael was spending on a piece about a new Miss America, he proceeded to lecture me on the verities of broadcasting.

"Do you realize," Michael said, "that one year the Miss America Pageant outdrew the Super Bowl?" And he recited the numbers and shares.

"Do you realize," I blurted back, "that Hitler was once the most popular man in all Germany?"

It was an absurd thing to say. Nonetheless, the control room burst into applause. Obviously the techs held Michael and his shticks in as low esteem as did I.

Sunday Morning:
Shad and Charles Kuralt

Stuart's departure left me sad and disillusioned about journalism, just as I was sad and disillusioned when Red McCann was forced out of the *Tribune* because he wouldn't compromise his professional ethics. Nonetheless two years passed before I was willing to give up *Today* and I did it for a brand new television news show. Before I left, Tom Brokaw wondered why I was making what seemed a risky move to a program that was not yet on the air. He pondered his own question, then said, "I guess you need to recharge your batteries." Looking back, I would say that Tom had it about right.

Early in the life of my new job on the new cbs News program *Sunday Morning* – in November of 1979 – the Iranian revolution broke out, a bulletin with consequences for the U.S. and the world, and for generations not yet born. It also signaled the start of a long relationship with a brilliant, bombastic, and tempestuous new boss.

"They've seized the police station," cried Brian Martin, my assistant, sprinting in from the wire room.

I was still not fully awake in the pre-dawn hours, but as the show writer, I was responsible for coming up with headlines for Charles Kuralt to give on the air. Mainly, the job consisted of re-writing matter-of-fact wire service prose into a more relaxed style for broadcasting. In Kuralt's case, one gave the news as one would chat over coffee with a neighbor.

So I listened hard, aware that network clocks moved faster in the small hours than at other times of the day.

"How do you know that?" I demanded.

"It's on the wire. A bulletin," said Brian, flinging his arms about wildly. "The Iranian revolution's started." He was a high-strung kid in his twenties, bright and pushy.

"I said, how do you know that?"

"They seized the police station. That's the first thing they do in third world countries."

He was steeped in Mao Tse-tung.

"That's what they've done here," he continued, hopping around as if he were going to burst a blood vessel. "Yes, the revolution has started. You can say so."

Brian ran back for more bulletins and I began writing furiously.

Once or twice he got so impatient that he tore the copy out of the typewriter before I'd finished and sprinted for the stairs leading to the studio.

"You always told me this was the way you did it in Eureka," he shouted before disappearing.

He was a smart ass, too.

Bud Lamoreaux, as senior producer, kept calling down from the control room.

"Anything new? Give us whatever you have as soon as you get it."

The phone again. It was Bud: "Keep us posted."

And again. Bud: "Let us know whatever you have."

The moment we were off the air the phone started ringing again.

"Now what?" I said.

"It's Shad Northshield," said Brian.

"Shad? What the hell does he want?"

"You sonofabitch," *Sunday Morning*'s executive producer cried joyously. "You did it, kid. You came through with flying colors. I owe you a blowjob, the whorehouse of your choice. I'm buying. You crazy, wonderful, *pro-fesh-ee*-nal, *extreme*-ly *comp-ah-tent son-of-a*-bitch. If you were here right now I'd do it myself!"

Shad!

•

Outrageous, irascible, absurd, petty, caring, lordly, vain, foul-mouthed – insufferably so – a bully and a screamer, yes, but also a genius – if a mad genius. All in this described Robert (Shad) North-shield.

I'd known him for years, going back to my NBC days. Shad was a tall, dark, loud, robust figure, with a reputation for never forgetting – or ever forgiving – a slight. He'd produced the prestigious *Huntley-Brinkley Report*, the *Today Show*, and a number of brilliant documentaries during the late 60s and early 70s. But he also was someone to be wary of. If you said the wrong thing, you could set him off. He was volcanic, but he was also artistic.

Once when I was languishing in local as a writer on the *Sixth Hour News*, I strode into the *Huntley-Brinkley Report* and made so bold as to ask him for a job.

The formidable executive producer had been sprawled on a couch watching television.

I stammered an introduction but Shad waved off any explanations. "We've had our eye on you, kid," he said. "One of these days something will turn up. Just keep after me."

•

In the fall of 1978, I was writing and producing segments for NBC's *Today Show* then hosted by Tom Brokaw and Jane Pauley. By now Shad was over at CBS. One day, word crossed town that he was hiring staff for a new show and pursuing a colleague of mine, Ric Ballard, to sign on as writer.

With twenty years at NBC's *Today Show*, Ric was a journeyman writer, facile and fast, with plenty of skills. Shad's mandate was to put a news show on the air that would be known for its good writing.

At first Ric was eager to make the move but then began calculating the risks. Should the new show be dropped after the obligatory thirteen weeks, Ric would be unemployed. He wanted some iron-clad guarantees, namely that if the show failed he would be guaranteed three years' salary. The deal stalled. The salary – $45,000 – was stupendous for the times, nearly double what *Today* writers were making. Ric, with his asthmatic wife, his daughter's ballet lessons, monetary obligations, and debts, backed off.

Shad had pounced on him. In his panic, Ric remembered I'd spoken of a need to recharge my batteries; Shad's show might well be my ticket.

So Ric sicced the cacophonous Shad on me, saying that I just might be in a temper to jump ship. Shad sniffed, "Hmmph, so let him call me."

And I did, after great soul-searching.

"I'll take the same deal you offered Ric," I said.

"You got it," said Shad.

Got it? A done deal? Oh, my gosh!

Anxious to keep nothing from him, I said, "I lecture, Shad. Go out once or twice a month and give talks. Out of town. You might not like that."

Executives don't like to be told things like that. They may say they don't mind but they really do. They want control – total control – of their underlings. They may not admit to it, but they do.

"I like it fine," said Shad. Later I would learn that – like most people – he was at his most charming when he wanted something from you.

"You don't mind?"

"I'm happy for you."

"Sometimes I'm gone up to three days."

"Not a problem."

But did I know what I was doing? I could still back out, I thought to myself, right? It was only a phone call. I hadn't put anything in writing, so I wasn't open to litigation if I didn't follow through.

I'd been growing restless at NBC. Stuart Schulberg, the executive producer who'd hired me, was long gone, let go, the proud marine of World War Two a casualty of falling ratings.

•

Before I left for CBS my friends at NBC were pleading with me to give up my deal with Shad.

"Did I hear right?" one said. "Are you really going to work for Shad?"

"You can't do this to yourself," another reproached.

"When I heard the news I refused to believe it. A nice guy like you going to work for a screamer like Shad Northshield? Why, the man doesn't see just one psychiatrist, he has two."

An old friend of Shad's sought to allay my fears.

"Oh," she said. "It'll probably be fine. Shad's bark is worse than his bite. You just have to stand up to him. Don't let him bully you. Once he knows he can't, he'll behave himself."

I began having second thoughts.

"What am I doing?" I'd say, waking up in the middle of the night. "I'm giving up a perfectly wonderful job for the unknown. No one has ever tried to put a news program on the air on Sunday morning before. What am I trying to prove? I may be working for a crazy man."

"Oh, Melvin, shut up and go back to sleep," my wife would say.

During one particular night, I said, "You don't care. You haven't the slightest interest in what happens to me. I could be out on my ear, on the street in thirteen weeks for all you care."

"I thought you were sick and tired of your job," she said.

"That's true."

"I thought they're doubling your salary."

"That's true."

"Then have a little faith in yourself. And let me go back to sleep."

•

"We've been saved!" Shad shouted with excitement over the phone one fall afternoon in 1978. "Guess who's going to anchor *Sunday Morning*? You won't believe it? Guess who they're giving us, and who's agreed? It's fucking amazing!"

"Fucking amazing?" I thought.

"This is the best news ever, the best possible." He sounded greatly relieved.

Other than, say, Walter Cronkite, cbs names were unfamiliar to me. And I must admit I hadn't expressed the least interest in who the host was going to be, as if it were of no consequence. In my haste to embark on a new adventure (and work under a notable producer), the thought had never crossed my mind. So great was my innocence (and greed) that I'd blithely signed a contract that bound me to cbs for three years that included, of course, a clause that said I could be let go at the convenience of the company with just thirteen weeks' pay.

Shad's provoking call came while I was shooting my last story for the *Today Show*, a sequence at the American Ballet Theater with Cynthia Hayden, the company's beautiful prima ballerina, and I wanted it to be perfect. I thought, why was he pestering me with such tremendous trifles? Why should it matter who the host or anchor was going to be? The important thing was that CBS was going to put on a show; that Shad Northshield no less was going to produce it; and that I was in line for a huge raise.

"I have no idea, Shad," I said.

"Charles Kuralt!"

"Charles Kuralt?"

"No shit! Can you believe it?"

My picture of the amiable traveler was pretty faint, mainly due to the fact that I loyally stuck with NBC's *Nightly News*. But, yes, Kuralt's was a familiar name. But if I regarded him at all it was as a minor figure; his was certainly not a name to be drawn in the same breath as, say, Barbara Walters.

"That's great," I said.

"Son of a bitch, we can't miss now."

•

It was not long before I came face to face with Shad's darker side.

You'd bid him a cheery good morning and he'd come back with, "Fuck you!" The next time you'd say nothing and he'd bellow, "What's with you? Too proud to say hello to the sonofabitch who picked you up from the gutter?"

I'd be in an editing room and Shad would swagger in. Addressing the tape editor, he'd say, "You know this fucking Lavine is a Jew, don't you?" A moment later he'd address me and declare, "These tape editors, they're assholes, really!"

He'd damn a piece in one breath but, not satisfied, heap epithets on its producer. ("Faggot!" he cried as he chased one poor fellow out the door.)

He once denounced a staffer as an incompetent for having the temerity to propose ideas for the show.

And he betrayed confidences.

When a producer discovered his wife's adultery, he poured out his heart to Shad who assured him the story would go no further and that he could take all the time he needed to put his affairs in order. But once the producer had left the office Shad began spreading the story.

Similarly, Shad broadcast the news of a desk assistant's decision to undergo a sex-change operation though he'd promised the young man that no one would learn his secret from Shad.

Indeed, after joyfully spreading the news, Shad paced, lamenting within everyone's hearing, "Oh, why does everything happen to me?"

•

Despite its producer's proclivities, *Sunday Morning* was an innovation when it went on the air in January of 1979.

Nothing like it had been seen on television since *Omnibus* in the 1950s and '60s during TV's so-called Golden Age. *Omnibus* had tapped into art, music, theatre, and the like, a rare and welcome aberration in a medium often described as a wasteland. With the return of the arts on *Sunday Morning*, the serious painter, composer, or playwright once again had a niche on commercial television.

Shad's strategy was to create the perfect show for the unique time period. On the one hand there'd be pieces – glorious pieces in many instances – about theater, music, dance, painting, or sculpture; on the other, stories about the fragility of life, of human suffering and want, with inspirational characters one cared about – people to root for, people who won out over the odds.

The broadcast was venturing into territory yet to be explored by network news. In this respect it was like the *Today Show* before there was any other morning television and the *Tonight Show* before there was any other late television. But it was even more daunting given the fact that Sunday morning had been the preserve of preachers, notably evangelists and faith healers. It was territory; territory that the networks had long feared to tread.

And so Shad took his cues both from the preachers and the proprietors of the great Sunday newspapers: faith, hope, and charity from the former; features, commentary, and entertainment from the latter.

At the outset he committed a revolutionary act. He killed all the reporters. Well, not exactly killed them, but downsized them, kept them at arm's length. Heretofore the reporters dominated every newscast with wall-to-wall narration. But this would no longer be permitted. *Sunday Morning* was not the venue for reporters parading their pomp.

He wouldn't let them sign off with the usual, "John Smith, CBS News, Washington." Such vanity was verboten on his show!

Further, he felt that a piece had to "breathe," have pauses in the narration. He loved it when we produced a rare piece without a reporter. It got him to bragging, "Fuck the reporters; who needs them?" But of course we did and he knew it and he truly valued some of them but whenever he could he rendered them all but invisible.

·

Above all, he raised up silence to an art during the last piece on the show each week.

The inspiration for the endpiece went back to a day when Shad was in charge of NBC election coverage. It was November 1968. The presidential race was very close, so close that people went to bed not knowing who'd been elected president, Richard Nixon or Hubert Humphrey. NBC extended the news the following night from a half hour to an hour to bring viewers up to date on all the major races.

With every contest accounted for Shad still found himself short by a few minutes. How to fill the extra time? Footage of birds – ducks in a national refuge – lay on the shelf. Why not run out the time with them? (Shad, a nature photographer, was especially crazy about birds.) And so he showed the pictures to David Brinkley who said, "What do you want me to do with it?"

"I want you," said Shad, "to write a brief introduction. The pictures will tell the rest."

The next day more people talked about the birds than NBC's coverage of the election.

Some day, Shad thought, I'll have a show where I can do things like this all the time.

He got the opportunity ten years later with *Sunday Morning*.
Still, he hesitated.
He was already taking criticism from news traditionalists for

giving undue amounts of time to the arts and so-called "soft" news. It wasn't the hairy, he-man journalism for which CBS News was renowned.

Nonetheless he put together pictures of whooping cranes, birds formerly facing extinction but now thriving, in a national refuge in Texas.

"You want me to talk about them?" Charles Kuralt asked.

"No. Do an introduction and shut up," said Shad. "They'll be at the end of the broadcast. Something different. And then you can say goodbye."

There were no complaints. The next Sunday he ran another nature piece. Again, no complaints. Another Sunday, ditto. And so on.

Then, when Pope John Paul II made a triumphal return to his native Poland, Shad decided to forego wildlife and focus on faces, in this case mile-long rows of adoring human faces.

"Show me a million faces," he directed from a New York studio thousands of miles from the frenzied scene.

"Holy shit," Shad recalled in later years. "Did we get it! Especially from Catholics, of all people. 'Where were the wildlife, the flowers, the lakes and mountains, and the rest?' Their one moment of bliss in the week and we took it away!"

Never again would he tinker with the end of the show.

•

Charles Kuralt was not the sort of TV star I'd been prepared for. He didn't look or act like a TV star at all. He looked and acted like a newspaperman, like the men I'd known when I was running copy at the AP in Boston. Like many of them, he was rumpled, fat, and smoked and drank too much.

He was born on September 10, 1934, in Wilmington, North Carolina (David Brinkley grew up in the same hometown). Charles probably knew even as a child where he was going. His father was a traveling social worker, his mother a teacher, and sometimes the father took young Charles along on trips. In this way Charles began his apprenticeship learning the things a writer has to know.

When he was fourteen he won an American Legion "Voice of Democracy" contest, went to Washington, met President Truman, and heard Edward R. Murrow, his idol, read his essay on CBS radio. (Reynolds Price, one of the country's finest novelists and short story writers, also competed in that contest. He came in second to Charles.)

Charles edited the college newspaper at the University of North Carolina at Chapel Hill, moved on to a reporter's job on the *Charlotte News*. When he was twenty-three CBS brought him to New York and at twenty-five made him the youngest CBS News correspondent in the network's history.

Charles made several trips to Vietnam during the war; he reported on the 1960 presidential campaign. He covered Latin America.

But he found his voice with his "On the Road" series on the CBS *Evening News* from 1967 to 1980.

At first Walter Cronkite was opposed to the series. He feared it would take precious minutes away from coverage of the tumultuous news of the day: Vietnam, the Middle East, the political wars at home, civil rights. Walter suspected the network was kowtowing to the affiliates who wanted "good news" because good news was good for business.

Charles intended to show that the beauty in nature was just as legitimate news. His first piece was done in Vermont in the fall of 1967 when the leaves were turning.

He said, "It is death that causes this blinding show of color, but it is a fierce and flaming death. To drive along a Vermont country road in this season is to be dazzled by the shower of lemon and scarlet and gold that washes across your windshield."

From that time on nary a contrary word was heard from Walter Cronkite.

Indeed, Walter said, Charles' upbeat "On the Road" stories turned out to be a welcome relief from the din of violence; people were given to realize that life went on and sometimes it was beautiful.

For example:

Charles discovered a butcher who could hold thirty eggs in one hand, a swimming pig in a water-ballet, a light bulb that had stayed lit in a firehouse since 1901.

A hundred-and-four-year-old entertainer who performed in nursing homes.

Unicyclists, gasoline-pumping poets, lumberjacks whittlers, farmers.

He once compiled his list of America's best: its best slingshot artist, its best bean shooter, its best holder of hens' eggs, its best runner at the age of one hundred and four (Larry Louis of San Francisco).

His work won three Peabody Awards and twelve Emmys. He wrote more than a half dozen books.

•

Sunday Morning started out over a tire retailer on 11th Avenue, the network equivalent of being born in a log cabin. For more than a year (before we'd proved ourselves and moved to the 555 Building across from the Broadcast Center) we were refugees, if you like, from the rest of network news.

Every now and then an executive from the Broadcast Center would show his face, look embarrassed at the rude surroundings, and say, "Oh, so this is where we've stuck you. Well, really, it's not as bad as all that."

Shad avenged himself by installing a toilet for his personal use, the perk of perks in television news. When we moved to the glass palace, he had to give up his private toilet but was given a vast office with two picture windows. But I always thought it a little sad that he had to share the bathroom down the hall with the rest of us.

All this of course was still in the future. When, in late 1978, Shad was asked to invent a Sunday morning show, there was no staff, no Bud Lamoreaux, above all, no Charles Kuralt.

Kuralt was reluctant to do *Sunday Morning*.

Whenever management called him in, as Charles told me years later, it always spelled trouble.

"They would always want me to do something I didn't want to do."

He loved his life on the road – "this nice little thing," as he put it. He hated to give it up. With his on-the-road series, he'd found his niche. Charles reported the stories of ordinary people as if he were speaking with neighbors over a backyard fence.

Sure enough, Bill Leonard, a network vice president, wanted to assign Charles to the new *Sunday Morning* program. The executive told him about the failing religious and arts shows and the decision to replace them with a news broadcast.

Charles refused. He did not want to give up his life doing the road pieces for the cbs *Evening News*.

But when Dick Salant, the president of cbs News, pressed, Charles listened. The chief of news was a personal friend. Nonetheless, Charles demurred. Salant argued that, except for showing up on Sundays to host the new broadcast, Kuralt could stay on the road.

At least, pleaded Salant, talk to Shad Northshield.

.

There's some confusion as to where Shad and Kuralt met. Shad thought it was at a West Side restaurant. Kuralt was equally sure they'd met on the East Side.

Wherever the place, as Kuralt recalled, they had a long lunch. "Shad was at his eloquent best. Without knowing me, he wanted me. He thought that if I agreed to do it, the show was bound to succeed."

They drank a lot of Calvados, a French brandy Shad revered from his World War Two days.

By the time "we'd staggered out of the place," Charles said, he had agreed to do the show but only for the first four months and with a clear understanding that if it messed up his life he could opt out of *Sunday Morning*.

Shad remembered that when they parted, Kuralt announced that he was off to see Gordon Manning, a cbs executive.

"What's with him?" said Shad.

"He got a new hip. They did the surgery today. New York Hospital. I'm going to see him."

Shad said, "Listen –" but Kuralt was already on the move. Shad had managed, however, to press his card on him before he fled.

The next part of the story is all from Shad. (One can surmise how he came by it.)

Kuralt, Shad said, wandered through the hospital in search of Gordon Manning. He went from room to room until he finally found the right one, but it was unoccupied. Befuddled, Kuralt slipped and fell. When he got to his feet he knew it was time to go home. It grieved him, though, that his friend would never know that Charles had been there. Before heading out the door, he left Shad's card on the bed, mistaking it for one of his own.

"Kuralt," Shad said, revelling in telling the story, "never got credit for his good deed, but Gordon Manning no doubt loves me to this day."

Sunday Morning went on the air the last Sunday of January 1979. As it turned out, the fourteen years – from 1980 to 1994 – that Charles presided over *Sunday Morning*, with its ninety minutes of unhurried news about the arts, nature, wildlife, sports, politics, etc., proved to be the crowning period of his career.

It was a show carved out of Kuralt's own heart, one that favored victims over victors, the anonymous over the famous; it covered books and music and dance and art as serious news, and making silence something to listen to. Those precious seconds of wildlife, natural sound, and silence at the end of every broadcast remain its popular signature to this day.

Writing scripts for him proved to be an agony for me. I tuned in to his basso profundo whenever I sat down to write. But in the end he always re-wrote my stuff, making it better. Now and then I would come up with a winning line, but even these he spurned in favor of ones of his own.

Looking back, I wonder if Kuralt resented me. (Shad had trumpeted my qualifications so extravagantly that Charles may have seen me as a rival. Astonishing hyperbole on Shad's part, since he hardly knew me.)

In the first year of my new job, Charles had re-written me so completely and so frequently that I got to feeling punch-drunk. I rose up from the mat countless times and gamely fought on but almost always with the same stupefying results at the hands of Killer Kuralt.

I got so despairing that I begged for a chance to go on the road. Shad listened with sympathy. My argument was I'd be out shooting with a crew during the early part of the week, and get back to New York in plenty of time to write the script (in time, that is, for another plastering.) Shad listened with sympathy. "Look," I said. "*Sunday*

Morning won't be losing anyone. It'll actually be acquiring an extra hand to help with the producing."

In the end Shad gave his assent.

On the road I was Charles' legs, as were all *Sunday Morning* producers. We were his surrogates across the length and breadth of America.

He made our life easy.

One mention of his name and doors flew open, an unusual experience in the pursuit of news. Be they rich and famous, poor and unknown, redneck or bleeding heart, white or black, or something else, everyone seemed to be a fan.

"You work for Charles Kuralt?"

"Is he really as nice as he seems on the air?"

Everyone trusted him.

Everyone thought they knew him.

And that's the rub.

For as warmly as people thought they knew him, nobody did.

People would ask me what he was really like. And I would have to say, "I really don't know. Charles is a very guarded person."

Though some things he kept very private, some things you couldn't miss. In all the years I'd known him, Charles feasted too well, smoked too much, and didn't exercise.

Surely doctors had warned him about his reckless life-style. If they did, Charles ignored them. I often heard him railing at the health police.

Some have suggested he might have had a death wish. Who can say? When he was recovering from quadruple by-pass heart surgery a year and a half before his fatal illness, his old "On the Road" cameraman Isidore (Izzy) Bleckman paid him a visit. The nurse took Charles off his oxygen respirator and left the room so the two friends could talk. As soon as she was gone Charles lit up a cigarette.

•

When Shad was given *Sunday Morning* he'd told his CBS bosses he needed a co-producer, someone who knew the inner workings of the network, above all someone he could trust.

"I'm not from here," he reminded them.

He was provided with the names of several candidates. The one he settled on was Ernest (Bud) Lamoreaux III.

"Bud impressed me very much," said Shad, years later. "He was very straight and knew everyone at the Broadcast Center." Most important, he knew "where the talent was buried." In short order Bud brought able tape editors and producers to *Sunday Morning*.

Lamoreaux's recollection of their meeting has Shad saying, "I need a friend at CBS."

They were the odd couple. Where Shad was the visionary, the artist, Bud was the proverbial city editor, a nuts and bolts man. Shad would rhapsodize over a finely honed line. Bud would ask the producer, "OK, but what's the picture?" In other words, what would the viewer be seeing when he heard these pretty words?

Their physical makeups were at odds as well. Where Shad was a loose-limbed, towering figure, Bud was thickset, squarely built.

Shad was in his late fifties, Bud ten years younger; both were married with grown children. But where Shad, a spiffy dresser, gloried in a reputation as a lady-killer, Bud was a faithful husband and doting parent.

Shad told many stories about his early years, and it was difficult to know what was fanciful and what was not. He'd told some of us that he'd been raised by the Navajos, which would help explain his near-encyclopedic knowledge of Native Americans. But when I raised the subject he said no, asking where I'd ever heard that. He'd never been near any Navajo reservation as a kid. He and a sister were raised by an elderly, childless, Protestant couple in Chicago after their Jewish parents died in a car crash. He didn't know any fucking Indians when he was growing up.

Shad attended Knox College in Galesburg, Illinois, and was planning to go to medical school when the Japanese attacked Pearl Harbor. He saw action in France and Germany as a first lieutenant. After the war he thought he was too old to start a career in medicine and drifted into journalism.

It would seem he lost almost every news job he ever had. But far from hiding the fact, he would urge visitors to his Croton-on-the-Hudson home to go view the dozen or more pink slips that papered the walls of the guest toilet.

One said: "Don't bother to come in. Your check is in the mail."

Another: "Please, Shad, go in peace."

A third promised severance on condition he never returned to the office.

In a sudden burst of candor Shad once told me that he was the opposite of Kuralt who, he said, was terribly vain. "People think I'm conceited but the truth is I hate myself. That's what pisses me off so – the fact that I *am* so stupid."

•

Bud Lamoreaux had only one employer – CBS – throughout his career.

Of French Protestant ancestry, he grew up in Westchester county, operated an amateur radio station as a kid, and majored in journalism at the University of Missouri. After a hitch in the post-war army, he began his CBS career in the mailroom, rising to news writer, then producer, then executive producer of the CBS *Weekend News*. When Shad and Bud's paths crossed, Bud's career was at a dead end at CBS sports.

•

Theirs was a fast friendship, a rare spectacle in an industry where personal loyalties, generally speaking, were dangerous to one's professional health. They were all but inseparable, doing lunch together, swapping raunchy stories, gossiping behind closed doors. You almost never saw one without the other.

"We're brothers, Bud and I," Shad made clear. "And don't ever any of you try something. Like playing one of us against the other. What you tell Bud you're telling me and vice versa."

They produced the show with little or no input from Charles Kuralt, though Shad later claimed he'd have welcomed ideas from Charles. Charles learned early on to be circumspect in his dealings with Shad.

"OK, Mr. Smart Guy," Kuralt remembered Shad saying when Charles complained that the cover stories were getting soft. "Suppose you tell me how to produce this show?" The tone was threatening enough to stymie the thought.

"I didn't want to get into it. I wasn't brave. Not by nature. And not where Shad Northshield was concerned."

"Could Shad take criticism?" I asked.

"No," Kuralt said.

•

Shad's windows in the glass palace, where we were eventually quartered, looked out on Hudson River traffic and the New Jersey Palisades. The spacious walls were filled with his own magnificent photographs of birds, the one of the puffin being to my eye the most striking. As often as not one found Shad sprawled on a sofa, his hands clasped behind his head, a picture of sovereign insouciance.

And to there we'd all troop, led by Bud Lamoreaux, who, as Shad's number two, ran herd over correspondent, field producer, tape editor, researcher, and script.

It was a solemn moment, Shad's first look at a piece before it went on the air. (Once, when I had the temerity to liken a Shad screening to the Holocaust, the remark brought an undeniable smile to his lips.)

As soon as the principal players were assembled, the door – which served executive producers in the same way the moat once served knights of old – was firmly shut. Shad took no calls, received no visitors, brooked no interruptions. No one was allowed to speak, whisper, comment, betray emotion; note-taking was not permitted. Only the executive producer had license to breathe easy.

"Someone has to represent the fucking viewer," said Shad.

As the piece played on his monitor, his reaction was raw, unfettered. "Why, that's horse shit, that line, I hate it," he'd cry, or, "That's a beauty, that shot," or "Where the fuck did you find that asshole?" When something was funny, he'd roar with laughter, and when it was piteous, he'd be close to tears.

Frequently he raised a piece out of mediocrity by simply re-arranging the furniture, so to speak; moving a shot here, changing a line there, dropping one sound bite and replacing it with another.

We have no rules, Shad liked to say. The only rule was what worked.

When Shad dumped on a piece you wanted to die, go through the floor, take an overdose and be done with it. Conversely, when he was pleased you were reborn and would gladly have followed him to the ends of the earth.

But sometimes Shad overreached himself.

Once, when I had a piece ready for screening, Shad kept putting me off. Now he was off to lunch. Now to a meeting. Now (or so he'd lead us to believe) to a tryst.

His lofty behavior was maddening. My wife and I were on the point of leaving on vacation for California. If Shad wanted changes I had to know as soon as possible.

"Don't worry," Shad said. "I'll get to it."

But the week wore on.

The piece was about a young Methodist minister and his wife, struggling to keep a camp for youngsters from broken homes from going under.

By the time Shad finally deigned to see the story it was Friday afternoon; my plane was taking off in a few hours.

A solemn Shad stroked his gray beard after the screening.

"With a little more work, it could be terrific. What do you think, Bud?"

"It needs a little more work," said Bud.

"Exactly," said Shad.

"Then it will be terrific," said Bud.

I spoke up. "How much do you want changed?"

Shad began enumerating. Fixing the things he wanted fixed would require an entire day – probably longer.

"I've got a problem," I said.

"No," said Shad. "We've got a problem. You're on vacation."

"We're all packed," I said, pleading for amnesty. "Donna's waiting at the house."

"It's going to be fine."

"But I got to fill you in. You've got to know some of the background. With luck we could talk on the phone from the airport."

"We'll take care of it, Bud and I, personally. Have yourself a great vacation."

"Forget this place," said Bud.

"We'll see you in a month," said Shad.

The piece Shad and Bud put on the air bore little resemblance to the one I'd produced. Theirs was an idyll of galloping horses, laughing children, and pretty farms. No one would ever have guessed that the kindly couple were teetering on the brink of bankruptcy and in desperate need of help.

Sometime later I learned that the couple were forced to sell the camp and disperse the kids among different foster homes. I'm not claiming my piece would have changed the outcome. But at least it would have told the story. In any event, I thought it too late – and unwise – to make any mention of this to Shad who, at every turn, lorded his achievement over any of mine.

·

By this time, of course, I'd been producing on the road for three or four days and then flying back to New York to work up a script for Kuralt, which he, in turn, would re-work beyond recognition.

When a job in the field was finished, the weariness lifted from my shoulders as I swept along the countryside toward the airport and home, providing a moment of enchantment that was recaptured after I'd slogged through the cycle again in some other place at some other time.

Every now and then Shad tore off on the road himself with a *Sunday Morning* production crew to do pieces for the show. (Art and nature were favorite subjects.) I almost always thought Shad's pieces were better than the ones the rest of us turned out. A Shad segment was somehow grander. Less self-conscious, more outspoken, they asserted a real sense of authorship; such license was a freedom denied the rest of us. But then the entire show was a reflection of Shad's personality, all of us being, to one degree or another, lesser stars in his firmament.

·

While I was with *Sunday Morning* I got a phone call from the vice president of the Eureka branch of the Bank of America. It was about Drivers Alert!, Hodge's most successful brainchild. By now Hodge had been dead a few years. The publisher, Don O'Kane, had died some years earlier than had Hodge, and the newspaper had changed hands, had been taken over by a British chain. Hodge had been elbowed aside, a new editor installed in his place. With little to do, and shorn of authority, Hodge started drinking again and having amours. He was sixty-seven when kidney failure caused his death.

For years, I'd worried about people finding out how Hodge, Al, Ernie, and I played fast and loose with Drivers Alert! It wasn't right what we did, tapping the shoebox stuffed with Drivers Alert! membership money as if it were our own personal bank. If word ever got out, people surely would condemn our behavior as criminal, a betrayal of the public trust – though we redeemed every last IOU before ever turning the money over to the committee of respectable citizens.

"You called about the money?" I said. Like an animal frozen in the headlights of a speeding car, I thought I was a goner. No use playing games; cop a plea.

The banker was indeed calling about the money.

He'd sought in vain to bring the matter to the attention of people who'd served on the committee. Several were deceased, some too ill for him to visit, a few left no traces. Then he had remembered me.

The funds, now totaling several thousand dollars, had gone unclaimed for more than twenty years. Drivers Alert!, long defunct, no longer could be carried on the books. The money had to be liquidated.

"What usually happens in cases like this?" I asked, greatly relieved.

"The money goes to charity. Do you have a favorite charity?"

"Yes," I said, remembering how proudly Hodge spoke of the Indian blood he'd inherited on his mother's side. "The Arapaho Indians."

"Are you sure?"

I was sure, and sure it would have been OK with Hodge, too.

●

In the fall of 1981, I began work on a profile of Virgil Thomson, the composer and critic. He would soon be turning eighty-five and New York's music world was in a dither.

I'd also begun the legwork for a story on a lifelong hero of mine – FDR. But more immediately I had a sports story to do in Minnesota where the Vikings were playing their last game outdoors. Next season they'd be on Astroturf inside a new Hubert Humphrey Stadium.

"The fans, they're the story," Bud said. "Tailgate parties, squareheads baring their hairy chests, swigging fire water, feasting on roasting pigs. Oh, a few shots of the game, sure, but mostly we want to capture the madness. Mood counts for everything on *Sunday Morning.*"

Before I even boarded the plane the media was reporting a vast arctic front "strangling" the Upper Midwest. Ferocious winds, it said, dangerous cold, altogether a misery quotient that caused ancients to scratch their heads and wonder if there ever was a winter as wicked as this one.

My fear was virtually paralyzing. I imagined myself sliding in my rental car on great sheets of ice, nothing between me and a crackup.

I arrived on a Friday. The flamboyant Heywood Hale Broun, Jr., whom we knew as Woodie, was coming the following day. Woodie, a *Sunday Morning* correspondent, had been assigned to the story. At the moment he was in bed in New York nursing a cold, yet insisting on flying out. I didn't think it a good idea and told him so.

By now the press was waxing apocalyptic: freezing temperatures (twenty-five degrees below zero with the wind-chill factor) had brought Minnesota life to a standstill and plunged neighborhoods into darkness.

Then I was hit with a real crisis. The heater in my room refused to kick in.

"Please try again, sir," the clerk said.

"I have and I'm freezing to death."

He gave me another room.

"This heater isn't working either."

"We don't know what to say," said the clerk.

"Has anyone else complained?"

"Well, yes. But there's nothing we can do. It's the weather, sir. An unusual cold snap."

I got into my thermals, put on my ski mask, slipped into my snow boots, wrapped myself in my great leather sheepskin coat, buried myself under a pile of blankets, and prayed for sleep.

Next day Woodie turned up, sluggish and feverish.

"You shouldn't have come out," I said.

He shook his head, recognizable only by the pair of blue eyes in the recesses of his arctic hood. In sunnier climes Woodie favored vivid plaid jackets, his trademark. With Norsemen pawing over him, Woodie perked up a bit and began to show flashes of his irreverent old self.

For the most part I kept up with the camera crew and lodged Woodie in a heated room, running him out only sparingly to deliver an on-camera line or quick interview.

We flew back on the first flight we could catch after the game. By now I was getting worried about Woodie. He was still running a fever. I should have been adamant and not let him come out. At the same time, I wasn't feeling so hot myself and thought I might be coming down with something. But Woodie really looked bad.

As it happened, he recovered but I was not so fortunate.

Four days later, on Thursday, December 24, Christmas Eve, I was sitting on the toilet at home feeling lousy, with aches in my neck and shoulder and arm, thinking it was a bug I'd picked up in Minnesota. When I experienced a burning sensation in my right arm, I suddenly took sick.

It was a heart attack, subsequently described as minor by the doctors. Damage was minimal; the arteries, for example, were "virginal." The doctors, puzzled over what triggered the attack, asked a lot of questions about the Minnesota cold. They said I should recover fully and be able to resume normal activities within a month or month and a half, but they remained puzzled.

·

That terrible night of the attack Donna reached Shad at home from a phone in the hospital lobby. He was genuinely shocked. I'd looked so healthy and trim, he told her, and had lost weight, watched my diet, exercised vigorously, wasn't drinking. He was kind, careful talking to her. He may have felt guilty for working me so hard: my spending the week on the road, weekends in the shop, writing. Was there anything he could do? Please don't sit on ceremony, he said to her. Anything you need.

As soon as I was out of intensive care and in a room, Shad was on the line.

"Were you scared?" he asked.

"Scared?" I said. The question struck me as odd coming from someone as lordly as he. But, of course, he was scared. He was of an age when men begin realizing that they are mortal. He asked about symptoms. Did I know I was having a heart attack? What did it feel like? When did it start? What did I do? Bud asked the same questions, as did other men of a like age. Only Charles never asked, but then he never called, never so much as inquired about how I was doing. I thought that strange. But except for a friend or two, Charles remained enigmatically silent during the illnesses and travails of people who worked on the show.

I never told anyone, doctors or colleagues and especially not Donna, what might have been the cause of the heart attack. I'd withheld the piece of information that probably would have solved the mystery for them. That same day, though weary and sleepless from the Minnesota trip, I ignored what I felt were symptoms of the flu and had sex with a young woman with whom I'd been having an affair. We eventually went our separate ways, but not before I'd spent many months in therapy.

•

On a mid-February night, the day before returning to work and after an absence of six or seven weeks in Florida convalescing from the heart attack, I made my way to Low Library on the Columbia University campus where *Sunday Morning* was receiving a Columbia-Dupont Award. Stepping into the foyer, I immediately came across Bud Lamoreaux, who complimented me on my Florida tan.

"I'm in the pink," I said. "The best in years."

"Nobody's going to pressure you," he admonished. "The only pressure you've had you've brought on yourself, asshole."

He broke into a grin. "You're seething inside, I can see it. You're thrashing at the bit. You're ready to go back in the field tonight."

Then Northshield came up and immediately enclosed me in a bear hug.

"You son of a bitch," he said.

The next morning Shad made a show outside my door by clasping his hands over his head. When he came in he gave me an assignment, a music piece, in Chicago. I was stunned. I thought I'd spend some time in town before having to go on the road again.

"You'll enjoy it. It's music."

I gave him a funny look.

"Don't you want to do it?" he asked.

"Sure Shad," I said, and thanked him.

On paper it looked like a winner: a profile of a businessman who went around town raising money to help young musicians develop as artists. As it turned out the benefactor was mostly talk, a self-serving publicity-seeker.

"I don't think he's going to work," I told Shad and Bud on the phone at the end of the day I spent with him.

"What's wrong with him?" said Shad.

I gave my assessment.

"Stick with it, kid." The guy was someone Kuralt had heard about and whose story he thought worth doing.

"It's not getting any better," I said the next day.

"He's that bad?" said Shad.

"That bad."

On the third day Shad said, "What the hell is this?"

"The guy's just awful. Worse every day."

"I think," said Shad to Bud, who was on the other line, "he wants to come home."

"I think that's what he's telling us," said Bud.

"Is that what you're telling us?" asked Shad.

"Yes, Shad, that's it exactly."

"Well, for Christ's sake. Why didn't you say so?"

"You got to speak up," Bud admonished.

Shad was laughing.

"What about Kuralt?" I said.

"Fuck him," Shad said.

"What'll I tell this guy?"

"Fuck him, too," said Shad. "He's an asshole, isn't he? Come home, kid."

•

There was Shad's iron voice striking terror within everyone's hearing. He was complaining to Estelle Popkin, the office manager, about Jo-Marie, Shad's secretary.

"Where is she?" he roared.

I could not hear what Estelle said but presumably she replied that Jo-Marie was busy getting my airline ticket for Miami. My mother had just passed away and I was rushing to tie up loose ends before leaving town. She died at eighty-seven on April 28, 1982 in the afternoon, in a Miami hospital. My aunts had gone to lunch. Her illness had been so depressing and they were anxious to be away from the hospital for awhile. In her delirium my mother kept asking for my father, a man long dead whom she'd divorced some forty years before. When the aunts returned, my mother was dead. She'd suffered no pain and looked at peace.

"It was the best she'd looked in months," my Aunt Rhoda said.

A little time elapsed and then there was the volcanic Northshield's voice again. Where was this hare-brained secretary of his? Why wasn't she at her desk? She wasn't worth a shit, always screwing off. He had it with her and was going to fire her ass. Then, some minutes later, he exploded.

"This fucking place!"

In the seclusion of my office I raised my eyes and wished my mother had not inconvenienced Shad so.

"He is a very important man, my senior executive producer. For heaven's sake, Mother, couldn't you have chosen a better time for all this?"

To tell the truth, I did feel guilty.

•

Sunday Morning was a success. Everyone said so: the critics, people on the street. Best of all, the ratings said so.

Shad could hardly stand it; he certainly could not keep his mouth shut, could not keep from crowing.

He expected everyone to cheer.

But not everyone inside CBS was cheering.

There always have been rivalries among shows for "resources," the best correspondents, producers, tape editors, camera crews, and so on.

Shad's swaggering revved up the competition.

"(Dan) Rather would see our show and say, 'Holy shit, why didn't we have that story?'" Shad recounted to me in one of our interviews. "And then he'd see one of our guys and say, 'Oh, when did he get good?' and grab him for the *Evening News*."

"We were getting somewhere and all of a sudden they put on the brakes," recalled Bud Lamoreaux when I spoke with him. "Dan Rather wouldn't let good people work for us ... Once we went to Charles Osgood to get him to voice a narration but Osgood said he couldn't do it. Dan Rather didn't want him to ... Before we knew it we were down to the bottom of the barrel in crews and correspondents."

Even so, Shad's show proved amazingly durable.

And then one day, Shad was gone.

Management may have been gambling on Shad's quirky genius to score a coup in television's most hotly contested hours, as some claimed: or, as others contended, management had hit upon a way of getting rid of him. Whatever the reason, he was given a show to produce in prime time, one hosted by Charles Kuralt and Bill Moyers.

Bud was now in charge of *Sunday Morning* and he subsequently moved into Shad's office.

•

Several months into his tenure Bud picked up the phone to learn that Shad's show was being cancelled. The ratings for *American Parade* with Charles Kuralt and Bill Moyers were respectable, but not respectable enough to keep the show in prime-time.

Shad was out of a job unless ... was Bud willing to take him back on *Sunday Morning*?

"It's your call," said the executive on the other end of the line.

The thought of Shad, his proud, bearded benefactor, hitting the bricks at age sixty-five was a fate Bud could not contemplate with equanimity. It just so happened that Bud was negotiating a new contract, one promising a hefty raise. In such circumstances, how could he not afford to be generous?

"You can't fire him," said Bud.

"Do you want him back or not? You have to make a decision."

"I'll take him back," Bud said with finality.

In all of Shad's years in television, he said at a staff meeting on his return, he'd never seen anything like it. It was probably a true first. This was not the way things were supposed to work out. We're supposed to hate each other. (Laughter.) Frankly, he went on, if the circumstances were the other way around he probably wouldn't have taken Bud back. (Very nervous laughter.)

So, said Shad in the uncharacteristic role of penitent, that tells you something about this overweight, hard-assed, sonofabitch Lamoreaux before whom Shad, dammit, was obliged to grovel until his last gasp.

Bud, in turn, was characteristically self-effacing. He'd asked Shad to return because, frankly, we'd put out a better show with him than without him. Shad brought certain things to the broadcast that, frankly, we've missed.

SHAD (*reviving his old self again*): Bud's our boss, that's the good news. But the rest of you assholes still have Shad to contend with, and that's the bad news. (*Laughter and cheers.*)

Had we been able to read Shad's mind we probably would have been treated to a different speech, one that said: That sonofabitch Lamoreaux, he's gotten too big for his britches. If he had any sense of propriety he'd have let me reclaim my old office. It's my office, dammit, not his. The asshole just doesn't know his place.

At the time Shad returned to *Sunday Morning,* Lawrence Tisch, the financier who'd gained control of CBS, was bent on downsizing the once great network. People were being let go in droves. Everyone wondered whether his or her turn was going to be next. (In the end Tisch took leave of a downsized company with a reported billion in profits.)

Shad, with a sixth sense for corporate survival, began separating himself from Bud. "I'm not talking to you," he'd snort whenever Bud drew near.

"The poor bastard. Bud needs direction, needs help, doesn't do anything, always fucking off," he'd complain to anyone who'd listen. "I've tried to warn him but he's stubborn, doesn't realize how much trouble he's in. I'm sorry to say this but he's become a liability to the show. I thought there was more to the guy. I really did. I misjudged him terribly."

Bud learned of his dismissal upon picking up the phone one day. Heartfelt apologies and all that, old boy, said the executive on the other end, but there it was. Damn shame, etc. In simple fact the company no longer could afford the luxury of two executive producers, together hauling in six-figure incomes, on *Sunday Morning*. Nothing personal, Bud was told, but Shad, the old rascal, had out-politicked his good friend.

·

It was one of those maddening summer days, furnace heat on the streets below, arctic temperatures in my office.

"Have you been here all along?" Shad said when he spied me.

"All day," I said.

"Why didn't you come in this morning to say hello? Did you see the letter? Did you hear about the letter I got this morning?"

Having said no to all questions, he led me into his office where I immediately noticed the temperature was more merciful. He removed a single sheet of paper from his desk. It was in Bud's hand, addressed to Shad.

"Go ahead, read it!" he said, putting the letter into my hand.

I hesitated. Shad kept insisting.

"Congratulations! You have won," Bud's letter began. "You deceived me. You are an evil spirit; I befriended you, let you come back to *Sunday Morning* after the *American Parade* debacle and you did me in. You must feel pretty good about yourself. But look around. Look into the eyes of those who remain and that will tell you all you need to know about yourself."

Shad drew so close I could hear him breathing.

"Now let me look into your eyes," Shad said. Was he missing something? Was Lamoreaux right? Was there something in people's eyes that Shad had failed to catch?

"Let me look into your eyes," Shad said again, making an elaborate business of it.

·

Bud spent a week in the hospital in a state of depression. Eventually he was recalled by the network after the bookkeepers discovered that CBS was obliged to pay Bud's salary for the years remaining on his contract.

On his return – he was put in charge of a documentary unit created for Walter Cronkite – Bud was buttonholed by Kuralt.

"Do you know why you were fired? First, you took Shad's office away. Second, your wife introduced Shad at a party as a colleague, not as your boss. That's why you were fired."

•

Shad, meantime, set about purging the staff of Bud's hires and other people forced on him.

Firing Heywood (Woodie) Broun, the raconteur and Bud's close friend, probably gave him the most satisfaction. But he derived pleasure as well by hopping a plane to New Orleans to dismiss a producer on the spot and, in another instance, by delivering the coup de grace to a fellow recovering from a car crash.

Yet another producer – a favored Bud hire – described for me his moment of truth.

"Shad was all smiles – I'd just been summoned. He was smiling the whole time he was telling me that my work was no good, that he had no use for me, that, in fact, he despised me, couldn't stand the sight of me. And all the while he was saying this he was beside himself with joy. Ecstatic. I swear the man was having an orgasm."

•

Like a great cat Shad stole into the studio early one Sunday and upbraided a writer in language so violent that Kuralt himself turned ghostly pale and shook uncontrollably. A technician who witnessed the outburst feared that Charles might not recover in time to do the broadcast.

When I interviewed Kuralt for this chapter in late November 1995 – the year after he'd retired from CBS – I told him that people believed that he had been behind the network's decision to remove the volatile Shad Northshield as executive producer of *Sunday Morning*.

Charles denied this, and told me of an invitation to lunch with

Howard Stringer, the president of CBS News, soon after Stringer had learned of the early morning incident.

"I hear that Shad is behaving badly," Charles quoted Stringer as saying.

Charles acknowledged a problem but (as he told me) he didn't make a point of it with Stringer. It was Stringer who pressed him about Shad.

What Charles remembered saying was that Shad was "a genius, but a mad genius. Always blows up. A volatile character. Volcanic."

But he wasn't telling the news chief something he didn't already know. Charles merely acquiesced. Stringer knew about Shad, said Charles.

●

Shad was gone from *Sunday Morning* again, this time to father yet another broadcast for prime time. But no one seemed particularly interested in the project and hardly anybody ever called or dropped in at his office in the 555 Building across from the Broadcast Center. In the end, nothing ever came of the idea.

His pay was cut by two thirds – down to $100,000 – about what mid-level assignment editors were paid. The network was telling him to go. Then, after doing nothing for seven years, Shad retired in 1995.

He was in his early seventies and in pretty good health.

During the years when Shad was idle no one ever came to his aid to say, "Hey, give this guy a break. He's great. One of the greatest. You don't find his kind every day!"

The show, though, was still going strong. It wasn't as sharp as when Shad was running it but, as Kuralt noted when I last spoke with him before his death in 1997, "a lot of the original *Sunday Morning* is still there."

And so it is even today, as the broadcast will soon be marking its thirtieth year.

As for the creator of the broadcast, Shad Northshield died on August 21, 2000. In the last year or two of his life he suffered several strokes. Near the end he fell in the garage at his home, but was not discovered until the next day. He lingered on at a nursing home until his death at seventy-eight.

I'd gotten word of Charles Kuralt's death of complications from lupus just before setting out on a camping trip with two fellow Bay Area journalists on the morning of July 4, 1997. We were on our way to the California gold country, a Kuralt kind of place, with places named Hangtown, Fiddletown, and Angels Camp.

In Sutter Creek, where we'd stopped for supplies, people mourned his death as if Charles were one of heir own.

One merchant said she still missed him on *Sunday Morning*, although he'd left the broadcast and gone into retirement in 1994. Someone else still missed him on the CBS *Evening News* although he'd given up his "On the Road" series to do *Sunday Morning* nearly twenty years before.

I ran into another Kuralt fan, an author and photographer, in a museum where he was autographing a new picture book on the California gold country. Once he'd taken note of my CBS T-shirt, he started talking about Charles.

"Did you know Charles Kuralt very well?"

"Well, yes. I worked with him for many years."

Kuralt, said the author Leslie Kelly, was not only someone he admired but was one of the four idols in his life. The others were his parents and Thor Heyerdahl.

"I'm honored to make your acquaintance," he said, thrusting a complimentary copy of the expensive coffee-table book into my hands. "Because of Charles Kuralt."

Obese, jowly, bald, and long past middle age, Kuralt was atypical for a TV star. My camping companions were curious. How did I account for his wide appeal?

"I've thought about that for years, as have many of my colleagues," I said. "It was an ongoing subject of conversation with us. He had one of the great voices in broadcasting. Second, credit his skill as an actor. Third, he was a terrific writer. Fourth, credit his technique as an interviewer. He listened patiently, cordially, and sympathetically to people and the strangest things happened. Ordinary people began saying extraordinary things. And fifth, he was never one to patronize or upstage others with a smirk or smart remark. The overall effect was that viewers believed that he was one of them, a man whom they could trust."

Kuralt's gifts as a journalist got us to speculating around the campfire. How many other TV news personalities today would be missed as much as he?

Surely Walter Cronkite, we readily concluded.

But, after naming Cronkite, we stumbled over all the other names that came to mind, even though we pondered far into the night.

•

A few weeks after Kuralt's death, his oldest friends and admirers packed Alice Tully Hall in Lincoln Center to pay him tribute.

Speaker after speaker noted Charles's unique contribution to journalism and their affection for him, but none could say that they really knew him. Dan Rather said as much, as did Walter Cronkite and Mike Wallace.

His oldest friend at CBS, Phil Sheffler, a senior *60 Minutes* producer, was one of the speakers. He came as close as anyone in explaining the man behind the mask.

Some years earlier Sheffler and Kuralt had bought a place in Connecticut for their families to share. (Kuralt was married twice, had two daughters, and was a grandfather.)

One morning Charles came downstairs, poured himself a mug of coffee, and sat down. Sheffler's wife, no doubt meaning well, put a place mat under his coffee.

"When I saw her do this," Sheffler said, "I knew the end was in sight." A month later Charles told him, "Phil, why don't you buy back my half and I'll go find a place of my own.'"

Which is what happened.

Charles didn't like to be regimented. This is why he had been so reluctant to host *Sunday Morning*. He feared the loss of his independence. All the years he was on the road, the network had left him alone. In the seemingly trivial matter of the place mat, Sheffler's wife had trespassed on his privacy.

•

A month after the memorial in New York for Charles, Robert Pierpoint, a long-time CBS correspondent and a colleague of Kuralt's and mine, accidentally stumbled upon the secret of Charles's personal life.

An avid fly fisherman like Kuralt, Bob remembered Charles telling him some five years before of his fishing retreat in Montana. It sounded ideal. Charles had moved an old schoolhouse onto the property, and turned it into his living quarters. Bob was eager to see it. But when Bob asked Charles about it, Charles begged off, saying he discouraged visitors. All he had put there, he said, was that shack in the woods.

Charles wanted to keep it that way, a place where he could fish, read, and write his books in solitude.

For some while, Bob and his wife had been thinking of acquiring land in Montana. When Charles died, Bob remembered their conversation.

He turned to Kuralt's longtime secretary. She provided Bob with information about the property and its location, but warned there was a problem. She didn't say more.

When Bob and his wife were next in the state they drove to Twin Bridges in southwestern Montana, and got directions to Kuralt's property. When they spotted the schoolhouse, they knew they'd found the place. But they were amazed to find something else on the site, something grander: a beautiful cottage fifty yards upstream from the fishing retreat.

When Bob got back to town he told a realtor that he was interested in the Kuralt place. From her he learned that he would have to talk to Kuralt's girlfriend, Patricia Shannon. While Bob looked on open-mouthed, she rang up her aunt and asked, "Where's Pat?" Then, turning to Bob, she said Pat had left town. Nobody knew where she was.

Some months later, Shannon filed court papers in an effort – one that eventually proved successful – to claim the Montana property for herself. Suzanne (Petie) Kuralt, Charles's wife of thirty-five years, who probably had never known of Shannon's existence, contested Shannon's right to the real estate. When Petie died in 1999, Kuralt's two daughters by a previous marriage kept up the legal battle. By this time the story of Kuralt's double life of twenty-eight years with Shannon was in the papers, first spread by a supermarket tabloid in January of 1998.

In the last years of his life, Kuralt and Shannon reportedly were not as close as in times past, but during his last illness Kuralt sent a note to Shannon from his hospital bed. He told her that he was sick and that the doctors were still trying to figure out what was wrong with him. But if he should die – "if it came to that" – he wanted Pat to have the Montana property he'd promised her. The lawyers were coming by in the next day or so to make the necessary changes in the will. But Charles died before they ever arrived.

Early in the relationship Charles had persuaded Patricia Shannon to give up her job as a federal government employee so they could spend more time together. Over the years Charles supported both Shannon and her three children, a son and two daughters. They had shared a home in Ireland as well as in Montana. The legal battle for possession of the Montana property was re-enacted on a national television show. Viewers were asked to choose between Kuralt's family and Shannon. A majority voted in Shannon's favor.

From what Bob could learn in the Montana town on that August day in 1997, Kuralt used to show up with Shannon around Twin Bridges in the late summer, especially in September. The town left them alone. People knew Kuralt was famous for his celebration of homespun American values and no one attempted to peddle the scandal to the media.

When Bob told me of his discovery, I was as nonplussed as he had been. We knew the story was bound to come out; in the meantime, we had agreed to keep the secret of Twin Bridges.

•

I'd long suspected that Charles was an unhappy man, trapped in his own conceit, his own successful recreation of himself.

An old London-based movie, *Night and the City*, could well serve as a parable.

In one of the film's stories, a young working girl has a crush on a stage personality, a ventriloquist. Night after night she sits in the gallery enthralled, fantasizing about the handsome entertainer. At length, she summons up the courage to go backstage, but the custodian drives her away.

One night, however, she succeeds in evading the old fellow, getting as far as the dressing room. Her heart freezes when she opens the door. The ventriloquist, she discovers, is actually the dummy and the dummy the ventriloquist.

There was something of that in my sense of Charles Kuralt.

I saw a side of the man but it was only one side and was always the same side. I never saw the whole man. I never got beyond the public persona; neither, as I've suggested, did many others who were his friends.

When, in one of the darkest periods in its history, CBS News, under pressure from new corporate owners in the mid-1980s, was ordered to fire 215 reporters and producers in a Draconian budget squeeze, no one heard a murmur of protest from Kuralt. Other well-known CBS newsmen – Dan Rather and Andy Rooney come to mind – publicly denounced the cuts. But Charles remained silent, even though his own show, *Sunday Morning*, suffered crippling hits, losing more than half of its producing staff.

As I've mentioned, when I was sidelined for weeks after my heart attack, I heard from a raft of people but never heard a word from him, though this was in the early years of *Sunday Morning* when we were working closely together. Nor did he ever find a moment to express concern for a colleague in the five years that this gifted producer was dying of pancreatic cancer. (The man spoke bitterly to me about Kuralt's silence.)

No doubt Charles was caring towards some people but I suspect (and this may be terribly unfair) he couldn't handle bad news when it touched people he knew.

In fact, I am being unfair. Charles was entitled to his independence, to behaving in the manner suitable for him, just as I am entitled to see him without tears.

Kuralt was sixty-two when he died. He was younger than Mike Wallace; younger than Dan Rather and Charles Osgood who succeeded him on *Sunday Morning*. Younger than I was at the time.

In explaining the loner's life he led, he once likened himself to Dickens's description of Scrooge: "Oh, but he was a tight-fisted hand at the grindstone ... secret and self-contained, and solitary as an oyster."

He said it better in words of his own in his book, *A Life on the Road*. Kuralt wrote: "I didn't want a place to live. I had nothing to do there. I didn't want days off. I had no way to fill empty days. All I wanted was stories, the wilder the better."

All the same, the best story in his satchel of tales was the one he never told.

As a writer in *TV Guide* noted, in the last book Kuralt published, *Charles Kuralt's America*," Charles wrote about his twelve favorite places in the U.S. Twin Bridges, Montana, was his choice for September, but nowhere does he mention that he owned a home there.

Cronkite

In the spring of 1987 I was one of 215 writers, producers, and correspondents fired in the merciless assault by Black Rock – the nickname for the network's headquarters in a black skyscraper in another part of town – on the CBS budget.

At the same time we were losing our jobs, the *New York Times* published a picture of Laurence Tisch, the CEO of CBS, presenting a $10,000,000 check to the Metropolitan Museum of Art. I made a calculation. The money saved by firing all of us added up to a similar sum; in other words, a case could be made that 215 people were thrown out of work so that Tisch, following the example of the Pharaohs and Medicis, could be memorialized in stone on a new wing of the museum.

I was in Key West the day I got the news, March 7, 1987, a Saturday.

"Glorious sunlight until 3 P.M. when the shit hit the fan," my log reads.

Rumors of mass firings had been circulating for weeks. With a sense of foreboding I gave up fishing for the day to wait for the late afternoon arrival of the *New York Times*.

Sure enough, the story was right there inside my Florida edition: 215 firings at CBS News. But only a few well-known correspondents were named, no producers.

I began calling New York.

When Bill Moran, the *Sunday Morning* senior producer, came on he asked if I'd talked to anyone; I answered no.

Then I said, "Who got hit?"

"It was devastating, the worst possible."

He read the casualty list – from Brett Alexander all the way to

Howard Weinberg. And I was thinking, I've made it. The paper said five of nine *Sunday Morning* producers were fired and he'd named five, six including Amy Weinman, a researcher. And then Bill said, "And you."

However grotesque the comparison, I remembered my father once saying how it was when he was hit by sniper fire in the First World War. He didn't know he had been hit until he began seeing blood. Even then it took awhile for him to comprehend what had happened.

So this is what it's like, I thought. It's not happening to someone else!

"Very well," I said.

"Now, listen," Bill said. "Get in touch with Bud Lamoreaux. He may be hiring. I'd call him right now."

"Saturday afternoon?" The sun was blazing in Key West. It had to be shining in Westchester as well. "He's got to be out on the golf course. Got his number?"

I wrote it down.

"And call Linda, too." Linda was Linda Mason, the new executive producer of *Sunday Morning*. "She feels terrible. Please."

I took down more numbers.

"But call Bud first," Bill urged. Moran was a friend. He and I shared a Maine and AP background. Bud Lamoreaux also was a pal.

Bud picked up the phone on the second ring.

"I've been canned," I said.

"Yeah, I know," said Bud. He'd been canned in an earlier cutback at *Sunday Morning*. When auditors discovered that he would still be able to draw his six-figure salary for another year under the terms of his contract, the network put him to work as executive producer of Walter Cronkite's moribund documentary unit.

"I may have something. I'm not sure. But there is a possibility."

"Anything. Even an office without a window."

Quite late that night, Chris Brown, my oldest New York friend, was on the line.

"Well," I said. "I got my wish. I'm a free man."

It was an old joke.

Truth to tell I was feeling a little giddy, drunk on the prospects of a newfound freedom.

I'd been fired a few times before in my journalism career, and another time when I was trying to do some serious writing and living a hand-to-mouth existence in Santa Cruz, California.

As chance had it, I'd found a fanciful job as a mushroom cleaner, a welcome relief from the grunt labor I'd had to put up with at a local cannery and at an ice plant. But after I spent a week or so of cutting and pruning in damp, dark sheds guided by the light of my miner's cap, the farmer, a gentle older man, was in distress.

As market day approached he told me I had to go. "I'm sorry, son," he said, "but you have no flair for mushrooms."

Now, this time, thirty years later and at CBS, I was breaking into cold sweats. I twitched, my heart palpitated. I was a mess.

•

When I got back to the Broadcast Center in New York, I found the walking wounded: Peter Hereford, Lindsay Miller, Howard Weinberg, Mary Ann Grabavoy, Brett Alexander, and Amy Weinman. Amy had fled first, packed up and left without a trace. The others lingered, playing for time with pieces in progress.

While I was in my office contemplating the disposal of an accumulation of papers, books, audio- and videocassettes, and pictures of the past eight years, my phone rang. It was Bud Lamoreaux.

"You want to go to lunch?"

"You betcha." We set a time and place.

Meantime, I kept up an assault on Mark Harrington's office. (The number two executive in charge of news, Mark was someone I'd found approachable in the past.)

"I'm going out to lunch but will be back at two-thirty," I told his secretary.

"Try then, you'll have a better chance in the afternoon," she said.

On our way out of the Broadcast Center, Bud asked me my preference, Japanese or Mexican.

"Mexican," I said. "I'm always happier heading south."

Over tacos and beans Bud said things looked good. "I think we're moving towards an agreement to bring you into the Cronkite unit."

I said, "I have an appointment with Mark Harrington this afternoon. I'm going to say a few things."

"OK," said Bud. "But don't get him mad. Keep it within the parameters. It's OK to say a few things, but we need him and you don't want to alienate him. You can't afford to do that now."

I ordered two Johnny Walker Black Labels, one more than was my custom.

I'd spoken to Mark a few weeks before when I was protesting a measly offer of a 3 percent raise on a new contract.

Although I'd left empty-handed I had the satisfaction of being listened to. When Harrington argued that I already was making more than many evening and morning news producers I countered, "That's probably true, but I'm a lot older than most of them and have more to offer."

He was gracious enough to concede the point.

When we parted he reminded me that his door was always open. So now I was taking the man at his word.

After lunch with Bud, I was lucky to find Harrington in his office. "Why was I fired?" I asked, after Harrington waved me to a chair.

"We're consolidating," he said. Producers would have to do more than they do now; one day covering fast-breaking news for the evening news and the morning news, and the next pursuing art and nature pieces for *Sunday Morning*.

He went on. "Only a few *Sunday Morning* producers have hard-news experience. So, regrettably, we've had to let some of you go."

"You're joking," I said. "I've spent most of my career chasing fires, cops, robbers and politicians."

"No one knew. I'm sorry."

The tribunal of executive news producers and managers knew the amount of money Black Rock wanted cut; their task was simply delivering enough bodies to make the cut.

Nobody knew me. Working for the off-beat *Sunday Morning* was like living in a cocoon. Shad Northshield, who'd brought me to *Sunday Morning* from NBC, was overseeing other CBS broadcasts. His successor as executive producer of the show, Linda Mason, told me that she was the only person to speak up in my behalf. But she was drowned out. Evidently one snort and I was out.

I tried to keep my composure. "But whose fault is that?" I asked

Harrington. "You guys didn't do your homework. You didn't know who you were firing. You don't know the first thing about me."

The Black Label was talking now. What the hell, here was Lavine's lecture on creative management.

"But we didn't have much time," Harrington said. "Tisch didn't give us much time."

The boyish-looking executive belying his forty or so years was a model of cordiality, but I feared I had not made my case. Immediately I hit him with the notes I'd taken from Shad's counseling earlier in the day.

"Look," Shad had advised, striding into my office. "Tell him about Donna. Tell Harrington if you lose your job you'll lose your health benefits. Tell him how sick she's been. Tell him about her open-heart surgery."

I found the idea appalling.

"That's right," he pressed. "You have to say that you are not asking to keep your job for yourself, but that you need to keep on working because of Donna. I'm telling you, he'll listen."

Shad Northshield had held many jobs, jobs like Harrington's. And what he was saying was probably true.

Donna suffered from a deteriorating heart condition and one day probably would have to chance open-heart surgery for a third time. But I wanted to stake the fight on my merits as a writer and producer. I hated the idea of having to trot out my wife's infirmities. It was not journalistically relevant; it was unprofessional.

In the end I did as Shad counseled.

And when I finished I could see that it had achieved the desired effects. Harrington cleared his throat and finally conceded that "perhaps an injustice had been done after all." He promised to review my case personally.

"I'll get back to you with a decision as soon as I can. One way or the other."

"But there isn't much time," I said. It was already Tuesday. Those given the sack were to be packed, gone from the premises, Friday.

"You will hear by then," he said.

As I made for the door, I wheeled around. "There is also a question of morality here."

"Morality?"

"Certainly. Don't you remember? I just signed a new contract and a week later you fired me."

.

The next morning Shad poked his head inside my door.

"You must have shook up Harrington. He called me after you left last night. Wanted to talk about you. Called you La-*veen*. I put him straight. I said, 'It's La-*vine*.' Sounds very hopeful."

At 4:45 P.M. – I have the time indelibly recorded – I was skimming through a new picture book about China that had been lying around the offices and that I was contemplating keeping when Bud called.

"You want to go for a drink?"

"You betcha."

We trooped up in silence to Armstrong's on the corner of Tenth Avenue.

I ordered Black Label, Bud the Red.

When the drinks arrived Bud hoisted his glass, clinked mine, and, breaking into a wide grin, said, "Welcome to the Cronkite unit."

He went on. "Whatever you said to Harrington worked."

"I give all the credit to Black Label. Especially that second one. It gave me wings." I made no mention of Shad. Those two were no longer speaking.

Back at the office, I told Bill, and he looked happy, and I talked with Linda Mason on the phone at Bill's insistence.

"Everyone's taking credit for this," said Bill. Linda Mason needed her recognition.

.

On Friday Bud showed me my new windowless office, and introduced me to the Cronkite staff.

I dropped by *Sunday Morning* and thanked Linda again and we hugged. Later Bill passed on a suggestion from her that I contact Bud Benjamin, Walter's long-time producer, to learn about Walter's ways, especially on the road.

I never did and paid a price for my folly.

A month after joining the unit, I met Walter. He rose up from the couch in Bud's office. I found him somewhat diminished in stature from the personality I'd seen on the screen. But he was in the pink of good health, the familiar features clearly drawn.

"Welcome aboard," he said gripping my hand.

"Glad to be aboard, Walter," I answered, though it almost seemed more natural to address him as Mr. President.

If one were casting for an individual to play president one could hardly do better than Walter. There'd been no president in my time since FDR who's looked quite so presidential as Walter Cronkite. And, of course, for sheer resonance, he had no peer either.

He was a smart dresser, too. I took full note of the tasseled shoes, sparkling to a fare-thee-well.

The meeting in Bud's office, with its fine view of the West Side and the Hudson River, was for the purpose of pinning down Walter's availability for interviews in this country and abroad. Ever since he had voluntarily stepped down as the anchor and managing editor of the CBS Evening News in 1981, he still craved the limelight but, as we discovered, he had no appetite for work.

Sailing his yacht, lecturing for fat fees, and hosting TV extravaganzas monopolized Walter's days. Getting in touch with him was often difficult, sometimes nerve-wracking.

It fell to our researcher, Barbara Baylor, to warn of pitfalls lying in wait for us.

There were two big things to remember, she warned us.

"He's hard of hearing and he's forgetful, doesn't remember things very well."

She went on. "And so you have to keep reminding him, sending him notes, telling him in person, because he frequently forgets. 'Now, Walter, you have an appointment with so and so at three o'clock.' You can't remind him often enough."

Walter's doomsday clock had begun ticking as early as March 6, 1981, when he stepped down as anchorman and managing editor of the CBS Evening News after nearly nineteen years in that chair.

Everyone had been speculating – it was a kind of game – when Cronkite would relinquish his anchor chair and who would replace him. There were two major candidates, Roger Mudd and Dan Rather. For reasons best known to himself, Mudd thought he would be the anchor. So he bided his time.

Dan Rather, like Hotspur, could not wait.

And the hour was his. Rather's contract was running out. Stories surfaced in the papers: one day Rather was lunching with Roone Arledge, the ABC News chief, the next he was dining with Arledge's NBC counterpart. Rivers of ink were spilled in the press contemplating Dan's future.

Alarmed, the bigwigs at Black Rock set to work to keep Rather at CBS. Walter was still hale and still first in the hearts of most viewers. But, as he pointed out in his autobiography, *A Reporter's Life*, he'd been telling CBS management for at least two years that he wanted to quit as anchorman on the evening news when he turned sixty-five in November of 1981. He was tiring of the grind; for years he'd been taking ever longer vacations to sail his yacht and others, and to follow his fancy.

In the end a deal was crafted giving Rather the *Evening News*, Mudd nothing, and Walter a monthly magazine in prime-time along with a reported million-dollar-a-year contract.

Cronkite relinquished the anchor chair with good grace. In his incarnation as a special correspondent, he anchored a science series and several documentaries and, beginning in 1986, the *Cronkite at Large* shows. But his role as a network correspondent was steadily diminishing.

Indeed, according to Walter, Van Gordon Sauter, the president of CBS News, "believed his job was to build Rather's reputation at whatever cost." Walter said that while lunching with Sauter one day, "Sauter admitted that he was deliberately keeping me off the air because he felt that it would be easier to build up Dan's audience if I wasn't around as a distraction."

By the time I joined the Cronkite documentary unit in the spring of 1987, Walter was well on his way to oblivion, gasping, quite literally, for airtime.

By the time fall rolled around, his condition, so to speak, could be described as terminal.

One morning I found Bud in distress and laying siege to Nora

Boch, Walter's manipulative assistant. Whatever she had to do or say she must find Walter. It was urgent.

I followed Bud into his office.

"Did you see the *New York Post* this morning?" he asked.

I shook my head.

He picked up the tabloid, turning to page three. The headline yelped:

CRONKITE: I'D FIRE RATHER

"This could cook our goose," said Bud. "Can you imagine what's going on across the street, or over in Black Rock? Rather will go bonkers. He's got to be climbing all over Stringer and calling Tisch. Now we'll never get on the air."

Walter's outburst stemmed from a much-publicized incident a month earlier. Dan Rather, presumably furious over a network decision to delay the *Evening News* until the end of a crucial tennis match, walked off the set in protest. When the network was ready to switch to Dan (he was in Miami for the visit of Pope John Paul II) the anchorman was not in his place. For an unprecedented seven minutes CBS went black before its star correspondent could be found.

For days the network was swept by rumors: persons in high places were contemplating banishing Rather and restoring Walter to the *Evening News*.

Bud lost no time in sucking up to Cronkite.

"When I told Walter this place was not only leaderless but rudderless and something simply had to be done, Walter's eyes began to sparkle. Oh, I think he'd love to get his anchor chair back," Bud reported to me over lunch.

His face flushed with excitement, Bud broke into a nervous, high-pitched laugh. "When you think of it, the prospects are unlimited," he said. He meant not only for Walter but also for the two of us.

Just then Walter was setting off for Europe. Before he was airborne he made sure to leave his itinerary with news division executives. In the event of a restoration, CBS would know where to reach him.

Walter's return from Europe went as unnoticed as his departure. While simmering over his neglect, he made good on a commitment to speak before a journalism class at the University of Texas at Austin, his alma mater.

When a student wanted to know how Walter would have dealt with Dan Rather after the infamous seven-minute incident, Cronkite fired off the page one rebuke heard 'round both Black Rock and the world of broadcasting.

"If Walter had kept his mouth shut or said something trite or banal there would not have been any headlines," said Bud.

"But then he would not have been Walter," I said.

"The point is, Walter's right. Rather had no business leaving the show unprotected. But you don't carry your family fights into the street. And especially now when the *Evening News* is struggling so hard to get back on top, and Rather is under such tremendous pressure to make good. It doesn't add up."

Barbara Baylor, our researcher, contributed to our state of anxiety by prophesying, "We're doomed. We'll never get on the air now. We're going to lose our jobs."

Barbara, who'd worked for Walter since the inception of the unit, contended he was having "a temper tantrum, that's what it is. And the rest of us, not him, will be paying for it with our jobs."

Walter's impromptu outburst put her in mind of a time in San Francisco when she and Cronkite were on their way to dinner and he drove right up on the sidewalk of the Mark Hopkins Hotel.

"The big doorman came running over in a fury but stopped dead in his tracks as soon as he recognized Walter. Walter bestowed a tip upon him and said, 'It's all right to leave the car here while we eat dinner?' and the flabbergasted doorman said 'Sure, Mr. Cronkite. Absolutely.'"

"He enjoys his fame and likes to flaunt it," she went on. "He kept Johnny Carson waiting for years when Carson pursued him for his show. And he took his time, a week, maybe longer, before accepting Paley's invitation to lunch after Walter stepped down as anchor. William S. Paley, the man who founded CBS. Walter kept him dangling for more than a week. Imagine!"

Now it was Walter who was kept dangling, complaining, for instance, that Laurence Tisch, the chief executive of CBS Inc., and Howard Stringer, the president of CBS News, were not returning his calls.

Bud's phone rang. We exchanged glances after he picked up. It was Walter calling in from Austin.

"You know about the story in the *Post*?" Bud asked, then said, "I'm practicing damage control." Hanging up, Bud said, "Walter says the *Post* story's accurate, and that's what we're supposed to say if anyone calls. But Walter's got nothing more to add."

•

Looking back I must say we were all a little to blame for permitting the vicissitudes of life to distract us from a particular principal mission in life: reminding Walter of his invitation to William Ruckleshaus, the former administrator of the Environmental Protection Agency, and his wife to spend the Labor Day weekend with the Cronkites on Martha's Vineyard. My log entry for September 1, 1987, is painful proof:

"Terrible Tuesday," I write. "WC says he knows nothing of plans for the Ruckleshauses staying with him on the Vineyard!"

Nora Boch came flying into my office with the news that Walter was on the phone. He was demanding to know who put him into this predicament.

"Why, he did it to himself," I said.

"I know," whispered Nora. "But we can never tell him."

She led me into Walter's lavish office and put a pad and pencil into my hand.

"Hello, Walter," I said picking up. "How are you?"

"Fine," he croaked, "until a moment ago when I heard this terrible news. How could Ruckleshaus be staying with me? Who did this to me?"

"Why, you did, Walter," I said only to myself. I went on in my head: Inviting Ruckleshaus out to the Vineyard was your own idea. You wanted him to stay at your house. You wanted to take him on a sail. You and Ruckleshaus were old friends; you said so.

But all I could manage was, "Well, that was the understanding."

"Whose understanding?" he thundered. His mother was recovering from a heart attack and a fall. They were short on staff. How could he possibly have agreed to this arrangement? "Oh, God!" he lamented. "I tell you I feel like canceling this whole business and probably will." He wanted to speak to Nora.

She scrambled with pen and paper ("Yes, Mr. C." "No, Mr. C.") as he inundated her with the names of hotels and people on the island.

She spread the word. Rosie and Linda, the two secretaries, and Barbara, the researcher, and Nora and I were to throw "Mr. C.'s" name around as far and wide as we possibly could. Labor Day Weekend notwithstanding, the Ruckleshauses must have their room! Nora first checked with Ruckleshaus's law office in Seattle.

"What kind of room do the Ruckleshauses prefer?" she asked of his secretary. "King? Double? Queen? Do they have any feelings about the view?" Then, with the acquisition of the information, we ran roughshod over the hapless innkeepers of Martha's Vineyard.

Between calls, a motherly Nora wailed, "He forgets. The poor man forgets. And the rest of us have to pay for it."

"A man that senile ought not to be on the air," I asserted.

"Don't say that," snapped Barbara, a single parent raising a teenage son. "We'll lose our jobs."

My phone rang. It was Bud with his sixth sense for knowing when to be out of rifle range.

"Is it all over?" he asked.

"Walter's been trying to reach you."

"I know."

"Where are you?"

"On the links."

"When are you coming in?"

"Maybe tomorrow or the day after."

"Enjoy."

Bud stayed away for two days. When he showed up he went on a rampage of his own: the fiasco was all my fault.

"You should have confronted the 800-pound gorilla," Bud said. "When he's discovered he made the mistake he'll come back at you."

"At me, for God's sake?"

"It's your job to save Walter from himself. Walter will be trying to explain to Ruckleshaus why he's had to disinvite him from staying at his place and Ruckleshaus will be thinking, 'This fool, this idiot, he invited us himself; has he lost control of his senses?'"

Bud continued, "Your error was you did not see it was your role to save Walter from himself, even if it meant getting fired." (Presumably this was one of the functions of a CBS producer not spelled out in my contract.)

It happened I had just been reading a satirical portrait of Tolstoy's chief disciple in the Henry Troyat biography. The way Bud Lamoreaux described my duties recalled Troyat's words about the character Chertkov.

"He thought it was his duty," wrote Troyat, "to keep watch over the old man, filter all his rash remarks and writings, transform him into a statue, a public monument, and appoint himself custodian of it."

"My role?" I replied. "You're the chief disciple around here. You're supposed to be the man in charge."

Bud laughed. "Just so you remember the next time."

Later that day when I went back to his office I saw that he'd been in a sweat; there were large stains on the shirt under his ham-like arms.

"Everything's fine," he said hanging up the phone. "Walter's talked to Mrs. Rucklehaus. She and her husband are happy with the hotel accommodations. He's hosting a dinner for them at the yacht club Sunday night. Sue and me and you and Donna are all invited."

Bud had just given me a lesson in survival.

●

I woke up in Victorian splendor at the Charlotte Inn in Edgartown, and worked for three hours on questions for Walter's interview with Ruckleshaus. Before noon Donna and I ate a sumptuous brunch, and when we returned to our room there was a message from Walter.

He'd decided to switch the dinner from the yacht club to L'Etoile, a formal restaurant at the Charlotte Inn. (Bud speculated that Walter made the change from his private club to the hotel so that one of us would be free to pick up the tab and charge it to our expense account. Though this would have been a CBS expense, Walter was famous for his penuriousness. A story has him reminding an assistant of his share of a taxi ride when the young man was being dropped off at his building.)

I said, "It's Labor Day weekend. On such sort notice there may be no room at the inn."

Walter was sure L'Etoile would not fail him. But he was confused. He wasn't sure how many there would be for dinner.

"There's me and my mother, I mean my wife, and you and your mother ..."

"My wife, Walter."

"Sorry, I've had my wife, I mean my mother, on my mind so much lately. She's been ill."

He began again. "There's you and your wife and Bud and his mother."

"Not Bud's mother, Walter. Bud's wife."

"Bud's wife."

He was planning dinner for seven but wasn't sure whether Bud said his wife was coming. I wasn't sure, either.

"Well, then, will you take care of all of this?"

"Of course," I said.

•

The maître d' at L'Etoile didn't blink. When I invoked the great name, he replied that a table for two, or possibly four, for Walter Cronkite, yes, he would do his best, but a party for seven or eight, tomorrow night, at this late date, was out of the question.

"Mr. Cronkite will be terribly upset if you can't accommodate him."

"I admire Mr. Cronkite as much as anyone but he must be made to understand this is Labor Day weekend, our busiest time of the year. For this holiday people have made their reservations weeks, even months in advance."

"But you will try," I said.

He was becoming agitated. "We have just so many tables, just so many servings. I would like to help you and Mr. Cronkite. Another time there would be no problem, no problem whatsoever."

"Then I want to speak to the owner."

"It will do you no good. You have to talk to me. It is my restaurant."

I was beginning to panic. "Look," I said, "my job is on the line. Another plate or two at the table, that's all I'm asking for."

The next morning Bud rolled up in front of the hotel in his Mercedes. He was grinning broadly and quipped, "Going my way?"

I said in alarm, "Where's Sue? Isn't she with you?"

He shook his head. "Has to work."

With the Cronkite unit's future as precarious as it was, Sue apparently thought it time to find a job herself. At least one of them would be working if rumors of more cutbacks proved true and CBS shut down the unit.

"That means seven, not eight at dinner tonight," I remarked.

"Yeah? So what?" said Bud.

"Well, Walter wasn't sure."

"But I told him."

"Shit."

"What's the matter?"

"Never mind," I said, marching back inside L'Etoile.

At dinner, the men were uniformly alike in navy blue blazers and pale khaki or gray pants. Walter was singularly resplendent in a red-and-white striped cotton shirt and navy tie. His wife, Betsy, was as pretty as she could be in a cotton dress and sweater and low-heeled shoes. I thought she was terrific – outspoken and direct in reining in Walter's ego.

Donna, who sat on Walter's left, told me later that he was polite and courteous but that he also gave her the feeling that she wasn't very important.

After dinner Betsy Cronkite and Jill Ruckleshaus expressed an interest in seeing our room. I'd referred to it, not entirely in praise, as "antique classic."

Walter put his foot down. "It'd only make me ill," he declared. He was fuming that while the Ruckleshauses had to make do in a second-best hotel on the outskirts of town, the likes of Donna and me were "living it up" at the Charlotte Inn.

He'd even talked to the inn's owner to get quarters for the Ruckleshauses. Shaking his head with dismay, he said for all to hear, "If I'd known those two were at the inn I would have had them trade with the Ruckleshauses."

Early the next morning when I got to Walter's waterfront home for the Ruckleshaus interview, I spotted him peering down from an upstairs window.

In a low voice he said, "This has been a very expensive weekend." He meant last night's dinner and the three-star hotel where the Ruckleshauses were staying. When L'Etoile presented the check, Walter amazed both Bud and me by signing off on his American Express card. I sought to reassure him about the hotel.

"I'll take care of their room," I said, "and see the Ruckleshauses off on the ferry to Woods Hole after the interview. You needn't concern yourself."

The next morning Donna and I escorted the Rucklehauses to the boat. On the way we learned that they and the Cronkites were not old friends at all. In fact the visitors were relieved when they learned that they were staying at a hotel and not with their hosts.

"The hotel worked out fine," Jill Ruckleshaus told us. "It's a terrible strain to be staying with people you don't know."

•

For months I struggled with a script. It was a harried, frustrating time.

Walter refused to give us more than a few days of his time in the summer. The fall was similarly restricted. In the winter he was weighing anchor for a Caribbean sail.

In princely fashion, however, he demanded a maximum effort from the rest of us. The last previous *Cronkite at Large* (which had aired just before I joined the unit) fared poorly in the ratings. Walter served notice on Bud that he would not be "humiliated" like that again.

The topics we were doing (pollution, the population explosion, gambling, hot-air ballooning) were all of Walter's own choosing, as were the exotic locations: Hong Kong, Macau, Singapore, Athens, Normandy. As the writer and field producer, I'd fly out to get, as my father would say, "the lay of the land."

In a few days the camera crews would follow, and then Bud. By the time Walter made his entrance we'd have choreographed just about every shot we ever intended making with him. Given his excitable temperament, Walter was not one to be kept in limbo.

The more years I've spent on the road drumming up stories for print or air, the closer I've drawn in spirit to my father. He was a traveling salesman riding out to territories that were new and strange. Like him I was facing unknown challenges – in his case making friends of strangers so as to sell lumber for a home or school or hospital, and in mine persuading strangers to share their stories with other strangers.

·

Walter treated producers, writers, and researchers with little regard. We were his hewers of wood and drawers of water. Bud, as I recall, turned purple to the point of apoplexy toting Walter's luggage up to his room in a Singapore hotel after Walter refused to wait any longer for a vanished bellman.

The same Walter was fond of saying how much he liked producers who were not afraid to stand up to him. And he named some who had screwed up their nerve to speak their piece. In at least a couple of instances, the people whom Walter cited were fired, whether for ruffling Walter's feathers or for other transgressions – Bud and I did not know which. But lack of information would not dissuade us from a doomsday theory.

I rarely saw Walter more provoked, however, than when he thought his eminence came under a cloud. Threading our way in a taxi through clogged Hong Kong for an interview with a shipping magnate, I let drop the footnote that Harry Reasoner had interviewed the very same businessman for *60 Minutes* several years ago.

The information, I thought, would help buttress the case that the man was worth doing.

Walter fumed.

From his perspective we were putting him in the position of playing second fiddle to the likes of Harry Reasoner, a journalist I am sure he respected well enough, but nonetheless one whose name should not be spoken in the same breath as Cronkite.

"Harry Reasoner," he said. "You mean to say you want me to do someone Reasoner's already done?" He was all for junking the interview and returning to the hotel.

"Walter," I countered. "Our story is different, totally different. I just mentioned Reasoner for background. This fellow is one of the most powerful figures in Hong Kong. I think he'll add something to the economic angle of our story."

"Mel's met him," said Bud. "He runs this town."

Walter grumbled but we sped on.

The interview was a disaster, in part because the magnate in question insisted on delivering an interminable speech that he read off a prompter before taking any questions, and in part because Walter was still pouting about following in the wake of a lesser star.

Later, an excruciating misunderstanding threatened to doom the entire enterprise.

We were dining at the florid Bellavista Hotel in Macau. It was a balmy night. Junks, giving off light from lanterns, glided on the river.

Walter spoke up, "What are your plans for me out here?"

Bud deflected the question to me.

"Mel's been working on it."

"Well, Walter," I began. "We want to do an essay."

I'd misspoken – knew it – but it was too late.

"Essay," in my television vocabulary acquired from fourteen and a half years at NBC News, meant a story in depth, running eight or nine or even ten minutes of precious air-time. In Walter's CBS lexicon the word stood for a cameo appearance by the correspondent, a mere minute or so on camera, a bridge to deliver a few incidental words between rivers of narration.

You could see the fire and smoke rising from the anchorman's silvery dome.

"Essay!" he pounced. "You mean to say you fellows dragged me half-way around the world to do an essay? Something I could have easily done back in Paris or New York?"

"Walter, you don't understand. I mean –"

"Don't understand?" He was beyond the reach of reason. "I understand only too well. Frankly, I'm appalled at your lack of direction and general state of unpreparedness." And he added, "It was unconscionable of you to lead me this far without more direction."

Bud looked sick. I was sure the end was near and that the two of us would be on the streets of Macau in the morning.

He raved on. "You fellows don't know what in the hell you're doing!"

Fortunately, it was late. Curtain time was drawing near for a Parisian revue that Walter was anxious to see. (He'd been told the first ten minutes were worth the price of admission.) I had all three tickets in my pocket. As Walter became more conscious of the hour, his rage began to splutter.

●

Walter turned out in an excellent mood the next morning, "all smiles" according to Bud, who'd met him for breakfast.

"The revue at the casino must have done it." I speculated.

Bud shook his head. "No," he replied. "What I think did it was Walter's realization that he needed us more than we needed him. Here he is in the middle of nowhere where his name doesn't count for shit. The son of a bitch would be easy pickings for all the shady characters in Macau. And he got scared. He'd be lost without us as his bodyguards."

"We also double as his gofers and porters."

"That, too," said Bud.

●

During the Macau shoot Walter borrowed my typewriter. He wanted to fine-tune a few lines. In the manner of many an ink-stained wretch, he didn't so much as type as attack the keyboard.

Take that, you sonofabitch, he seemed to be declaring, and that, and, believe me, brother, that's the God's own truth and there's not a bloody thing you can do or say to gainsay the facts. Just like that.

By means of such hallowed wire-service phrases as "shining example," "critical impasse," "swift reprisals" and the like, he drove his copy onward.

●

Bud was right. For a couple of days, trying to mend fences, Walter was a changed man. Over drinks and dinner, he charmed us with lively stories, setting each scene with a deft word or two, limning the actors, and engulfing us in laughter.

Whatever the occasion or the climate, Walter took pains to dress as befitted his standing as America's most famous anchorman. Although it was a sizzling day when I met his plane at the Athens airport, he emerged from the jet in a fresh shirt, dark suit, and dress handkerchief.

He cast a disapproving eye on my T-shirt and shorts.

"Don't worry," I said at once. "I'll be in a suit and tie tonight."

I suspect Walter took Charles Collingwood as a model. In Walter's opinion, the late CBS correspondent was "a man who knew how to live."

In his Vietnam novel, *The Defector*, Collingwood may have set a standard for globe-trotting journalists of Walter's generation by strongly advising them to wear suits – if possible, a dark suit and tie – in tropical as well as temperate climates.

"Whenever they go to a hot country," he wrote, "most Americans seem to think they are in a resort, and go around in espadrilles and loud sports shirts. This is not calculated to make a favorable impression on a cabinet minister or even a grade-three bureaucrat. He does not think he is in a resort."

That evening Walter was the guest of honor at a dinner hosted by Melina Mercouri, the actress and cultural affairs minister, and her husband, Jules Dassin, the film director. Everyone – Bud and myself included – sat spellbound while he held forth on the state of American politics on the eve of the 1988 election.

It was a Walter his viewers never saw, his talk unfettered by network restraints and taboos. He was outspoken, even passionate, in expressing a liberal philosophy; his analysis of the presidential campaign was nothing short of brilliant.

•

On a January night of snow and rain in 1988, my *Sunday Morning* colleague, Bill Moran, and I swiftly made our way up from the Broadcast Center. We were hell-bent for the bar at Days Inn.

What spurred us was word that the *Evening News* was airing a mini-documentary alleging Vice President Bush's complicity in the Iran-Contra scandal. Dan Rather planned to follow up in an interview with the vice president. Bush's insistence on going on the broadcast live rather than being taped (and edited) beforehand raised suspicions that something untoward was afoot. "There's bound to be fireworks," said Moran. We hurried to be at the TV with drinks in our hands.

We weren't disappointed. The documentary was tough, the ensuing interview a donnybrook.

Rather accused the vice president, who was the likely Republican candidate for president later that year, of hypocrisy, of knowing a great deal more about the scandal than he ever let on.

Bush protested his innocence, and Rather pressed in on him. They wrangled. It was a slugfest. Then Bush found the opening he was looking for.

How, he asked, would Rather like to be judged by a single incident, by, for example, his walking off the set last summer in Miami and causing the network to go black for seven minutes?

A solid blow. Rather's retort was lame. Bill thought the vice president had landed a crusher. He also thought Rather looked bad by acting so belligerently.

I said, "When I was a reporter, I wrangled with politicians. Haven't you?"

"Reporters can't behave like brawlers on TV," he argued.

I said, "It's got to be page one in the *Times*. If you were Max Frankel where would you play it?"

"Page one," said Bill.

"And above the fold?"

"Above the fold."

When I got home my wife said that Bud had been trying to get me. I called and he said in jubilation, "Rather has done it this time; he's gone off the deep end."

I wasn't so sure. Besides, I was impressed by Dan's performance, thought it gritty, and said so.

"He could have been more laid back and let Bush hang himself. That's what someone else would have done," said Bud.

"Maybe," I said.

"It's not an anchor's role to get into a pissing match with a vice president of the United States. A lot of people will resent it."

"Yeah, but it's terrific television."

"Terrific television, but after tonight's show Rather's out of there. How can they keep him in the anchor chair? Tisch isn't going to stand for it. This is the last straw. Rather's finished."

"What have you been drinking?" I said.

"You saw it in a saloon. You should have seen it in your living room where most people saw it. There'll be hell to pay. Mark my words," Lamoreaux declared.

According to Bud, Walter was down but not yet out. Our hopes for the salvation of the Cronkite unit had taken a sudden, sharp turn for the better. His argument was that Rather's embarrassing behavior increased the likelihood of management bringing Walter back to the anchor chair. In such a scenario Bud envisioned Walter taking Bud and me and perhaps others in the unit along with him to the *Evening News*.

In the *Times* the next morning the story ran inside on the TV page. The reporter, Peter Boyer, wrote that Rather was stunned by Bush's attack and had been momentarily at a loss for words.

When I walked into the office, Rose and Roz, two members of our staff, were on the phone reading the headlines to Walter who was out in Austin.

"In Living Color: Rather-Bush," Roz read from the *Daily News*. She went on.

Walter was loving every line.

At lunch Bud was anxious to tell me that this time Walter was lying low, letting Rather do himself in. No statements to the press, only "no comment."

"Stringer's got to be climbing the walls, I can hear him, 'This time Rather's gone too far.' As for Tisch, he must be calling for Dan's head."

Now Bud recounted what he'd told Walter when the latter solicited his views on the Bush broadcast.

"I told him Rather's support group (read executive producer) fell down. They should have warned him that Bush was no wimp, that he was tough and out to make some political hay at Rather's expense."

"It was the executive producer's fault, not Rather's?" I said. "An anchorman is entitled to a strong executive, one who anticipates ambushes, say, somebody like yourself."

"I couldn't put it better myself."

"You're kissing his ass," I said.

"You goddam right I'm kissing his ass, and I've only just begun."

•

Every day we waited for Stringer or Tisch, someone in high authority, to discipline Rather, to say, in effect, "This time, Danny boy, you've gone too far, putting the network at risk. You don't go after vice presidents as if they were perpetrators in a homicide.

"Even Murrow, your putative god, not ours for cripe's sake, was circumspect when it came to men in high office. Joe McCarthy, for instance. Sure he raked him morally, but if you bother to look it up, you'll see he did it by the rules, keeping his cool, the CBS way.

"Matters with you have come to a fine impasse, Danny boy, and the fact of the matter is we cannot afford the luxury of your bizarre behavior any longer.

"When Richard Daley's cops roughed you up out at the '68 convention in Chicago, you were our hero, a champion of the First Amendment.

"Years later when a cab driver in the same city took you on a wild ride, you said you were kidnapped. He said you refused to pay. We stuck by you, though, frankly, there were questions concerning the incident that linger to this very day.

"Just a few years ago when you were beaten up by two, or was it three, mysterious men, who kept raving, 'What's the frequency, Kenneth?' we were sympathetic, wholly sympathetic, but there were questions, Danny boy, questions that we asked among ourselves, though never raised in public. All this, however, has proved to be mere prologue.

"In Miami you abandoned the anchor chair and plunged the network into chaos. In the entire history of broadcasting nothing like this had ever happened before. You did the unthinkable, Danny boy, and believe us there were cries for your head, and not from Walter alone. Believe us you were on the razor's edge of extinction, and yet we spared you.

"But what transpired the other night is the last straw. We can't ignore it, can't excuse you, and we won't. This time there must be a punishment to fit the crime. This time, Danny Boy, you are finished, kaput. Courage, good night, and here's W-a-l-t-e-r!"

So Bud and I hallucinated.

During this period we witnessed a revived Walter. I caught a glimpse of him one day running out the door. He was on his way to keep a lunch date with Stringer.

What Stringer wanted, I subsequently learned from Bud, was to effect a reconciliation between Walter and Dan. Towards this end the president of CBS News called Walter to make the first move. But Walter balked. He proposed a compromise: Stringer should throw a Christmas party and invite both Rather and Cronkite. This time Stringer balked. He was going no further in his role as honest broker.

•

By Christmas, four months after we'd ended our travels, Walter had still not found the time to finish recording the narration for the broadcast. We were well into January of the new year, 1988, when this was finally done.

Walter was due in at two o'clock. He didn't make an appearance until three but it was just as well. The camera crew, consisting of a shooter, a soundman, a tech to run the prompter, and a makeup woman made good use of the hour getting ready for him.

The taping went astonishingly well. Walter read with intelligence and force. His pitch was just right for television. There were no flubs, not one, and no retakes; he gave a full half-hour of flawless on-camera takes. I had never seen anything like this before. It was exciting to see him in action. He was the same Walter, alternately peevish, fuming, even apoplectic, but the moment the red light came on he was transformed.

For months he'd been a bully mourning the loss of his glory days, or a pathetic septuagenarian looking for a merciful word from snickering bureaucrats, or a somewhat desperate man in pursuit of a vainglorious balloon sortie with Malcolm Forbes over Normandy. He had been raiding the lecture circuit or hosting TV specials.

The year went by. Time passed. The show crept forward. In most instances the footage was superb. The script took shape and even began to look credible. Editors were hired, pieces began to breathe, but Walter was still off somewhere, out of reach, or else scolding us, petulant and faultfinding.

At length the day came when Walter recorded the final segments of narration for the broadcast. It was in the afternoon in his office in the 555 Building and within shouting distance of the Broadcast Center across 57th Street with his father's shingle, "Dr. Cronkite, Dentist," of St. Joseph, Missouri, hanging from the wall. He stood up and waited for his cue from Keith Kulin, the cameraman, and there was a silence. And then he said, "Hello. Every once in a while I am privileged to gather you all together like this to report on some matters that have caught my interest and that I think just might interest you. This time ..."

The shock of recognition of a life-long calling chilled my spine. A journalist, one of the greatest in television, was being recreated before my eyes. I saw the Cronkite of Dallas ("President Kennedy is dead"), of that first landing on the moon ("Oh, boy! Whew! Boy!"), of Vietnam ("The only rational way out then will be to negotiate, not as victors but as an honorable people"), of the assassinations of Martin Luther King, Jr. and Senator Robert F. Kennedy, of Watergate, of the Israeli-Egyptian peace, of virtually every major news event in our time. He was again the Cronkite of old.

·

On the morning the president of CBS News was to screen our documentary, I examined the twitching in my bathroom mirror. If it didn't stop soon, I would be unable to accompany Bud to the executive suite.

Donna was in the next room plaintively searching for my navy blue pants. I shaved with a trembling hand.

"Pipe down," I shouted. "Can't you appreciate the state I'm in?"

"If I can't find them, what are you going to wear?" she fired back.

"It may be academic."

"You've had this before when you're under stress. Stop carrying on so and it will go away."

"What if it doesn't?"

"It always has," said Donna.

A moment later she let out a squeal.

"You found them?" I said.

"Yes," she sighed from deep in the recesses of the closet.

"Only what? What's wrong?"

"They're ruined; there's food stains on them." And once again the familiar cry was heard at 320 Riverside, apartment 4C: "Why don't you leave your clothes on the floor when this happens, when they wind up in this condition?"

Presently, thanks to my wife's ingenuity with cloth, cleaning solution and iron, I was able to go forth into the world in a suit fit for the executive suite.

"Just remember to comb your hair after you remove your hat," she admonished. I'd put on a black cap from Saks, which I delighted in wearing at a rakish angle.

"One more thing."

"What's that?"

She was smiling. "Don't take any shit off them."

I said, before tramping out, "Why aren't I president or something?"

"You were president of your journalism class at Columbia, and you were president of the Eureka Jazz and Chowder Society," Donna replied.

It was a sunny February morning, the temperature in the forties. I'd set out early enough to walk the two-and-a-half-mile jaunt along Riverside Park. My mind was as clear as a bell. I'd consumed no booze the night before, or the day before that. I was ready for the bastards.

At 11th Avenue and 59th Street I actually spied a shiny penny and put it in my pocket.

Bud breezed in at 9:10.

"Hello, Scoop."

"Hey, Chief, how're you doin'?"

"Walter's going to call in Friday to see how the screening went," he said.

That was two days from now.

"Where is he?"

"Bimini."

"Shit."

Before we left for the Broadcast Center across the street, Bud warned me not to react in any way, shape, or manner when we screened; I was to comport myself like a stoic, or better yet, a deaf-mute.

"And don't speak unless spoken to."

"Don't worry," I said. "I learned to keep my mouth shut from you and Shad Northshield." (When they were running *Sunday Morning*, one had to sit as still as a mummy at a screening; no calls or visitors. Solemnity was the watchword.)

A male secretary rose up from a counter in the president's suite. We were expected, he said, and told us to wait in a small conference room. There was a big leather armchair at the head of the table, Howard Stringer's, I surmised. It turned out his office was in the next room. The door was ajar and we could overhear him on the phone. I was surprised by the nature of the conversation. He was making a reference to a figure in Greek history. I recalled being told by someone that Stringer had been a history major at Oxford. Then what was he doing in a job like this? I asked myself. What was the good of all that fabulous education?

Mark Harrington barged in. He had on a large, colorful scarf and looked the picture of a rosy-cheeked boy on a Christmas card.

"Good morning, gents," he said. He and Howard, he said, would be with us before too long.

When we were finally summoned, Stringer sniffed, "Wally's new hour? It's ready to be looked at? I don't know if I can stand the suspense."

He was a big man, in his forties, with curly, blonde hair, wearing a pink shirt and toying with something like a baton (or maybe a ruler) that he would wave from time to time.

His flippant manner came as a shock. He made no effort to conceal a lack of respect for Cronkite in the company of Walter's own men.

"Oh, Wally, you don't say?" he mocked Walter on the videotape, flourishing his pointer. "Really, Wally, so that's the way it is?"

My picture of Stringer already had been painted by people who knew him. ("The Welsh Sammy Glick," was how Richard Salant, a former president of the news division, put it.) I came away from the screening with a similarly low estimation of Stringer's character.

"Stringer wasn't watching," I said to Bud as we made our way back to our own office. "He was too busy making fun of Walter and taking phone calls. I couldn't believe it. He took every phone call. Five, six, seven, I lost count."

"Harrington was watching," said Bud. "His eyes were focused."

He was right. It was Harrington who critiqued the broadcast. Except for his proposing a couple of minor changes (he objected to my word "inscrutable" in a segment about Macau on grounds it was racist) the broadcast passed muster. It would be fair to say our auditors were not enthralled with what they saw, but they didn't hate it, either. The important thing was that they pronounced it fit for air. There were even one or two things they professed to like.

Bud was an old hand at screenings with the brass but for me it was a first, and I was feeling light-hearted. We had a show.

Once settled in Bud's office, I said, "When will they give us an air-date?"

"Walter is figuring not until March."

"March?" That would make it a whole year since we started. "What are they waiting for?" I asked.

"They're waiting for the network to make a time-slot available. Don't worry, it'll be when nobody will be watching."

A few days later we learned the program would air in two weeks on February 24, a Saturday night, at 11:30 P.M.

Though it was not that obvious at the time, we had come to bury Walter, not to produce him.

Throughout the year that we worked on the program Walter vainly tried to stave off extinction by impressing Larry Tisch and Howard Stringer with his continuing value to CBS. He made a big deal of his "drawing power." In despair he turned to Merrill-Lynch, one of the *Walter Cronkite at Large* sponsors, with an idea for a new series about politics.

"The boys across the street wouldn't hear of it," he complained to Bud, so he was fashioning an end-run, encouraging Merrill-Lynch to take the concept to Tisch and Stringer directly, in effect, presenting them with an offer they couldn't refuse. There was gall and wormwood in Cronkite's voice when he spoke of "the boys across the street" in the Broadcast Center.

Nothing whatever came of the scheme. The brokerage house

expressed a profound lack of interest. It was news that must have affected him deeply. On the day he learned of their rejection he tugged Bud's tie, saying, "See, I warned you it was going to end up this way."

Running into Stringer one day, Bud learned that the president of news "hated" the *Cronkite at Large* broadcasts. Stringer thought the stories Walter wanted to do were hardly memorable.

The executive preferred an hour's topic, say, on Cronkite in Australia, "Somewhere we could get something solid on."

Clutching at this straw, Bud bid me to get busy working up a proposal for just such an hour. We had visions of Walter, Bud, and me trekking across the subcontinent in the spirited company of Robert Hughes, the Australian-born author and art critic for *Time* magazine.

I reached Hughes in Sydney and he was more than willing to act as our on-camera guide. But "the boys across the street" no longer showed any interest in Walter Cronkite's Australia, assuming, that is, that they ever had. Our memos and follow-up phone calls were met by deafening silence.

Friends used to press me on my relationship with Walter.

"But there is none," I said. "Unless, 'Where's the script?' 'What time is the interview?' 'I have to be finished in time for lunch at the Jockey Club.' 'Can you arrange for a car and driver?' etc., constitute a relationship."

"It's quite possible," I added, "that he doesn't even know my name." A couple of times he called me Al. Such instances of absent-mindedness were not unusual for him. He frequently botched the names of people who served him. But when it came to the rich and famous or a Howard Stringer or a William Ruckleshaus, his enthusiasm raised the threshold of memory.

I could feel sorry for him and be critical of CBS for the shabby way they treated their most famous journalist. But I also have to remember he didn't want to work very hard and when *Cronkite at Large* went off the air CBS settled on him a reported annual salary of $500,000 for ten years (plus valuable perks); in exchange, Walter could not appear on ABC or NBC, the major competitors. He was, however, perfectly free to accept assignments from PBS, CNN, and other venues.

Still, it was too bad. There was work for Walter to do, serious work, and he could do it very well and, I believe, he was itching for action. He got very little of it.

He was virtually ignored during the 1988 presidential primaries, although once he did go out to Iowa to cover the caucuses. But not in the role of a CBS News correspondent; he went instead as a free-lancer for the *Paris Herald-Tribune*, a job that could have been handled by a cub reporter.

Walter was cast adrift like the Flying Dutchman, the sailor condemned to sail the seas until Judgment Day. However, his fellow crewmen, Bud and I, reached safe harbor. I resumed my old job at *Sunday Morning*. Bud returned to the show as a senior producer.

Linda Mason, the executive producer, called me in one day to talk about Walter.

"I don't understand him," she said. "He had it all, his own show and staff, and yet he proceeded to alienate everybody. So now he's off the air." What she meant was that no one else was to blame for his fall from grace but Walter himself. If he had been a team player and accepted his status as a supporting actor graciously, he would still be on the air.

I chose my words carefully. "Walter is a proud person and for him to act any differently would be out of character for him; it would not be Walter." I further suggested that his was a case of the often-told tale of the ageing star in an uphill struggle to remain in the limelight.

(Cronkite never got over his disdain for Dan Rather. Twenty years later, in March 2005, when Rather was forced out as anchor of the *Evening News* and replaced by the mild-mannered Bob Schieffer, Walter sniped that Schieffer should have been given the anchor job years ago. Rather's departure from the *Evening News*, and a short time later from CBS, followed a story he broadcast about President Bush's National Guard service during the Vietnam war. The report cited evidence that could not be documented.)

In the course of my thirteen years with CBS News in New York, I chanced to meet several members of that intrepid band of early CBS reporters led by Edward R. Murrow during World War Two. Over time I spoke with William L. Shirer, Charles Collingwood, Howard K. Smith, and Eric Sevareid, among others.

Instead of nostalgic old gentlemen sharing golden reminiscences with a younger journalist, I found, to my surprise, disillusioned and even bitter old men. They had few if any kind words for the profession that had made them famous, and, in one or two cases, prosperous. Their mentor, Murrow, died a bitter and broken man in 1965.

When I was saying goodbye to Shirer, who was then eighty-one, he shook his head, saying, "I don't envy you at all."

I wasn't sure what he meant.

He explained, "Working for a corporation."

Walter was of the same generation and, with the possible exception of Murrow, the most famous broadcast journalist of all. But not even Cronkite could escape the consequences of growing old in a big machine that had become all process and no heart, all business and no mission.

In his memoirs Walter remarked that a career can be called a success if one can look back and say, "I made a difference." He did not feel he could do that. "All of us in those early years of television felt, I'm sure, that we were establishing a set of standards that would be observed by, or at least have an influence on, generations of news professionals to come."

But it was not to be, at least not in his eyes. In each case, and particularly in Walter's, the discovery would come too late.

Epilogue

In the fall of 1991 when I was sixty-four, Donna, then sixty-six, persuaded me that it was past time to heed our physician's words and get away from the fetid air of New York and return to northern California. The Pacific winds made for a healthier environment. I struggled with bronchial asthma at times but as her health deteriorated – she continued to suffer from congestive heart failure brought on by rheumatic fever as a child and had had two open-heart surgeries during our New York years – Donna yearned for the natural beauty of California. She spoke often of the mountains and the sea. I missed the West, too, but her ties were stronger.

We settled in Berkeley and bought a small Craftsman's house made of redwood. It was within walking distance of stores and cafes and newspapers. I rented a small office in another part of town and continued to work for *Sunday Morning* as a freelancer. My health improved, but Donna's condition reached the point where she had to have further heart surgery. On the day she was being released from the hospital, just as I was getting ready to bring her home, I suffered a minor heart attack. But I mended rapidly, and within a week or so resumed my normal life. But Donna went from bad to worse. Before my eyes, she was slipping away. The day before she died she had great difficulty breathing, but insisted on showing me how I could look after myself in the kitchen. The next day, as I was leaving for a doctor's appointment in San Francisco, she implored me to call and tell her what the doctor had to say before I left for home. I called, but there was no answer. I hoped that Donna, who subsisted on multiple medications, was only asleep. When I got back to Berkeley, I cowardly went to my office first and phoned home from there. It rang and rang but no one answered. The house seemed strangely still when I pulled up. I went in through the back door, which, surprisingly, I found wide open. The weather was fine and the day very bright; I thought it extravagantly bright for a January afternoon. Then I went into the bedroom and found no one, and no one was in the living room, either. Very puzzled and almost by accident, I stepped into the bathroom and there I found her.

With Donna's death, I knew I'd dithered long enough. If I was ever to leave more than a myriad of illegible notebooks, old articles, and videos behind as a legacy of a lifetime in journalism, I'd better get serious. And so I stopped doing pieces for *Sunday Morning* and turned my attention to making sense of all that. Since I am a slow writer, I could not get started soon enough.

A Strange Breed of Folks